José Martí and the Global Origins of Cuban Independence

José Martí
and the
Global Origins
of
Cuban Independence

Armando García de la Torre

THE UNIVERSITY OF THE WEST INDIES PRESS
Jamaica • Barbados • Trinidad and Tobago

The University of the West Indies Press
7A Gibraltar Hall Road, Mona
Kingston 7, Jamaica
www.uwipress.com

© 2015 by Armando García de la Torre
All rights reserved. Published 2015

A catalogue record of this book is available from the National Library of Jamaica.

ISBN: 978-976-640-552-6 (print)
978-976-640-561-8 (Kindle)
978-976-640-570-0 (ePub)

Cover illustration: Carlisle Harris
Cover and book design by Robert Harris
Set in Adobe Garamond Pro 11/14.5 x 27
Printed in the United States of America

To all dreamers, wherever you may be . . .

CONTENTS

Foreword *Candice Goucher* / **ix**

Acknowledgements / **xiii**

1. The Global Origins of Cuban Independence / **1**

2. Transmitting Civic Values to Our Future Citizens: Martí's Global Histories for Children / **33**

3. The Hindu Inspirations of a Freedom Fighter's Spiritual and World Outlook / **67**

4. Martí and the Divine Nation-State / **85**

5. Martí and the African Diaspora / **103**

6. Transmitting Proper Government: Ulysses S. Grant and the US Civil War in Martí's Imagination / **143**

Afterword / **172**

Notes / **179**

Selected Bibliography / **201**

Index / **213**

FOREWORD

The Afro-Cuban divine messenger Eleguá sits at the crossroads, a meeting place of all directions, all intersecting forces. Like any busy intersection, this crossroads is a place of danger and confusion that arises with the opportunity to alter direction. Through drumming or divination, Eleguá will be called upon to assist with the deeper truths about nature and the ambiguities of human communication, opening up the paths ahead. The aim of this Yoruba-derived ritual reflects an ideal world of balance: humans are in balance with nature and the unseen forces of agency and energy; the past is in balance with the future. Nineteenth-century Cubans also lived in a period of uncertainty that they shared with much of the world and that came to be known as the *fin de siècle* (end of the century). Feelings of despair, discomfort and uneasiness accompanied the possibility of tectonic shifts in the cultural meanings and identities of the modern world.

Long before the nineteenth century, Cuba was situated historically in the crucible of globalization, where the peoples, foods, sweat and dreams of five continents met and mingled. Historians have recognized that Europeans, Africans, East Indians, Asians and North Americans shared a history of interaction and commonalities of identity. Yet the nineteenth century offered Cubans something more: participation in the global marketplace of ideas. Armando García de la Torre stages his study of the Cuban martyr José Martí in precisely this setting of the modern crossroads.

Under García's close scrutiny, Martí has one foot in the old Cuba and another in its future. Standing at a crossroads where Martí tried to balance these worlds, nationhood became the perceived pathway to modernity. García notes that nationalist sentiments evolved from below, yet Martí was born to white parents. Both a twist of fate and his considerable intellect and natural curiosity provided exposure to a world library. He read the ancient *Bhagavad-Gita* but also closely studied the current news of independence movements in India and Vietnam. The early streets of Havana offered African resistance and models of syncretism. Clandestine political associations brought Martí the Masonic ideals of fraternity, equality and liberty derived from the French Enlightenment, while encouraging an ecumenical embrace of a selfless and divine search for perfection within a brotherhood of select men.

Like other contemporaries in exile, Martí used his distance from home and the metropole to gain global perspective and achieve personal nuance. It was not only Cuba's past and present that offered Martí an opportunity to engage with new ideas; world history, the American Civil War, the ancient writings of the *Bhagavad-Gita* – all provided moments of insight and reflection. The global movement of people and capital had affected Cuba, hurtling potential elites together with a new influx of Chinese labourers and American investment in the nineteenth-century crucible.

Afro-Asian teachings – both Afro-Cuban and Hindu philosophies – transcended the divide between sacred and secular worldviews. For Martí, even the pragmatic document of political independence, the *Manifiesto de Montecristi*, extolled the mission in profoundly spiritual terms. The nation-state was divine and duty not only was divinely sanctioned, it demanded sacrifice. Yet Martí transcended the limitations of nationalism. The national agenda needed to be understood as a process of honing a populist cultural sentiment rooted in the local. At the same time, nationalist ideas jostled in a world of Hindu, African and North American thought and competed in the larger world. Both inspired by the past and conceptualizing a rebirth of revolutionary fervour while facing towards the modernity of a new century ahead, Martí began to perceive war as a sacred duty. Ultimately, Martí became a martyr for his cause. This sacrifice would be meaningless without its spiritual component. The other divide Martí crossed was intergenerational. His writings for children recognized his own experience in the library of a teacher and his early, influential exposure to the world's great ideas. These and other experiences led him to believe in the perfectibility of the human endeavour.

Quintessentially world history, this study of Martí bridges the familiar and the individual with larger global patterns and processes. Martí has been celebrated for his nationalist project. The peculiar brand of nationalism in

Latin America has leaned on the cult of the individual, even debating the necessity of populist sentiment in its construction. In this study, Martí's martyrdom for the cause of an island state swims in the global currents of a broader world, a global experience.

V.S. Naipaul once suggested that everything was destroyed in the Caribbean and nothing created anew. García presents another Cuba, one whose context of creating a modern world – from the angst of mobility, the passion of encounter, the working with words – is situated at a crossroads of history. This study is world history not only as a consequence of revealing the global breadth of philosophical groundings to which Martí was exposed, but also because, quite simply, Martí without the broader historical and cultural framing of the wider world now appears shallow and incomplete. As with any classic historical work, one can no longer imagine Cuban nationalism or any nationalist biography without this same global perspective.

Eleguá's crossroads is an apt metaphor, signalling danger and opportunity in the change of direction. Martí might have heard the batá drums as he walked the streets of the Havana of his youth. Although Martí eschewed the bitter racism and racialized world inherited from slavery as a challenge to the inclusivity of the nationalist enterprise, can it be argued that he inherited anything from its culture of orality? The African diaspora offered Martí the camaraderie of anti-colonial and anti-imperialist activists. Besides a penchant for storytelling, Martí also gained the vocabulary of a religiosity of daily life, where the ancestors intersected the struggles of the living. Armando García de la Torre brings his readers to this intimate crossroads faced by one extraordinary individual. He brilliantly balances the ideas and forces of change operating in Martí's world, and in so doing gives birth to a modern Cuba understood from a truly global perspective.

Candice Goucher
Washington State University, Vancouver, Washington

ACKNOWLEDGEMENTS

As a boy in Miami in the 1980s, while playing in my Little Havana neighbourhood YMCA, I wondered about a large, white plaster head, beside a Cuban flag, that overlooked the yard, a tribute to José Martí. From that early memory, the interest in who he was and in his relevance has grown and benefited from experiences and from individuals around the world. I thank my mentors and former graduate school companions in the master's programme of Florida Atlantic University and in the World History doctoral programme at Washington State University, where the ideas in this book first took shape, and Graciella Cruz-Taura, John Kicza, Heather Streets-Salter and Patrick Manning, for their guidance. I also thank Bill Youngs and my former colleagues in the Department of History at Eastern Washington University and Dean Vickie Shields. A visiting professorship at Portland State University, encouraged by Linda Walton, allowed me to develop the African dimensions, particularly with the support of Kofi Agorsah. My colleagues at the University of the West Indies, St Augustine, Trinidad, Rita Pemberton, Bridget Brereton, Michael Toussaint, Claudius Fergus, Nicole Roberts and Dean Heather Cateau, provided commentary, support and encouragement. I am thankful to the Centro de Estudios Martianos in Havana and to Esperanza B. de Varona, Lesbia Orta Varona, Gladys Gómez-Rossié and María Estorino of the Roberto C. Goizueta Cuban Heritage Collection at the University of Miami for their support during several research visits. Funding from a 2009 Eastern Washington University Faculty Grant for Research and Creative Works and from the University of the West Indies allowed for additional research and writing of the manuscript. Scholar colleagues of the World History Association and from the Association of Caribbean Historians also provided commentaries on my presentations of book chapters. Other scholars I wish to thank for their critiques, suggestions and support are Pedro Pablo Rodríguez, Marlene Vázquez Pérez, Reinaldo Funes Monzote, Marnie Hughes-Warrington, Kenneth Pomeranz, Louis A. Pérez Jr, Ada Ferrer, Richard Blakett, Jane Landers and Jeffrey Kerr-Ritchie. My friends and family in Miami, Fort Myers, Spokane, New York, Portland, Madrid, Havana and Trinidad all gave me the inspiration and encouragement that I needed along the way. I also thank Barbara Kitchel for her valuable assistance with the initial editing and the Trinbagonian artist Carlisle Harris for dedicating his artwork for the book cover. I am indebted to Candice Goucher for setting this book on its final path and for helping me to fulfil this "cosmic cause" – without her support, this book would not have reached its destination. To Linda Speth, Shivaun Hearne, Nina Hoeschele and the editorial team and anonymous reviewers of the University of the West Indies Press, I am grateful for their work in this project from initial contact to publication. Finally, I began the book in Miami, continued it in the Pacific Northwest of the United States and in Cuba. I had the satisfaction of finishing it on the island of Trinidad, in the Caribbean, where Martí set his sights and where his spirit remains.

St Augustine, Trinidad and Tobago

1. THE GLOBAL ORIGINS OF CUBAN INDEPENDENCE

Plenamente conocedor de sus obligaciones con América y con el mundo, el pueblo de Cuba sangra hoy a la bala española, por la empresa de abrir . . . la república independiente que ha de ofrecer casa amiga y comercio libre al género humano.

Fully aware of its obligations to America and to the world, the nation of Cuba bleeds today the Spanish bullet, in an endeavour to usher . . . an independent republic that will offer friendly shelter and free trade to [all of] humanity.[1]

– *Letter from the battlefield to the New York Herald, 2 May 1895*

In 1895 José Martí, the leader of the Cuban Revolutionary Party, affirmed how Cuba's recently reignited independence struggle was also an act of service to the Americas and to the world. The above excerpt from a letter to the *New York Herald* dated 2 May 1895, written on a Cuban battlefield, is testament to how this leader was entirely aware of the global origins of Cuba's independence.

José Martí (1853–95) is widely celebrated as Cuba's national hero. He is credited as a founding father of the modern nation and as a seminal articulator of pan-Latin Americanism. He was the prime agent who organized and was instrumental in relaunching the Cuban War of Independence in its final confrontation with the Spanish empire in 1895, a struggle which was ultimately overwhelmed by US intervention in 1898. For his early anti-colonial activities, he suffered hard labour imprisonment in Cuba and deportation to Spain at the age of seventeen. He remained in Spanish exile from 1871 to 1874. In Spain, he earned law and philosophy degrees, and he advocated and published

Figure 1. José Martí in 1894.

in support of an independent Cuba. Through his speeches and writings, he made a largely unacquainted Spanish public aware of their government's despotic rule over Cuba. Two seminal essays published in Spanish newspapers, "Political Prison in Cuba" ("El presidio político en Cuba", 1871) and "The Spanish Republic Faces the Cuban Revolution" ("La república española ante la revolución cubana", 1873), date from the period of his first Spanish exile.

Martí left Spain in December 1874, travelled through France and Britain, and arrived in Mexico City in 1875, where he would remain until 1877. In the Mexican capital, Martí emerged as a respected poet, orator, playwright and journalist. He lambasted the budding dictatorship of Porfirio Díaz and left Mexico for Guatemala where he held a professorship, and then returned to Cuba in 1878 under a general amnesty proclaimed by colonial authorities. While on the island, he was deported a second time to Spain in 1879 for his pro-independence activities. He finally settled in New York City in 1880, remaining there for the last fifteen years of his life. During his extended stay in New York City, Martí worked and campaigned on behalf of Cuban independence in Florida, Jamaica, Venezuela and throughout the circum-Caribbean. Moreover, New York provided him a window to the modern world. In the booming US metropolis, he exposed himself to the greater global currents of an increasingly globalized late nineteenth-century world, through its scores of newspapers, books, events – the opening of the Brooklyn Bridge, the Statue of Liberty, expanding railroads and masses of immigrants arriving, to name a few. At the age of forty-two, on 19 May 1895, barely two weeks after writing the letter to the *New York Herald,* he died on the battlefield, fighting for Cuba's right to be free of colonialism.

Martí and Modern Theories of Nationalism

Martí's life personifies the forces of late nineteenth-century global technology and thought, particularly the transnational forces that resisted the oppressive character of nineteenth-century European colonialism. Martí's efforts to fight imperialism by extricating foreign, imposed ideologies, such as racial prejudice, predate anti-colonial struggles that later appeared in the twentieth century. Martí's ideological formulation and promotion of nationalism complicates an accepted understanding of late nineteenth-century nationalism as being ethnocentric and exclusionary. For during Martí's lifetime, ethnocentric doctrines of nationalism proliferated in the Western world; indeed, to this day, nationalism in Scotland, Ukraine, Catalonia and other areas of the world is based on the idea of a homogeneous ethnicity with a common shared history deserving its own nation-state. Although Martí was a child of Europeans, he led a nationalistic independence movement that, as I demonstrate in the following chapters, had a profoundly intentional, globalized conceptualization of the Cuban nation and state building. He had innovative ideas for a nationalist living in his time, visibly evident when he declared that "there is no racial hatred, since races do not exist . . . for in the justice of [Mother] Nature . . . the universal identity of mankind emerges with a turbulent appetite and in triumphant love".[2]

Any scholar currently writing on nationalism and state building must confront the leading theories developed by social scientists on this modern phenomenon and, specifically, regarding Martí, one must also consider how he viewed *patria*,[3] a term he employed extensively. Although this historian acknowledges that the social science approach to dealing with nationalism may often lack essential historical awareness[4] – and, according to another historian, social science even "prefers idealised facts, abstract and constructed data, conceptual categories and parsimonious theories to the ambiguities and complexities of the past"[5] – theories of nationalism may nevertheless assist in examining modern nationalism. The following chapters, however, are not a broad study of nationalism as it emerged in different societies and how they relate to Martí's independence programme, nor do I attempt to make an overarching claim on how or why nationalism developed in the nineteenth and twentieth centuries. Rather, I delve into a major late nineteenth-century Cuban nationalist's conception and promotion of independence and the nation-state and reveal this conception's hitherto largely ignored global origins, against a backdrop of anti-colonialism and abolition. In line with Cuban scholar Pedro Pablo Rodríguez, I argue that Martí's independence programme "went beyond the framework and objectives of the first Cuban War of Independence (1868–1878)"; his struggle was not one to merely expel Spain from Cuba, but instead "was connected to the idea of national liberation".[6] Therefore, I seek to illuminate in this work the global, transnational connections of how Martí conceived and promoted national liberation.

Scholars have developed theories on how and why modern nationalism emerged. Nationalism, based on the idea of nation, is a sentiment that unites individuals beyond the level of community and may or may not be tied to a specific state. One leading theorist of nationalism, Anthony Smith, considers the nation as indeed being connected to a specific state. Smith argues that notions of rights, duties and a common economy play critical roles in the development of nationalism. Smith's theory is based on the idea of "ethnie", a human population with myths of common ancestry and shared memories linked to a homeland and a sense of solidarity among at least some of its members.[7] Another theorist, Ernest Gellner, views nationalism as the product of social homogenization processes undertaken by the state in its attempt to forge a labour force suitable for industrial society. Gellner emphasizes the modernity of nationalism.[8] Another major theorist, John Breuilly, defines nationalism as a form of politics – specifically, a structure of political behaviour in the context of the modern state and the modern state system.[9] And yet for another scholar of nationalism, Liah Greenfeld, beyond factors of language, territory, history and levels of civic and/or economic development, nationalism is a drive for recognition and is defined by its concern for status and equality vis-à-vis other nations.[10] Another theorist, Craig Calhoun, argues that nationalism is a "way of constructing collective identities that arose alongside transformations in state power, increased long-distance economic ties, new communications and transportation capacities, and new political projects".[11] Martí's nationalism indeed emerged in a similar way to the nationalism Calhoun describes as "constructed [in opposition to] the oppression of the imperial, controlling state, [and by] the inability of the state to address the aspirations of political, economic, and mobile freedom".[12] In Martí's case, as he extensively argued, it was Spain's inability to provide for Cuba's welfare and its economic, political and social development that also prompted Cuba's struggle for sovereignty.

Martí's ideological construction of the nation, as Cuban historian Rodríguez argues and I add, was also based on responding to the real problems caused by foreign domination and economic hegemonies. Both were equally the foci of Martí's perspectives and ideas regarding nation building. Also, the Cuban independence leader's nationalism was based on notions of cross-ethnic fraternity and an aspiration for freedom, particularly from the external pressures of Spanish imperial rule and from the likelihood of an impending US intervention in the affairs of Cuba.

The theorist of nationalism whose work has received the most recent attention is Benedict Anderson. Anderson considers the nation to be an "imagined community", facilitated by the rise of "print-capitalism" that allowed new loyalties to be established by people who had little, if any, day-to-day contact with each other. Anderson recognizes that all communities larger than primordial villages of face-to-face contact, and perhaps even these, are imagined.[13] Anderson views the construction of nationalism as facilitated by the rise of newspapers and of literary novels.[14] For Anderson, the entropy and the various technological by-products of the modern age provide "the genesis of the nation-form and its ensuing modulations".[15]

Two key themes run throughout Anderson's writings on nationalism: first, that the nation is imagined; second, that the imagined nation exists in comparison to others in the wider world.[16] Anderson is particularly concerned with the rise of this new form of consciousness, the identification with the nation and the way nations have imagined themselves. Partha Chatterjee, by contrast, is perhaps the most avid critic of Anderson's theory of nationalism. Chatterjee considers his theory a sociological-determinist one that fails to "respect the specificity of Third World nationalism",[17] especially since Anderson promotes the notion that modern nationalism is a legacy of the Creole independence movements in the Americas that then spread back to Europe, and from there emanated to the rest of the globe. Anderson's leading work, *Imagined Communities* (1983, 1991, 2006), also affirms that sovereignty is a necessary condition when thinking of the nation.

Regarding nationalism in Latin America, historians of the region have considered that the state preceded national consciousness, as opposed to nationalism motivating state formation. In essence, the Latin American state was created before citizens of the state felt national attachment to it. Several reasons propelled this; for instance, the wars for independence in Spanish America at the turn of the nineteenth century were not clearly defined struggles. Conflicting loyalties existed throughout the mainland American colonies of Spain. In no single Spanish colony did an overarching sense of being "Mexican" or "Peruvian" exist, much less in regions where nation-states were created from more recent colonial territorial demarcations or contested as a result of the wars themselves, such as in Bolivia or Argentina.

Few major theorists and comparative historians of nationalism, according to scholar Nicola Miller, have focused on Latin America. Leading theorists of nationalism such as Ernest Gellner, Anthony Smith, John Breuilly and John Hutchinson "have either ignored Latin America altogether, or relegated it to an uneasy footnote, acknowledging that it does not really 'fit' any of their schemas, but not modifying their frameworks to accommodate the region's experiences in any significant way". Miller believes that the real difficulty presented by Latin America is "not that it is wholly different from the implied but [rather] that everything *partly* applies".[18]

One notable exception to this relative neglect by theorists is Eric Hobsbawm, who considers that nations are politically constructed and therefore capable of sustaining themselves, notwithstanding the malleability and changeability of ethnic identities. Hobsbawm argues that from the early twentieth century onwards, Latin American nationalisms have drawn upon a rhetoric of inclusion, which may, in some cases, have opened up possibilities for the marginalized to renegotiate their positions. I argue that the rhetoric of inclusion emerged even before the twentieth century. Haiti in the early nineteenth century is surely an example of a state that emerged inspired by a rhetoric of inclusivity.

Moreover, delving into the global origins of Martí's search for an independent Cuba reveals that the discourse of inclusion in Latin America can be traced to earlier than the Mexican Revolution of the 1910s, and instead to the revolution spearheaded by Martí, specifically by his organizing the pro-independence Cuban Revolutionary Party in 1892 and promoting a racially blind republic that also included women – quite phenomenal for a nation builder living in the 1880s.[19] Martí's independent Cuba would be a thoroughly inclusive nation, as I demonstrate in the following chapters.

This work therefore sheds light on an episode of Cuban, Caribbean and Latin American history that is not known for its global connections or for how it further discloses the linkages of global ideological trends in the late nineteenth century. This book therefore complicates notions of what is generally understood about late nineteenth-century nationalism as ethnocentric and exclusionary. It also problematizes notions that liberal approaches to nationalism, such as Martí's, emerged in "cultures with strong traditions of tolerance, such as India".[20] I seek to move away from generalized hypotheses and indeed reveal in the following pages the "ambiguities and complexities of the past".[21] For as this study of the global origins of José Martí's independence programme shows, Cuban nation building was neither a result of the rise of "print-capitalism", nor did it emerge after the formation of a republic as in the case of mainland Spanish-American independence, nor was this nationalism born in a land with a strong tradition of tolerance. I affirm that Martí did not create a new Cuban nationalism, for he was following a long line of existing Cuban nationalist thought that can be traced to the late 1700s. Indeed, the nationalist leader considered himself heir to the decades-long struggle and understood the reasons for previous failures, as the pages that follow demonstrate.

Martí's nationalism is nonetheless compelling, for he was a modern nation builder who was inspired not only by his Cuban or Caribbean or larger Spanish-American homeland, but also by the history and the ideological currents of our planet. Delving deeper into Martí's quest for an independent Cuba reveals that he imagined the Cuban nation and conjured its independence programme in a global, historical context. He envisioned the mission to free Cuba as culminating in a successful anti-colonial war that would establish a free nation. While developing this mission, he deeply considered the struggles of the colonized world of his time.

Latin American scholars have taken Anderson to task regarding *Imagined Communities*'s assumptions that modern nationalism emerged with Creole bureaucrats who developed an elite consciousness of the differences between Spain and its colonies, and how this spread back from the American lands to Europe and then to the rest of the world. Anderson's other main argument, regarding the significance of print-capitalism and of the role of late colonial newspapers in creating proto-national consciousness, according to some scholars of Latin America, seems to be based on limited evidence.[22] Closer scrutiny of historical evidence lends more credibility to the notion that Creole independence fighters at the turn of the nineteenth century were imagining a republic more than a nation.

Yet, in the case of Martí's nation building, he was imagining both a republic *and* a nation – and both intrinsically as being one and the same, and as ethnically inclusive and sovereign. How could one imagine a republic and a nation as one, yet have the nation be heterogeneous? The chapters that follow delve into this question and do not provide definitive answers, but convincing ones, based on readings of Martí's speeches, written works and actions. Martí promoted the need for an independent Cuban nation-state at quite a different historical moment than his mainland Spanish-American predecessors and even his Cuban liberation precursors. The world Martí lived in, the 1880s and 1890s, was remarkably different from that of the 1790s to 1810s of Miguel Hidalgo's Mexico or Simón Bolívar in Gran Colombia, a fact Martí knew. He also understood how colonialists used the history of Haitian independence as a means to undermine Cuban freedom fighters, unpacking their subjective assumptions. And he too, like Bolívar before him, benefited from the support of Haiti in his fight for independence.

Scholar of Mexico Claudio Lomnitz is perhaps the most visible critic of Anderson's theory of nationalism regarding Latin America. Lomnitz considers Anderson's assumptions flawed, for they do not consider the different ways in which the term *nación* could have been used in the period preceding the independence movements. According to Lomnitz, the term *nación* had several connotations in late colonial Mexico. It could be employed by European descendants in New Spain (colonial Mexico) to identify with Spain, or by others to differentiate themselves from Spain, or yet by others to "distinguish his [or her] territorial space in New Spain from that of the indigenous communities, which were designated a separate *nación* with distinctive legal privileges".[23] Lomnitz's second major argument against Anderson's theory is that, to Anderson, nationalism entailed a "deep horizontal camaraderie". Lomnitz argues that nationalism, not only in Latin America but in general, inherently entailed "bonds of dependence" between full and part citizens. Lomnitz affirms that "although nationalism always invokes fraternity, or horizontal bonds, it is in practice built upon hierarchical relations of paternalism and clientism".[24] Lomnitz's third argument is that Anderson had made a fundamental error in associating nationalism with secularization. In Spain, Lomnitz emphasized, national consciousness was stimulated at least in part by religious expansionism in the New World and the sense that to be "Spanish" was to enjoy a privileged connection to the Roman Catholic Church. In independent Mexico, according to Lomnitz, Freemasonry also played a crucial role in converting regional leaders into national ones.[25]

Lomnitz further problematizes Anderson's theory regarding nationalism in Latin America by applying it to the case of Mexico and finds that it does not entirely fit. In the case of Cuba, since Martí was building a nation-state at a different time than the mainland Spanish-American leaders of the early 1800s (such as Mexico's), Lomnitz's points do not entirely apply either. Although it is true that *nación* in Cuba, like in Mexico, could have been used in different ways, one specific way that it was used by Martí's contemporaries, the *autonomistas*, was as the notion of a Spanish nation that bridged both sides of the Atlantic, the peninsula (Spain) and the island (Cuba). Basing their arguments on notions that the Spanish *nación* was not limited to the Iberian Peninsula but encompassed the island of Cuba, the *autonomistas* fought for reforms, equality and democratic practice in Cuba, albeit under a Spanish imperial framework.

Lomnitz's point that *nación* was also employed to "distinguish territorial space"[26] by indigenous communities with distinctive legal privileges is absent in the Cuban case, for unlike Mexico and other regions of the Spanish-American mainland, Cuba lacked any large, cohesive, self-identifying indigenous populations at the time of Martí's independence efforts, as these peoples had been decimated by centuries of European colonialism. Nevertheless, the Cuban leader wrote extensively about the first peoples of the Americas as well as on indigenous issues, and he often employed the idea of indigeneity when promoting Latin Americanism.[27] A vivid example is his 1887 Spanish translation of Helen Hunt Jackson's novel *Ramona* (which he compared to Harriet Beecher Stowe's *Uncle Tom's Cabin*), a work highlighting racial discrimination and the plight of indigenous peoples through the life and loves of a mixed-race indigenous orphan girl in the southwestern United States following the Mexican-American War.[28] To Martí, Cuban independence and its nation building were also firmly rooted in a larger Latin American consciousness, one that embraced its vibrant and diverse mixed ethnic heritage and would not turn its back on America's indigenous peoples.

Other ways that Cuba's case diverges from Spanish-American independence, complicating theoretical rebuttals to Anderson, is that on the island, nation indeed came before the state – whereas in Spanish America it would be continually contested. Martí understood that the bloody conflicts in post-independence Spanish America were ideological battles based on nationalism and *caudillismo* (loyalty to strongmen rulers). Moreover, Cuban nationalism had no issue with disputed borders or communities arguing for regional identifications; as an island, Cuba was more limited in scope, and the conception of Cuban nationalism was linked to a fixed, clearly defined geographic entity.

Although scholars of Latin America have since complicated Anderson's theories regarding the region and of how "modal nations" first appeared there, and how they moved from there to the rest of the world, notions of globalization in Latin American nationalism have not been thoroughly investigated. I argue that Martí's conception and promotion of Cuban independence was neither derivative of other nationalisms nor a model for others worldwide.

Rather, Martí's nation building is an example of how imported ideas and experiences are grafted onto the local; of how a hybrid conception of nation was constructed by influences and inspirations beyond the West – indeed, a global, modern version of nation building emerged in the struggle to decolonize a European colony in the Caribbean and to establish a sovereign nation-state. As I reveal in the following chapters, Martí indeed acted upon his idea that "the world [may] be grafted onto [the tree of] our Republics, but its trunk must be [our own]",[29] which leads us to consider what renowned Cuban scholar Roberto Fernández Retamar has written on the matter:

> The other great [nation] builder of Latin America, Simón Bolívar (1783–1830) had already seen that "we [Latin Americans and Caribbean peoples] were [our own] small human species"; that we are not an extension or echo of Western Europe, but rather something quite different, [we are] another world. Martí goes even further than Bolívar in not only acknowledging this distinction, but also [by identifying] the structural kinship that unites a society to others throughout [our] broad planet: in this sense, [Martí] was perhaps the first to identify the common cause of the man who "is not from Europe or from European America".[30]

Martí's nation building, and his sense of nationalism, thus emerge as a modern construction that compared Cuba's problems with ones of larger global imperialism. For as the late, eminent Latin American thinker Leopoldo Zea suggested, "Bolívar initiated the liberation efforts that culminated in Martí." Yet, the Cuban leader, unlike Bolívar, lived in a fully modern world of industrial factories, steamships and locomotives, and of instant telegraphic communications – and especially during a time when "the Western European expression", according to Zea, "of the unrestrained acquisition and partition of Africa and Asia took new forms, with the United States debating whether to do or not the same with [Latin] America and [the Caribbean]".[31] In this sense, Martí's prime objectives were to expel Spanish colonialism; to prevent a budding US one from establishing itself on the island; and simultaneously to build and promote a free, democratic and sovereign nation. In order to achieve this, he found inspiration in and disseminated ideas and histories from not only our America – as scholars have hitherto demonstrated – but, as I amplify, from different regions of our world.

In this context, Martí's independence project diverges from previous Spanish-American nation building ones; it did not emerge in the context of a struggle to rebuild legitimacy following Napoleon's invasion of Iberia, for Cuba remained "the ever-faithful isle", a colony that stayed loyal to the Spanish monarchy. While the mainland waged wars for independence and leaders sought to gain legitimacy vis-à-vis their populations in the early nineteenth century, decades later Martí sought to gain legitimacy on modern notions of full democracy and of undermining imperialistic ideologies of racism and the superiority of European civilization. As I later show, he moved others to think of the new Cuban republic belonging to a "mother America" and not to a "mother" Spain. In fact, scholar Nancy Raquel Mirabal affirms that

> fundamentally distrustful of Spain and the United States, Puerto Rican and Cuban *independentistas* geographically reconfigured the islands so that they would have no connection to any form of colonialism present or future. The use of the term Antilles signified an association with the Caribbean devoid of any outside influences. In other words, instead of looking to Spain and the United States, Puerto Rican and Cuban migrants would now look to Jamaica, the Dominican Republic, Haiti, and the West Indies to inform how they would define community and identity. As a result the impact and importance of Africa, the African diaspora, and the history of the African slave trade in the Caribbean could no longer be avoided.[32]

Cuba's independence movement was linked early on to the abolition of the system of slavery on the island. Cuban nationalism grew within the confines of a bounded territory, an island, unlike the mainland Spanish-American states that emerged with contested territories and boundaries and with republics seeking to unwind existing colonial rights for distinct indigenous communities. While in Spanish America individuals could identify with various alternating loyalties of indigenous, Spanish or whichever local republic was envisioned, in the case of Cuba, where indigenous populations had been decimated, existing options to subscribe to "national" loyalties were more limited. Individuals in Cuba had basically two options when it came to national identification: either Spanish or Cuban. Since African descendants had no possibility of returning to Africa – but nevertheless maintained vibrant African ethnic cultural, linguistic and spiritual connections – to be part of a Cuba, independent from Spain, was perhaps the most appealing option for the Afro-Cuban community. Nevertheless, some African descendants would continue to identify with Spain, as not all Spanish loyalists were of the conservative kind. Several Spanish supporters attempted a construction of nationalism that was broad enough to include a multi-ethnic sense of Spanish nationality within an empire.

The United States cannot be excluded from this study of José Martí's efforts. Although during the period that this book covers, roughly from the 1870s to the early 1890s, the US had not emerged as the hegemonic power on the island, Martí lived for most of his adult life in the US, was aware of the major social issues and knew the politics of the US's limited democracy and expansionist foreign policy. Martí worked for Cuban independence and promoted Cuban nationalism not only in contrast to Spain's cultural and political claims to the island, but also in confrontation with US designs. Martí counteracted pressures from pure Spanish loyalists, from the reform-minded *autonomistas* and from those Cubans who believed that the island would be better off joining the North American union. Nevertheless, Martí's nation building was not marked by hatred for the US, nor did he discard all North American influences in the promotion of Cuban independence. This book shows that Martí's views on the US were complex. Interestingly, Cuba's first president, Tomás Estrada Palma, a close associate of Martí's, was also a US citizen who lived in New York during Martí's exile.

Martí employed his North American connections and close associations to promote the cause of independence. In fact, a close associate of his, the North American attorney Horatio Rubens, lobbied the US Congress to pass the Teller Amendment, which stipulated that the US would not retain Cuba as a result of a war with Spain. To Martí, North America could serve as a model of what to emulate or not, but through Martí's writings it remains clear that he envisioned a Cuban independence victory negotiated directly with Spain, not by the United States, and a nation-state as a sovereign republic, not as history had it.

This Cuban republic, along with an independent Caribbean, would play a fundamental role for Martí, as Cuban scholar Pedro Pablo Rodríguez has affirmed, "in that *fin-de-siècle* conjecture. The Spanish Caribbean had a particular geopolitical value in the face of the soon-to-be opened Panama Canal, and its real independence would contribute to the US not becoming the antithesis of its principles as a nation, indeed, a democratic republic dedicated to the expansion and control over its Southern neighbours."[33] Cuba's independence – and, in a larger sense, the Caribbean's – could serve as a counterbalance to North American power in the region. Unfortunately, when the 1895 Cuban War of Independence against Spain concluded, the peace treaty was not negotiated by the Cubans, nor was Cuban independence established at the time. I expand this line of thought in chapter 2 in a discussion on the Cuban leader's view of a nation's right to self-determination, considering this as a globally inspired theme of Martí's nationalism.

Although nineteenth-century nationalism had strong exclusionary tendencies, Martí's nationalism stood in sharp contrast.[34] A close examination of Martí's independence efforts reveals that he diverged from other late nineteenth-century nationalists, for he did not believe that a nation needed to be based on a single, clearly identifiable ethnic group, and much less one based on pseudoscientific notions of race. The *patria* (nation) to Martí was a living, spiritual entity, divine in nature, and composed of a large community of individuals that loved and identified with Cuba's well-being. In fact, Martí's concept of nation resonates with that of a later nationalist, India's Mahatma Gandhi. Martí, like Gandhi, conceived of the *patria* (nation) as godly, and this divine conception of *patria* stems from Martí's personal views of the human soul as divine. Since, according to Martí, both the human soul and by extension the *patria* were inherently divine, human individuals were also intrinsically connected. In a larger sense, so too were the nations of the world. Therefore, Martí's concept of *patria*, though deserving independence, was not entirely disconnected from a wider community of nations. The Cuban nation composed of the spiritual essence of all those who loved and sacrificed for Cuba was innately linked to its Caribbean home, and in a larger sense to its Latin American sister republics. Therefore, Martí's efforts to liberate Cuba from imperialism and to establish an independent, democratic republic on the island were an exercise of furthering the freedom of the world's spiritually and intrinsically linked nations.

The Global Nature of Martí's Nation Building

Throughout his travels, Martí frequented fraternal lodges, political circles and reading clubs and he actively engaged in charitable groups and speech giving for the cause of Cuban independence. In a globally charged intellectual climate, especially considering the political tensions of the "Cuban question" – whether Cuba should push for independence, maintain its status quo as a colonial dependency of Spain or attempt annexation to the United States – Martí engaged a variety of global intellectual trends. This book reveals that

Martí tapped from these late nineteenth-century currents – a global market of ideas – to nurture a strong nationalist and pro-independence stance regarding the issue of Cuba's future.

As a child of working-class Spaniards, his father a colonial agent and police officer, his mother from the Canary Islands, Martí nonetheless developed a strong sense of Cuban nationalism at a young age. Through his mentor and schoolteacher, the Cuban-born and ardent nationalist Rafael María Mendive (1821–86), Martí became acquainted with Cuban nationalist tradition, particularly by reading Cuban thinkers and reformers such as the Roman Catholic priest Felix Varela (1788–1853), intellectuals such as José Antonio Saco (1797–1879) and others. Both his close reading of Cuba's nationalist and reformist thinkers and his exposure to Mendive's circles of pro-independence-minded intellectuals nurtured Martí's outlook as a youth. This early exposure, and a personal desire to right the wrongs in his own world, would lead to his early anti-colonial activism. The Havana of Martí's youth was the capital of a colony in the midst of a major colonial rebellion, the first independence war (1868–78), and of concomitant repression by colonial authorities as they attempted to suppress it. According to Cuban scholar Reinaldo Suárez Suárez,

> The scaffold was the symbol of colonial power; the first and final tool that the metropolis used against the colony; the peninsula [Spain] against the island [Cuba]; the Spaniards against the Cubans; parents against their children and violent or coercive measures were so extensive in family culture at the time that in Valencia – where Mariano [Martí's father] was from – or in Havana – where they came to live – or in the towns and cities of the peninsula and of the island, the extensive practice existed of parents taking their children to the public square to witness, with absurd pedagogical intent, the [punishment and] suffering of a criminal.[35]

Martí was arrested during this period of Cuba's first major colonial uprising and sentenced to six years of hard labour imprisonment for defending Cuba's right to self-determination. While serving his prison term in rock quarries, Martí sustained injuries that afflicted him throughout his adult life. In 1870, his sentence was commuted to deportation to Spain as a result of his father's colonial connections.

From the time of Martí's first deportation to Spain in 1870 until his death on the Cuban battlefield in 1895, Martí lived most of his adult life outside of Cuba. In his places of exile, whether in Spain, Mexico, Guatemala, Venezuela or New York City, Martí engaged in the major intellectual debates of the time and participated in politically and socially progressive circles. Martí explored the moral reasoning of Freemasonry that transcended specific religious and cultural affiliations. He avidly read and discussed ideas from India and beyond. In New York City, he visited Masonic Temples, Theosophical Societies and attended public lectures by North American progressive preachers and visiting foreign intellectuals. He read an extensive array of magazines, newspapers and community periodicals. He knew about the latest trends within the Italian and Irish immigrant communities in New York City during the 1880s, and he involved himself in causes that promoted equality for African descendants. Martí's independence and nation-building project took shape in this milieu, in a late nineteenth-century world that felt to him increasingly interconnected as he traversed its continents, intellectually and physically.

Martí's writings have often been considered impenetrable. Readers not fully understanding some of Martí's declarations regarding nation building have attributed them to the musings of a literary genius, or to the fact that Martí was an idealist dreamer, or have concluded that he was somehow ahead of his time. Readers and scholars have indeed labelled him a genius and due to this categorization of gifted intellect, certain assertions that cannot be fully understood or defined have been uncritically accepted or have been glossed over. I believe that the apparent limitations in understanding Martí's work are equally a result of the Western/Eurocentric constraints that scholars have employed in reading Martí. This failure to more fully understand Martí's writings and speeches has motivated me to search beyond traditional Western frameworks in analysing Martí's conceptualization and activities of nation building. By abandoning a Eurocentric approach, it can be seen in Martí's work that he promoted nation in terms of sacrifice, selflessness, abnegation and even racial blindness because of largely ignored, globally derived relationships and Eastern-inspired ideas of the nation-state as divine. His personal views, including of the divine nation-state, were nurtured by Asian philosophies, albeit distilled through writings from Spanish and German thinkers, North American Transcendentalists and even his own personal exposure to Hindu thought, while his conception of the nation as racially blind was nurtured by his African-derived relationships.

By pursuing the global origins of Martí's work for independence, I have found that his calls rallying Cubans to serve the nation in battle, and if need be sacrifice their lives, were not mere political strategies that played on his male audience's notions of masculinity in defence of home and country. Instead, his calls to service were motivated by his spiritual convictions that envisioned the nation as a divine entity and the human soul as inherently godlike. Pursuing the global connections of Martí's inspirations allows for an understanding of his view of patriotic duty as a journey of purification, leading to an ultimate Godhead through the same selfless and sacrificial actions. Supporting the cause of national independence thus would not only serve to politically sever Cuba from Spain but would also facilitate the spiritual, evolutionary growth of Martí's own soul. Hence, the revolutionary leader dedicated his adult life to serving Cuba. These are not the only insights made possible when searching for the global origins of Martí's Cuban independence.

The literature on Martí in the Spanish language is vast; less has been written on him in English. Literary studies have focused on Martí as a member and even herald of *modernismo*, the late nineteenth-century poetic movement in Spanish-American literature. Cuba has perhaps the unique distinction of having its major independence activist, organizer and national thinker also be a renowned writer and poet in his own right. Martí, despite his role in Cuban independence and nation building, has a place in history as a major Spanish-American writer of the late nineteenth century. Scholarly attention on Martí has therefore focused on his poetry and his writings in terms of their literary value. His political efforts have been examined profoundly through a local lens. The national lens that scholars have employed for the study of Martí's political activities has been expanded in recent decades to include a wider pan-regional Latin American framework. Traditional studies of Cuban independence and nationalism have also focused on Martí as a heroic martyr cast by the events of the anti-colonial era. A global framework, as I employ in this book, brings together these multiple viewpoints.

Martí has figured prominently throughout contemporary Cuban political and cultural landscapes. For regardless of political persuasion, in the Cuban imagination Martí is considered to embody what it means to be Cuban, personifying an ardent nationalism. Ironically, the Cuban passion for Martí has made him somewhat of an insular figure, little known for his breadth, and his ideas are not clearly understood beyond Latin America or the Hispanophone world. Only recently has Martí been studied by English-speaking scholars, and then mostly in a regional, hemispheric context for his work on Latin American unity. In the end, even these regional studies have been lacking a truly global perspective and significance beyond the boundaries of the nation-state in its Latin American setting.

A holistic, transnational perspective on the study of Martí's efforts requires a wider lens than the local. Martí was a cosmopolitan individual who lived in several international locations, spoke several languages and had cosmopolitan spiritual views. He built bridges between Cuban, Caribbean, Latin American and other global cultures. Indeed, in the words of Martí scholar Carmen Suárez León, he served as a cultural mediator (*mediador cultural*).[36] Martí took a holistic approach to ideologically building and promoting the new nation. He crafted an ideological premise to establish an independent state that included traditional political rallies and speeches, but he also founded newspapers, wrote a children's magazine, composed biographies of figures that served as models in teaching governance and established a decentralized political organization, the Partido Revolucionario Cubano (PRC, the Cuban Revolutionary Party), where he united Cubans of diverse social, ethnic and economic classes into a common cause while minimizing hierarchical tensions – all quite innovative for his time.

The chapters that follow are a globally oriented approach to the study of Martí's holistic efforts at independence. The global approach of this study also enriches the understanding of how Martí conceived the nation and how he advocated against Eurocentric or Western-centric constraints in his conception. In this way, an alternative interpretation of Martí's declarations and actions is based on evidence derived from establishing their global origins. The following chapters analyse Martí's words in the context of the events occurring in his life, the relationships he had and the wider intellectual world in which he lived. The global historical perspective of this study thus avoids interpreting Martí in a vacuum. Martí's nation building reflected that he did not bifurcate his writings into the spiritual and the political, just as he did not dichotomize the activism that was political (to free Cuba) from the social (to eliminate racism). Even though this was not achieved in post-1898 Cuba, the murder of the leaders of the Partido Independiente de Color (the Independent Party of the Coloured) in 1912 is a vivid testament of later generations' failure to implement Martí's vision. And neither did Martí dichotomize his private and public lives; the private Martí was largely indistinct from the public one, a transparency he sought to transmit.

Yet I do not seek to elevate the pedestal that he has been placed on, for from a global, modern perspective, Martí was neither unique nor extraordinary. His ideas may seem singular and exceptional when compared to other late nineteenth-century Europeans or their descendants in the Americas, but when employing a more global scope, as in the following chapters, Martí emerges as exceptionally adept at transferring, translating and transplanting ideas and experiences that had previously existed in different world regions for the cause of Cuban independence. This holistic, world approach to the study of Cuba's independence leader reveals the ways in which he tapped and employed subjects from indigenous America, Africa, South and Southeast Asia, Europe and North America to promote a project that was Cuban, Caribbean and Latin American in character. He was aware of the major anti-colonial movements of his time, such as the 1857 Sepoy Rebellion in India, the Taiping Rebellion from 1850 to 1864 and the uprisings in Egypt against corrupt and expansionist powers. According to British historian C.A. Bayly,

> The state across Europe and the Americas, now empowered by railroads and new military capacity, strengthened itself enormously, especially after the unification of Germany and Italy and the American Civil War. The colonial state over much of the rest of the world also entrenched itself violently for another two generations: in India in 1857, and through the French conquest in Indochina, for instance. One small sign of the future was the creation of a new state in Japan consequent on the Meiji restoration of 1868–72. Broadly, then, we may think of the "age of revolutions" of the years from about 1760 to 1840 as framed in turn by a longer period that stretched from 1720 to 1850, including a phase when the state was unusually dominant stretching from about 1850 to 1914. The expansion of the state was in turn matched by the ideological and military challenges to it.[37]

Martí lived during this time that C.A. Bayly discusses; a time when Spain, if it did not consolidate its control over Cuba after the first failed independence war of 1868–78, at least thought it had, for the Spanish struggle to preserve its Cuban colony was also an attempt to not lose prestige vis-à-vis the other expansionist European colonial powers. With a global perspective, Martí's independence efforts indeed fit into "the ideological and military challenges" to expanding and colonizing states.

Delving into the global origins of how Martí presented the waging of the independence war reveals that the Cuban leader considered the decades-long separatist movement as having a greater impact than just the establishment of a sovereign nation-state on the island of Cuba. To Martí, the struggle would continue the liberation of the Caribbean archipelago. With this in mind, Martí, well aware of the plight of democracy in the United States at the time and cognizant of the uneven independence trajectories of Cuba's Latin American sister republics (as succinctly articulated in his 1895 letter to the *New York Herald*[38]), created a new national vision and organized a successful final confrontation against the Spanish empire.

Although Martí's independence project was nationalistic, its inspirations and impact stretched beyond the island of Cuba. His transnational engagement of ideas and subjects in crafting a modern way of thinking about nation situates him as personifying the increasingly globalized and modern nature of the late nineteenth-century world. Even though revealing the global origins of Martí's work demystifies him by stripping away the notion that he originated these ideas, it nonetheless allows his legacy to gain greater modern-day relevance and to speak across generations.

Hagiographies have been written on Martí's conceptions of the Cuban nation and his life has been interpreted and reinterpreted by Cubans from divergent political persuasions at different times of Cuba's history since independence: after the 1912 brutal suppression of Afro-Cuban political demands; in the mid-1930s, at the fall of Gerardo Machado's dictatorship; during the conventions that crafted the 1940 Cuban constitution; in 1953, at the centenary of his birth, under the cloud of Fulgencio Batista's coup d'état; at the rise of the 1959 Cuban revolution; and in divergent visions of the island's future. The biographies and studies of Martí reveal more how people have perceived him than how he perceived himself. The task of the historian must be to understand individuals and events in their historical contexts, including how people viewed themselves and their own actions. This book is therefore motivated by an interest in the way Martí perceived himself and how he conjured his political programme, considering the world he lived in at the time, and how and why his struggle against colonialism and for a sovereign republic in Cuba was an act in his ultimate quest to "balance the world".[39]

Major Arguments for the Global Origins

In this book, I present the following arguments: first, Martí's independence efforts had significant, yet overlooked global origins beyond the national, regional or hemispheric. Second, these global origins reveal that Martí conceived the Cuban nation-state as divine, a "God *patria*",[40] and not as a distinct entity composed of homogeneous ethnic, historic or linguistic elements, in contrast to other nationalists of his time. Third, his conception of a divine nation-state was a product of his personal spiritual and world outlook, which was influenced by non-Western thought, particularly Hindu-derived notions. Fourth, Martí promoted in spiritual terms his programme to free Cuba from the Spanish empire because he perceived the nation-state as divine, and because it fulfilled his personal spiritual objectives of purifying his own soul. Fifth, Martí should be considered an ally of the pan-African cause in the Americas due to his radical positions against racial ideologies for his time and for his work in improving the conditions of African descendants. His fight against racism was not merely a political strategy, but a perceived personal spiritual mandate.

I also argue that, through global intellectual and physical cross-cultural borrowings, Martí paradoxically employed the "modern" tools of late nineteenth-century global empire-building – such as the steamship, railways, telegraph and newspapers of mass publication – to oppose the propagation of empire. Additionally, his revolutionary politics addressed and gave remedies to the rise of strongman politics (*caudillismo*) in his future, imagined republic. Martí's nation building aimed to create a thoroughly modern nation as a result of a modern ideological and physical war, one that, according to him, would avoid the failings of previous Cuban independence struggles and the pitfalls of the North and Latin American republics. I also argue that he undermined cultural and gender stereotypes of his time, including his idea of the role that women, men and children should play in the future independent nation in order to promote Cuban independence. I also demonstrate how Martí understood and presented the reasons why previous Cuban independence struggles had failed and how he not only identified the problems on a local level, but addressed them in global, humanitarian terms.

The next chapter, "Transmitting Civic Values to Our Future Citizens: Martí's Global Histories for Children", demonstrates that the world history narratives Martí wrote for children in his magazine dedicated to young readers, *Golden Years* (*La Edad de Oro*), constitute critical and innovative components of his programme for national liberation and nation building and encapsulate his nationalist ideology. I argue in this next chapter that Martí wove three major themes throughout his history narratives in order to promote love for Cuban, Caribbean and Latin American identity: the right to self-determination at the national level, the right to self-determination at the personal level and a sense of global humanitarianism. I demonstrate how, remarkably for a child of Europeans writing in the 1880s and early 1890s, Martí considered and portrayed non-European cultures equally, if not as more exemplary. I show in the next chapter ways that Martí affirmed the non-superiority of European civilization and undermined the European civilizing mission that was so much in vogue at the time. In equipping young readers with the moral values that would make for responsible citizens of a budding republic in the Americas, Martí conveyed the history of indigenous American and Southeast Asian societies as a way to familiarize children with global cultures and to intellectually nurture them with alternative cultural traditions, quite striking for the 1880s.

Liberating Cuba was Martí's lifelong dream. He considered that struggle as connected to humanity's search for greater freedom and progress. Although he fought for a nationalist cause (and arguably for a regional one as well), by defending Latin American and Caribbean societies against foreign encroachments on their independence and by undermining ideologies that compromised home-grown culture, Martí looked to the world for inspiration. Martí translated books from English and French into Spanish, beyond *Ramona*, even translating Victor Hugo's *Mes fils*. The next chapter shows how Martí translated, beyond foreign-language books, ideas from distant global regions in order to improve the world of Latin American children. In chapter 2, I therefore examine Martí's role as a translator of global cultures and history and how he presented them to Cuban and Latin American children as a way of transmitting nation-building values that would ultimately serve to strengthen Latin American awareness. In his global history narratives, Martí encodes connections between anti-colonial struggles in French Indochina and Cuba's colonial predicament in the larger context of a struggle for humanitarian causes.

In chapter 3, "The Hindu Inspirations of a Freedom Fighter's Spiritual and World Outlook", I reveal the Eastern ideas that influenced Martí, specifically

Indian thought. I employ the *Bhagavad-Gita* as a tool to juxtapose and disclose these Hindu inspirations. Since Martí's efforts and writings were a product of his personal beliefs and these personal beliefs motivated him to act, one must understand Martí's general outlook on the world and how he considered and related to his existence. In his conception of the world and of his own life, there is a strong component of spirituality that diverges from traditional Roman Catholicism or Christianity. I demonstrate in this third chapter that employing the *Bhagavad-Gita* reveals Martí's spiritual ideas as inspired by Hinduism, particularly through his exposure to the philosophical current of *krausismo* in Spain and in Mexico, and through the Transcendentalists in North America. I also delve into a little-known component of Martí's spiritual outlook, his belief in reincarnation, and uncover Martí's views of the spiritual nature of man; the essential unity of all of humanity; and the journey of the human soul as it purifies itself and ascends to ultimate union with the divine Godhead. These ultimately Hindu-inspired personal beliefs that Martí held have not been adequately addressed or disclosed, and much less in connection with his efforts at Cuban independence.

In chapter 4, "Martí and the Divine Nation-State", I explore how Martí conceived the nation of Cuba as a divine entity and I examine his ideological promotions of the war that would establish that independent state. I employ in chapter 4 a perspective facilitated by Hindu sacred wisdom, again through the *Bhagavad-Gita*, to reveal why Martí considered and promoted the Cuban nation-state as divine – and not merely for the political purpose of gaining foot soldiers for the cause. Further, I analyse the historic *Manifiesto de Montecristi*, considered to be Cuba's declaration of independence to the world, which was signed in the Haitian-Dominican border town of Montecristi on 25 March 1895 as the war against Spain (largely organized by Martí) ignited in Cuba. This fourth chapter situates the *Manifiesto de Montecristi* not only as a Cuban document but as a Caribbean one. I demonstrate, through a globally inspired analysis of the *Manifiesto* and other political writings and speeches, the ways in which the Cuban leader's programme for an independent Cuba was influenced by Eastern traditions, beyond Western philosophies of natural rights, positivism or Roman Catholicism.[41] Therefore, chapter 4's Hindu perspectives disclose the underlying meaning of Martí's declarations as not merely seeking the fulfilment of material objectives, but reflective of Martí's conceptions of the Cuban nation as divine, and service to it as a spiritual task. In this sense,

I explore how Martí preceded India's Mahatma Gandhi, despite the obvious divergence of Gandhi's non-violence and the Cuban leader's promotion of war, as an independence leader who conceived the nation as a divine entity that required selfless devotion and unconditional love.[42]

In chapter 4, I also demonstrate that examining Martí's beliefs in the ability to purify the soul through sacrifice, in the fulfilment of duty and in the spiritual merits of selfless actions – all major tenets of the *Bhagavad-Gita* and Hindu thought – provides a more authentic understanding of how the Cuban leader conceived and portrayed the *patria* (nation). I therefore argue that exploring the relationship between Indian sacred wisdom and Martí's construction of nation enhances the understanding of the struggle for Cuban independence. Such an investigation places Martí's writings in a context beyond recent hemispheric studies on him. By juxtaposing Hindu notions as they relate to Martí's conception of nation, I place the Cuban nation builder, a major Latin American and Caribbean historical figure, in a global, if not globalized context.

In chapter 5, "Martí and the African Diaspora", I address the scant attention paid to the role African descendants played in Martí's life and in his formation of a successful independence programme by exploring his interactions with the children of the African diaspora. Chapter 5 is an African-centred narrative that brings African descendants to the foreground and considers the issues important to the African diasporic cause, such as the elimination of racial ideologies that included notions of adopting white culture for upward social mobility. I also examine Martí's views on race and how they diverged from his Latin American counterparts. More importantly, I argue that Martí's avant-garde notions of race were not merely political strategies to rally Cubans of diverse backgrounds into supporting the independence movement. Rather, his anti-racism was a result of his close interactions with African descendants and, building on my discussion in chapters 3 and 4, also a means to facilitate his own spiritual evolution.

I also present in chapter 5 how Martí perceived the reasons for the poverty and economic deprivation of African descendants in his time: as a consequence of oppression and not as a product of race or biological predetermining factors, as many of his contemporaries argued. In chapter 5, I bring forth again the arguments I made earlier in chapter 2, "Transmitting Civic Values to Our Future Citizens", regarding how Martí undermined ideologies of the European "civilizing mission" and of white superiority. Chapter 5 also sheds light on Martí's relationships with African descendants, particularly his interactions with three historic figures: Antonio Maceo (1845–96), Rafael Serra (1858–1909) and Juan Gualberto Gómez (1854–1933). The relationships that Martí had with these three black Cubans and the way they perceived Martí offer a snapshot of the close working and affective bonds Martí had with people of African descent, and how they affected his anti-racism and his pro-African-American activism in the broadest sense. Through chapter 5's discussion, I demonstrate that Martí worked to correct the wrongs against African descendants as one more way to "balance the world".[43] Moreover, my discussion in chapter 5 serves to situate Martí as an ally of the African cause in the Americas and as a radical democrat for his time.

In chapter 6, "Transmitting Proper Government: Ulysses S. Grant and the US Civil War in Martí's Imagination", I examine a critical, yet little-known biographical essay on former US Civil War general and US president Ulysses S. Grant (1822–85). I demonstrate in chapter 6 how Martí considered and portrayed the US Civil War and its significance to him as a nation builder. The US Civil War may be considered a war of independence or separation by the South from the North, yet to Martí, independence without freedom meant nothing. Therefore the South's overarching objectives of (re-)establishing independent states under a Confederation in order to maintain its system of slavery, its unique social system, were countervailed by the North's goal of expanding freedom. I argue that the North's war had a special relevance for Martí's own independence programme. It allowed him to promote four major themes that were critical to his programme: forgiveness and reconciliation; sacrifice and selflessness; the respect for personal freedoms; and the need for knowledgeable governance. In chapter 6, I reveal that the cause of the North represented an analogous struggle to the one Martí prepared for Cuba and that he conceived and promoted it as a struggle to free a part of humanity in bondage that had suffered gross injustice, much like Cuba under Spanish colonialism. To the nationalist leader, Cuba's independence movement resonated with the US Civil War and with what he considered to be the North's noble struggle. I also present how Martí portrayed the Civil War in spiritual terms, for he considered it to be one that advanced the cause of liberty, much like Cuba's would promote the freedom of the Caribbean, complete that of Latin America and secure that of the Western Hemisphere. In this sixth chapter, I show the complexity of Martí's representation of Grant by depicting the former US president in positive and negative lights, and particularly by using Grant as a model for governance and with the future government of an independent Cuba in mind. In chapter 6, I disclose Martí's visionary critiques of US expansionism into the Caribbean and decipher his prescriptions on how nation-states should be run.

I also argue that the essay on Grant and the Civil War served as an exercise for Martí in writing "national" history. He had an interest in writing a history of Cuba's own great national epic, its first major independence struggle, the Ten Years' War (1868–78).[44] He envisioned the new Republic of Cuba as a product of a noble and sacred war of independence. Therefore, the experiences of the new American republic, the US that emerged after the Civil War, were important to him as an example for the new Cuba that would also rise in the wake of an independence war, where Spaniards, white and black Cubans, along with other ethnicities, would need to reconcile and govern their nation – much as Martí believed the post-Civil War United States attempted to do. I assert that his critiques of Grant are powerful and are particularly instrumental in deciphering what Martí envisioned for the Cuban republic as it emerged from its noble war of liberation. I therefore complicate scholar Ricardo Rojas's assertions that "[Martí's] objective was to 'hand the entire country a free *patria* [nation]'. What would come later is something that is not in his texts and that can neither be comfortably inferred nor deciphered from his body of work."[45] I argue, however, that one should not assume that what exists today as Martí's body of work is what he intended it to be. His untimely death at the hands of the Spaniards in Cuba's independence war put an end to that corpus. I thus present that what Martí considered as proper state practices are encoded in his descriptions of the US Civil War and of Grant's presidency, particularly since he told a close friend in a private letter that he wrote the essay thinking of Cuba and Mexico.[46]

In promoting an independent nation, Martí was aware that the means of establishing the new nation had to be holistic. The process of building the nation would have to cover as many spheres as possible, and particularly take advantage of the techniques and technological tools of the modern world. In ushering in a new world in Cuba, he not only had to convince fellow Cubans of the political and economic viability of independence, but also had to build on the line of Cuban nationalist thinking, particularly in ideological terms. Martí knew that he had to create new national foundational myths and stories that inspired and nurtured the memory of the Cuban nation. He knew that his new nation required a history, a "national myth" of sorts. Martí's biographical essay on Grant is an exercise in history as national story. In this sixth chapter, I also demonstrate how the Grant essay reveals the influences that nineteenth-century European Romantic historians had on the Cuban nation builder, particularly Jules Michelet (1798–1874). Martí read the leading European and North American historians of the time. By knowing how Eurocentric historians constructed their arguments and created their historical narratives, Martí became better equipped at unpacking European racial ideologies and notions of the imperialistic "civilizing mission". Martí indeed admired Michelet's poetic presentation of historical events[47] and he emulated this type of historical writing with indigenous American and even non-Western subjects.

Through the chapters that follow, I aim for Martí's ideas to be better understood not merely as political statements, though in a literal sense they were, but more as spiritual, humanitarian declarations that speak to the essence of men and women everywhere. In fact, successful liberators throughout modern history have spoken to this spirit. Mahatma Gandhi in India and Martin Luther King Jr in North America are examples of freedom fighters whose projects were framed in larger, humanitarian terms. Despite both Gandhi and King basing their movements on non-violence, Martí may be considered in their league of liberators, for to the Cuban leader war would be the final sequence of a movement that had already been launched. He presented it in noble terms without hatred for the enemy. To Martí, the independence struggle would culminate in the "necessary war" (*la guerra necesaria*); it was unavoidable and inescapable. He did not give cause to it or initiate it, but he believed that through his efforts and new way of conjuring and promoting it, the final war would not only succeed but be justified by bringing freedom, sovereignty and agency to the Cubans.

The personal struggles that Martí endured in the course of organizing and campaigning for an independent Cuba brought him significant pain and suffering. He never fully established a home life. His wife left him in 1891 while he lived in New York City and she returned to Cuba with their only son, seeking "protection" from the Spanish consul general. In her eyes, Martí did not fulfil his duties as a husband, father and provider. He never saw them again, a profound blow to him, caused by his refusal to concede to her wishes of living a quiet, comfortable life as an attorney on the island. Martí experienced prison sentences, exile, alienation and loneliness. Beyond his avant-garde, visionary critiques of expanding US imperialism in the Caribbean and Latin America; beyond his struggle against racism and to improve the lives of the underprivileged; and beyond his organizational, literary and oratory talents at successfully uniting disparate ethnic and class groupings into a successful relaunching of Cuba's war for independence, Martí appeals to us because in his struggles we may see part of ourselves in him: how we are confronted with everyday choices that either lead to our physical comfort or to our emotional/psychological evolution, often at the price of that same perceived comfort. This inner side of Martí, a more human side of him, need not strip from him the roles of independence leader, nation builder and humanitarian. Identifying the global origins of his independence efforts facilitates this understanding.

In fact, Martí's messages seem to rise separately at later times, in different parts of the world, by different speakers and in different contexts. Mahatma Gandhi's views of *swaraj* (self-rule), of national autonomy requiring personal autonomy, are echoed in Martí's struggle against slavery and racial discrimination. A Cuban nation cannot be free on a larger scale, to Martí, if an individual in chains cannot decide his or her own future. Martin Luther King Jr's assertion that people should be judged not by the colour of their skin, but by the content of their character resonates in Martí's declarations that individuals come together by affinity of character and not by race. Political figures such as Gandhi, King and Martí nevertheless share a historic legacy as visionary liberators who were spiritually grounded. Gandhi, King and Martí's efforts were not only politically motivated, but all three sought to fulfil a spiritual call to duty of liberating their respective constituencies. All three sought to correct the wrongs of humanity in their part of the world.

Throughout Martí's writings, particularly in personal letters to friends and political associates, he described his struggle to free Cuba as an exercise in "balancing the world".[48] Martí considered his fight for a free Cuba to be inextricably linked to a larger humanitarian struggle. Cuba, as the largest island in the Caribbean, served as an example of the crucible that was the Caribbean region, a fact he mentions in the *Manifiesto de Montecristi*. As a colony of Spain, among the first where European imperialism established itself beyond the confines of Europe – and as, Martí hoped, Spain's last colony – Cuba represented a heterogeneous society suffering from enslavement and racial discrimination. Cuba also represented, to Martí, a fertile land in a geographically favourable position between North, Central and South America, wasting away under Spanish mismanagement and corruption. Martí viewed Cuba as a microcosm of larger humanitarian struggles of the world's peoples. He considered the fight for Cuba as part of the larger struggle to make the world more just and free. Without a free Cuba, neither the Caribbean nor the Americas would be truly liberated. As long as Cuba was a dependent entity, the Americas would not be a sovereign hemisphere. Indeed, in the *Manifiesto de Montecristi*, Martí describes how Cuba would serve to usher the freedom and independence of other Caribbean nations and establish a sovereign Americas. One can only imagine had Martí survived the Cuban independence war how his struggle would have continued; certainly Puerto Rico's liberation was on the mind of Cuban independence fighters. One can only speculate that the Dutch, British and French Caribbean possessions also possessed a possibly imagined drive to establish a fully free and independent Americas.

Martí and the Caribbean

Martí considered the war for Cuban independence, beyond a physical battle of two opposing armies, as a spiritual movement that was nurtured by the Caribbean. Dominicans, Haitians, Puerto Ricans, Jamaicans and Caribbean peoples from different islands and coasts contributed financially, physically, intellectually and spiritually to the cause of Cuban independence. In this context, Martí was not only a Cuban nationalist and advocate of pan-Latin American consciousness, but he was also a child of the Caribbean, born and raised in a Caribbean island that was fully integrated and that experienced the greater dynamics of the Caribbean world. The Caribbean as that crucible of the world, as Martí himself mentions in the *Manifiesto de Montecristi*, is a place where European wealth was derived from the forced work of hundreds of thousands of enslaved Africans and their descendants, as well as from Asian indentured labourers and from workers from all parts of the globe. The Caribbean provided products, markets and resources to European nations, the major imperial powers of Martí's time.

The significance of the Caribbean in this context has been underplayed in studies of Martí. The Caribbean, as the first "globalized" space of our planet, where Europeans, Africans, Asians and indigenous Americans coalesced – this Caribbean world, the by-product of a globalization begun in the late fifteenth century, plays a central role in Martí's work. Cuba, the homeland to be liberated, is a central place of that globalized "crucible" of the Caribbean, and contains a population having commercial and social relations that reflect the wider archipelago. Indeed, the culminating document of Martí's independence efforts, the *Manifiesto de Montecristi*, is foremost a Caribbean document. Martí wrote it on the island of Hispaniola, near the Haitian-Dominican border, not merely because it was the home of Máximo Gómez, the head of the Cuban Liberation Army, and because they were on their way to the Cuban battlefields, but also because Montecristi provided a suitable setting that underscored the significance of the Caribbean in Cuba's liberation. This further underscores that Martí's nation building was fundamentally a Caribbean project. The major themes of his work – confronting external political and economic control; transcending externally imposed ideologies of racism and subjugation; and embracing a unity in diversity – are all Caribbean issues that are present throughout Martí's work. Martí envisioned a liberated Cuba serving the greater Caribbean. Yet he has been known more as a Latin American figure than one of the Caribbean, in part because he wrote and worked mostly in Spanish and his legacy has faced the linguistic barriers of a Caribbean that speaks English, Dutch, French, Kreyòl and Papiamento, among others.

To balance the world, to rectify the injustices of the planet, to set right and correct the course of events, to free fellow humans from a life of misery, dependency and oppression – all were the diverse dimensions of the human struggle that Martí idealistically sought to amend and remedy in public and private spheres. The following chapters connect Martí's search to balance the world with his fight for an independent Cuba. Considering that his first exposure to the world was the violent and oppressive colonial Cuba of the 1850s and 1860s as a child, when he sought early on to right the wrongs of Cuban society, such as slavery and the island's despotic government, Martí supported independence as a way to set right his own world. His later political actions, such as supporting the first Spanish republic during his deportation at seventeen from Cuba to Spain, and later defending the plight of indigenous peoples in Mexico and Guatemala and that of African descendants in New York City, were also efforts at "balancing the world". Martí's struggle for independence was therefore connected to an even greater global and cosmic cause. In this sense, the global origins of his search for an independent Cuba, as I argue in this book, magnify the significance of his legacy, for his fight for Cuban independence was essentially a humanitarian struggle that, at the core, stripped of its Cuban character and paraphernalia, was a struggle motivated by the same sentiments that drove other freedom fighters throughout our world – namely, the right to live a life of dignity, free from political, social and economic oppression. In Martí's mind, to remedy the wrongs of the world required correcting the injustices of his own world first, his beloved Cuban homeland.

Figure 2. José Martí and María Mantilla at Bath Beach, New York, 1890.

2. TRANSMITTING CIVIC VALUES TO OUR FUTURE CITIZENS
Martí's Global Histories for Children

Esas cosas de niños son un trabajo del alma.
Those childish things are a labour of the soul.[1]
— *Letter to Rafael Serra, July 1889*

Renowned Cuban poet and scholar Fina García Marruz affirms how "Martí had a perception of the universal, of the world, and not merely a political, social or an artistic vision. It therefore should be articulated and the radii [of this vision] should not be seen independently from their centre. For all thought – and not his alone – is based on a vision of the world – whether implied or clearly stated, whether complex or simple – that explains it."[2] In this chapter I attempt to articulate one of the "radii" of Martí's vision of the world as it relates to Cuban independence. In my view, a major "radius" – the global histories in his children's magazine – may appear at first glance as separate and distinct from his struggle for independence, yet the children's journal he wrote while in exile in New York City is a microcosm of his thought, permeated by a strong desire to remedy the problems of the contemporary world and the intent to forge a new, imagined one. The children's magazine helped Martí to usher what did not yet exist, but was envisioned.

Golden Years (*La Edad de Oro*),[3] Martí's magazine for youngsters, written entirely by the Cuban leader, promotes his diverse ideas on how to improve relationships between parents and children and among children themselves. The magazine also serves to elevate the role of the child in society by teaching tomorrow's citizens, future government and business leaders what he considered to be the modern moral and civic values. Martí expected that, after having absorbed the conspicuous or implicit lessons in his magazine, a Cuban child would help forge, establish and sustain a new, free and independent Cuba, and all children would gain a stronger love and pride for the Latin American and Caribbean regions.

As a young man, Martí had a major paternal figure apart from his father. The Cuban-born educator and nationalist Rafael María Mendive (1821–85) taught and ran the school in Havana that Martí attended. As a teenager, Martí often visited Mendive's home, where he would study in the Cuban educator's personal library and engage in pro-nationalist discussions that most likely were not allowed in his Spanish parents' home. When the colonial authorities arrested Mendive in 1869, accusing him of inciting rebellion, Martí regularly visited his mentor in prison. Both were ultimately, separately deported from Cuba to Spain for their nationalist activities. Mendive's lectures and the informal pro-nationalist gatherings in the Cuban educator's home were Martí's first significant exposure to nationalist thought as a boy. Surely, when remembering Mendive, Martí realized the impact that childhood education could have in the evolution of an individual's political consciousness.

In this chapter, I argue that the world histories that Martí wrote to educate children in 1889 are evidence of the global influences and connections of Martí's independence programme. Unlike most late nineteenth-century nationalists who considered a nation to be a union of people who shared common ancestry, language and culture, Martí believed that people from diverse origins could form a nation. Since the nation, to Martí, could be heterogeneous, variegated ideas could also serve to promote, in his mind, the values that would build the new Cuban nation-state from a Spanish colony. Not surprisingly, to instil in children the civic values he believed citizens of a new nation should have, he looked beyond Cuba. Martí wrote global history narratives as a means to promote an inclusionary, racially blind, humanitarian form of nationalism that aimed to establish Cuba as an independent nation, completing the cohort of Latin American republics and setting it as a catalyst for the further liberation of the Caribbean. In this sense, the history of the world, acquired through extensive reading of books on history and science as well as historical fiction, and reflected in his published essays in Latin American newspapers,[4] provided a palette for Martí and a means to transmit to children the nation-building values he deemed critical for the envisioned republic.

In this chapter, I examine Martí's global histories in his children's magazine and reveal three main ideological themes that he wove throughout them. The three themes are strongly related to his notions of spirituality. Above all, the three themes demonstrate, in a visible way, the global origins or "globalism" of Martí's nation building. Throughout the global histories he wrote for children, Martí promotes, first, the right to self-determination at the national level, supported by a belief in the non-superiority of European races and civilization; second, the right to self-determination at the personal level, upheld by the belief in the need for citizens to be critical of authority and to subvert restrictive ideologies that legitimize undemocratic government; and third, an espoused humanitarianism that promoted the essential unity of humanity, emphasizing the importance of selfless actions and attitudes for sustaining a republic. Also related to the theme of humanitarianism was the need for citizens to be globally conscious individuals in order to transcend the Cuban nation's geographic insularity.

Martí's global historical narratives for children may have escaped the eye of scholars of nationalism for the same reason they eluded official Spanish censorship at the time: the implicit messages strengthening nationalist sentiment against imperialism and illegitimate authority are not plainly visible. They are encoded in a larger global narrative that aggrandizes the political mission of decolonization. Martí's messages simultaneously defied late nineteenth-century Western conventions by redefining what children should be taught in history lessons of the world's past.

Historians have neglected Martí's global historical narratives in part because Martí never presented himself as a historian. The global histories appear in a magazine written for children and may not have been taken seriously as history for this reason. Martí's repertoire of writings and speeches currently spans twenty-five published volumes and the critical edition of his complete works, currently under preparation by the Centre for Martí Studies in Cuba, is expected to reach over forty; two relatively short global history narratives may understandably be ignored. Nevertheless, these two narratives, "The Story of Humanity, Told through Its Houses" ("La historia del hombre, contada por sus casas") and "Journey through the Land of the Annamese" ("Un viaje a través de la tierra de los amanitas"), in the August and October 1889 issues of *Golden Years* should be considered a critical and innovative component of his independence programme.[5]

Like the Indian independence leader Jawaharlal Nehru (1889–1964) after him, who strengthened Indian nationalism through depictions of global history in his letters to his daughter, Indira Gandhi, Martí presented global history in magazines dedicated to Latin American children in order to edify Cuban national consciousness and promote love for the region – as he later did for adults in his seminal 1891 essay "Nuestra América" (Our [Spanish-] America).[6] Martí's pan-Latin Americanism has been well established in the literature on the Cuban nationalist.[7] Moving beyond his Latin American regionalism, I employ a global framework to focus on the globalism of Cuba's tripartite relationship with the Caribbean, Latin America and the world, a sequence that emerges when delving into his global history narratives for children. Moreover, Martí's Latin American– and Caribbean-based patriotism served to establish Cuba as part of a greater whole. This was an important way for him to think about space, belonging and politics in between the national, the regional and the global. On a practical level, shifting the *madre patria* (mother country) from Spain to a *madre América* (mother America) served to ideologically anchor Cuba in a spiritual commonwealth of Latin American and Caribbean sister republics, while moving the island nation-state away from the shadow of Spanish colonial despotism.

Global Histories for Children: Inspiration and Context

Martí's project to sever Cuba from the Spanish empire was intrinsically related to Cuba joining a free pan-Latin American concert of nations. It was also related to the furthering of the Caribbean's liberation, and ultimately to securing the freedom of the Western Hemisphere.[8] He echoed this sentiment in his letter to Francisco Henríquez Carvajal, a missive known as Martí's Caribbean testament, written in Montecristi, Dominican Republic, on 25 March 1895, days before he set sail for Cuba to join the newly ignited war against Spain.[9] The Cuban leader expressed that the liberation of Cuba and of the Caribbean would "serve to accelerate and [to] set the balance of the world".[10] Although Martí never specified that pan-Latin American unity would take the form of an overarching government like the former thirteen North American British colonies under a federal one, he nevertheless advocated for a united Latin American front against foreign encroachments on Spanish America, whether in the form of Spanish colonialism or motivated by the US expansionist politics he witnessed in the media and political milieu of the United States after his arrival in New York City in 1880.

He especially had in mind US efforts to expand economic hegemony in Latin America through a pan-American monetary conference (a convention to further a US-led hemispheric monetary and customs union) that began deliberations in Washington, DC, in October 1889, during the final month of publication of *Golden Years*.[11] Martí was well aware of the proceedings of the conference, since his secretary Gonzalo de Quesada was also the secretary for the head of the Argentine delegation, Roque Sáenz Peña, and the Cuban leader personally influenced the Latin American delegates through speeches and conversations with them. He witnessed first-hand US efforts to economically penetrate and even dominate Latin America, which he described in several 1889 articles to *La Nación*, a newspaper of Buenos Aires.[12] Regarding the conference, Martí warned his Latin American readers that

> there has never been in the Americas, from independence to this day, a matter requiring more thought, nor that compels the highest vigilance, nor [that] demands a more clear and detailed analysis than the invitation by the powerful United States, full of unsellable products and determined to extend the areas it [already] controls in the Americas, to lead the less powerful nations of the Americas who are linked by free and useful trade with the nations of Europe, to secure a league against Europe, and to end agreements with the rest of the world.[13]

He further urged, "Spanish America knew how to save itself from Spain's tyranny and now, after having witnessed with impartial eyes the circumstances, cause and motivations of [this] invitation, it must be said, for it is the truth, that the time has come for Spanish America to declare its second independence."[14] These words, written while he also published *Golden Years*, clearly reveal Martí's mindset regarding not only the need for Cuba to be free from Spain, but for Latin American nations to be independent from the United States. This sentiment is transmitted in the global history narratives of *Golden Years*.

Surely Martí had another conference in mind: the one held in Berlin in late 1884 and early 1885, where the major European powers partitioned Africa among themselves. European imperial powers, particularly France and Britain, and to a lesser extent Germany, began to increasingly accept Latin America as being within the United States' field of influence and expansion. Later in the 1890s, a similar posture emerged during the case of the Venezuela-British Guiana border dispute, when Britain, the world's major power at the time, allowed itself to be challenged by the United States; certainly, the United States interpreted this British acquiescence to the US stance on the border issue as European acknowledgement of US hegemony in its Latin American and Caribbean "backyard".

In the end, Martí's fear materialized when the United States intervened in 1898 in the Cuban War of Independence, an intervention disguised as humanitarian assistance to the Cuban insurgents that went unchallenged by the European powers at the time and ultimately resulted in the establishment of a protectorate over the island. Although the Cuban leader did not live to see this denouement, at the time when he wrote his children's global history narratives he was well aware of the political trends that increasingly favoured the United States influencing the destinies of the nations of Latin America and the Caribbean. This influence was not only based on economic considerations of searching for new markets for its growing industrial output, but it was also supported by ideologies of "manifest destiny" that dictated that for the good of the "white" race, the United States should expand into territories that "naturally" belonged to it. Martí agonized over these circumstances. With this in mind, Martí believed that the best way to contain US expansionism was to create a united front of free, democratic and sovereign Latin American nations that included a free Cuba and Caribbean. This strong desire to establish a sovereign nation, free of colonialism, motivated Martí to teach the civic and moral values that the free citizen of tomorrow, the child reader, needed in order to protect his or her republic from any type of threat to its well-being.

The two global history narratives that I survey in this chapter, "The Story of Humanity, Told through Its Houses" and "Journey through the Land of the Annamese", reflect Martí's desire to allow "other [world] areas" to "enrich the crop [of Latin American children]", yet as he explained to his lifelong Mexican friend Manuel Mercado, "the farming must be done according to our soil; our children, we must raise as men and women of their time, and as men and women of the Americas".[15] Martí's journal for children, *Golden Years*, also contained fictional stories, poetry and essays on current events, yet it carried throughout a pedagogical, thoroughly modern moralizing intent; its deep political purpose was affirmed by Martí separately in an August 1889 Uruguayan newspaper article stating that "to be a citizen of a republic is a difficult thing, and [it] must [be] exercised from childhood".[16] *Golden Years*, as Cuban scholar Salvador Arias has pointed out, may also be considered the partner publication for children to the later *Patria*, the official newspaper of the Cuban Revolutionary Party; both periodicals were edited entirely by Martí.[17]

The year 1889, when he wrote *Golden Years*, was one of significant activity for Martí. He published these children's global history narratives in the midst of heavy political campaigning, speech giving and fundraising activity for the cause of Cuban independence and while representing Latin American interests in the United States. Since 1886, he had reported extensively on North American subjects as a foreign correspondent for leading newspapers in Mexico City, Buenos Aires, Caracas and other Latin American cities. In 1889, he wrote twenty-five newspaper articles for Latin American newspapers, such as *La Nación* of Buenos Aires, *La Opinión Nacional* of Montevideo and *El Partido Liberal* of Mexico City.[18] On 25 March of that same year, Martí wrote a major rebuttal to the menacing US nationalist idea of manifest destiny, "Vindication of Cuba", in the *New York Evening Post*. On 10 October 1889, he passionately called for a free Cuba in nationalist rallies in New York City's Hardman Hall.[19]

In addition to these prolific writing and campaigning activities, he served as honorary consul general of Argentina, Paraguay and Uruguay in New York City. As mentioned earlier, the narratives in *Golden Years* were also written while he participated in the Pan-American Monetary Conference in Washington, DC. Regarding this conference, Cuban scholar Rodolfo Sarracino affirms that

> 1889 and 1890 were among the most trying years of his political mission. During the Pan-American Conference negotiations, he met the most talented Argentine and Latin American diplomats who were able to hold independent positions vis-à-vis an already powerful US. His efforts helped neutralize the US Republican government's actions, spearheaded by James G. Blaine, so that a group of Latin American nations would mediate between the US and Spanish governments to facilitate the purchase of the island of Cuba from Spain.[20]

While Martí drafted and published *Golden Years*, the real possibility emerged of the United States finally annexing Cuba, after several attempts –

an event that would have struck a mortal blow to his independence struggle.[21] Furthermore, Cuban author Cintio Vitier considers the years 1886 to 1891 as a pivotal "fifth stage" in Martí's political struggle. *Golden Years* was written, according to Vitier, during this period "of the maturing of political circumstances, emotional enlivenment and ideological definition".[22]

The pedagogical intent of intellectually strengthening individuals – what Fina García Marruz referred to as the edification of an honest individual[23] – also emerges later in Martí's work with *La Liga* (the League), a charitable institution that educated Afro-Cuban and Afro-Caribbean adults in New York City.[24] By 1891, he accepted the Cuban patriot Néstor L. Carbonell's "call of destiny" for him to speak to a group of Cuban immigrants in Tampa on the evening of 26 November in order to raise funds for the Cuban cause.[25] In the following year, 1892, he established the Cuban Revolutionary Party to channel all activities and resources for the Cuban independence war. "The Story of Humanity, Told through Its Houses" and "Journey through the Land of the Annamese" were therefore written during these intense political and philanthropic activities. Although many have ignored the political value of these global history narratives, Martí's stories contain strong political directives through his depictions of non-Western history, and they were written in the context of significant political efforts. The children's history narratives hence provide a concise overview of Martí's nationalist ideology.

After having earned a reputation as a gifted orator, political campaigner and organizer during the years preceding his publication of *Golden Years*, many contemporaries chided Martí for writing a journal aimed at children, a project perceived as infantile and distracting.[26] Nevertheless, since he wrote these narratives during a period of serious political activity, they deserve our attention for the political, nation-building values embedded within them. Perhaps his August 1889 letter to his friend Manuel Mercado in Mexico is the moment when Martí most reveals his intentions in writing the narratives. He expressed to Mercado that he had "entered in this [*Golden Years*] endeavour, for while [he] waited to die in another greater one" – referring to the independence war against Spain – "in this one . . . [he] could place, in an enduring and useful manner, all that had been maturing, in pure blood, through [his] soul".[27] It may be that the sense of his own mortality with an impending independence war made the need to educate the next generation all the more urgent.

Beyond the Cuban and Latin American children that would read "The

Story of Humanity, Told through Its Houses" and "Journey through the Land of the Annamese", Martí also intended the enclosed teachings to reach the adults reading the stories to them. Indeed, Martí had adults in mind when writing the children's narratives. In the same August 1889 letter to Mercado, he asks his friend "to please tell [him] honestly what [Mercado's] children thought of the magazine" and also what he "as an adult thought of it".[28] In this way, it may be that Martí conceived of a larger audience of illiterate or partially literate adults who might have benefited from the narratives.

The Cuban leader sent five hundred copies of *Golden Years*'s first issue to Mercado in Mexico and charged him with "finding a central agent that would distribute them throughout the largest cities"[29] so that local governments would use the magazine in primary schools, as well as to satisfy the hopes of the magazine's financial supporter, Aaron Da Costa Gómez,[30] for commercial success. Martí expressed to Mercado that he had received orders from Argentina for 1,250 copies of the first issue and that copies were also sent to Cuba.[31] The total sum of issues published or sold in Latin America is unknown, but through Martí's personal letters it appears that nearly ten thousand copies were printed for each of the four issues.[32] *Golden Years* proved popular in Latin America and received favourable reviews, particularly from leading intellectuals on the cutting edge of Spanish-American literature, such as the Nicaraguan poet Rubén Darío and the Mexican journalist Manuel Gutiérrez Nájera. Enrique José Varona, a renowned Cuban intellectual, affirmed at the time that although "it's a journal for little ones, [it] deserves the attention of all the grownups".[33]

The World of Late Nineteenth-Century Children's Journals

An analysis of the world of late nineteenth-century children's magazines enriches our understanding of the context and literary milieu that *Golden Years* emerged from, and of other factors that motivated Martí to write these narratives, such as a desire to modernize children's literature in the Spanish language. Inspired by late nineteenth-century English-language children's journals that he read during his fifteen-year stay in New York City, Martí also wrote *Golden Years* to challenge the manner in which traditional Spanish-language children's magazines taught youngsters. This sentiment is echoed in the view of *Golden Years* expert Eduardo Lolo, that the Cuban leader's magazine represented an example of the new line of modernist (*modernismo*) work, for

> Martí goes from the newspaper [journalism] genre to a literary one (traditionally distinct categories) with the same ease that he crosses other ones. The result of which (already developed by the author in his [separate] writings for adults), is [a type of] literary journalism, another characteristic of the Spanish-American *Modernistas* that for the first time [through Martí's work] made its appearance in narratives for children. All this is additionally very post-modern, since the [traditional] divisions between genres [and disciplines] are being increasingly blurred.[34]

This cross-borrowing of genres in his literary work is also linked to Martí's search, according to Lolo, for "what is new, appealing, unfamiliar, of immersing [himself] into other disciplines, by a constant urge to be original and by [a certain haste] in transcribing current events or what he recently read into a chronicle".[35] All this supports Martí's drive to modernize Spanish-language pedagogy.

Martí believed that English-language magazines, such as *Harper's Young People* and *St Nicholas*, could serve as models for his children's journal.[36] He patterned fictional stories in *Golden Years* after, and interspersed references to characters from, stories such as Frances Hodgson Burnett's *Little Lord Fauntleroy*, which appeared in the November 1885 issue of *St Nicholas*.[37] In other stories in *Golden Years*, Martí adopted tales and poems from Helen Hunt Jackson and Ralph Waldo Emerson.[38] Emerson's and other writings by New England Transcendentalists would be a major source of inspiration in Martí's ideological formation.[39]

The most popular children's journals sold in Spain and Spanish America in the late nineteenth century were *Los Niños* (*Children*), *El Camarada* (*Buddy*), and *El Museo de la Juventud* (*Museum for Youngsters*). These Spanish-language journals contained articles such as "The Lives of Saints" and "The Moral Sentiments" that urged children to submit to higher authority and to depend on adults for making their decisions. Martí emphasized the opposite, promoting the need for children to think freely and independently. While these moralizing Spanish publications were being imported into Cuba, Cuban authors attempted to write alternative narratives suitable to the island's environment, which indirectly fostered the growing sense of Cuban nationalism.

Press censorship in Cuba under the colonial regime, however, did not allow conspicuous challenges to Spanish rule. Cuban journals such as *La Niñez* (*Childhood*), emerging nearly a decade before *Golden Years* and to which Martí contributed, experienced heavy pressure and ultimately ceased publication.[40] Martí therefore knew not to directly antagonize colonial authorities and also how to carefully craft narratives with nation-building values encoded in histories of distant global societies.

The innovative North American, British and French children's journals that Martí read diverged from the prevailing Spanish children's magazines that carried messages for children such as "submission and dependency are so important in this world that going against them would be cause for innumerable evils".[41] Martí looked to the British, French and North American traditions of children's writings as an alternative source from the constraining Spanish ones. In this sense, Martí remained faithful to the views expressed in his letter to Mercado that "other [world] areas may enrich the crop [of Latin American children]", but Martí's final published product would be specifically designed for the cause of raising Latin American awareness through new perspectives for children.

Martí was inspired by the line of modern children's narratives, dating from the first English- and French-language stories written by Charles Perrault (*Tales and Stories of the Past with Morals*, 1697), Daniel Defoe (*Robinson Crusoe*, 1719) and Jonathan Swift (*Gulliver's Travels*, 1726), and continuing to the first early nineteenth-century journals created for children in England, such as *Boy's Own Magazine* and *Aunt Judy's Magazine*; and in the United States, *Juvenile Miscellany* (1827), *Harper's Young People* (1879–99) and the better-known *St Nicholas*, published from 1873 to 1939.[42] Other sources of inspiration were Lewis Carroll's *Alice in Wonderland* (1865), Louisa May Alcott's *Little Women* (1868) and Mark Twain's *The Adventures of Tom Sawyer* (1876) and *Huckleberry Finn* (1884).[43] Martí also found inspiration from the French author Édouard René Lefebvre de Laboulaye (1811–83) and from Hans Christian Andersen (1805–75), translating and adopting stories from these authors for *Golden Years*. Laboulaye was also a journalist and pedagogue who publicly criticized the policies of the Second French Empire, publicly defending the freedoms of religion, press and secular instruction. Laboulaye also wrote the introduction to *Reformes dans les îles de Cuba et Porto Rico* (Paris, 1869), a pro-Cuban treatise written by Porfirio Valiente y Cuevas, a Cuban independence fighter and consul general of the Republic of Cuba at arms in Paris.[44] Again, the link between the Cuban independence movement and educating children through imaginative tales emerges.

Martí also created the magazine to be visually stimulating. He incorporated the latest graphic techniques, as images in "The Story of Humanity, Told through Its Houses" and "Journey through the Land of the Annamese" demonstrate. He followed the graphic techniques developed by Nicolas Pellerin, director of the Épinal graphic studios in France, who substituted lithographs for literature from 1845 onward, ultimately developing the first comic strips. In writing "The Story of Humanity", Martí closely followed the weekly journal *L'Exposition de Paris de 1889*, published in forty issues beginning in October 1888. The French journal was entirely dedicated to the 1889 Paris World's Fair and included many drawings, sketches and graphics.[45] Martí's integration of different techniques from non-Spanish sources for his Spanish-language children's magazines underscores the innovative and global character of Martí's project to edify Cuban and Latin American children with nation-building values.

Sadly, though, Martí's innovative children's journal ran only four issues, abruptly ending in October 1889, despite material for many more issues. He ceased publication due to philosophical differences with the journal's financier who "for conviction or commercial apprehension wanted [Martí] to speak of 'the fear of God'" in his stories and not to challenge prevailing conventions, as he confessed to his friend Manuel Mercado in a November 1889 letter.[46] Martí suffered the pressure of his ideas being perceived as subversive by those invested in the traditionally moralizing tales of Spanish children's journals.

Despite Martí's long-standing desire to publish an innovative magazine for Latin American children, first expressed in an October 1888 letter to his friend Enrique Estrázulas, and notwithstanding his personal attachment to the magazine, Martí expressed to Mercado that "[this] is the first time, despite the hardships of my life, that I abandon something that I have truly endeavoured".[47] Conflicting ideological convictions prompted Martí to abandon the enterprise. Even though *Golden Years* assuaged his emotions of being an absent father (writing the children's journal relieved the longing to be with his young, distant son in Cuba), and despite the inspiration provided by his strong paternal affections for María Mantilla (the young daughter of the widowed Carmen Mantilla, owner and manager of the boarding house where Martí lived while in New York City), and though it earned praise from leading avant-garde intellectuals, Martí refused to readjust his writing in order to please the magazine's financial supporter's more conventional outlook on what to teach children.[48]

An Innovative Way of Transmitting National Pride

"The Story of Humanity, Told through Its Houses" and "Journey through the Land of the Annamese" promote Martí's unique elaboration of nationalist ideals that are void of the exclusionary politics that characterized late nineteenth-century US and European nationalist doctrines. Studies on European nationalism have represented the nation as a construct of ruling elites to gain the consent of people opposed to them on other grounds.[49] Mass nationalism developed in nineteenth-century Europe not as a "fixed product of economic and social developments but [as] an evanescent construct, rising in response to crises and elite campaigns to mobilise patriotic sentiment, dwindling away at other times, always in flux".[50] A recent study of the 1895 Cuban independence war that Martí ideologically shaped succinctly expresses the Cuban leader's unique sense of nationalism:

> Martí thought of nationalism as demiurge emanating from the people themselves. Like the Italian Giuseppe Mazzini and other romantic nationalists, Martí believed that the nation existed as an intuition, an internalized sentiment, before it became an institutional reality. A more fundamental category than the individual or state, the nation to Martí was the precondition not only for effective state formation, but for individual self-realization and the collective flowering of humanity in its constituent national communities.[51]

This sense of nationalism as emanating from within the people finds analogous sentiment in Ernest Renan's spiritual conceptions of nation, which Martí praised in separate writings, such as in his 10 December 1881 commentary to *La Opinión Nacional* of Caracas.[52] Martí's views of the "collective flowering of humanity in its constituent national communities" also compare favourably to the view of Immanuel Kant, who also suggested a league of nations as a way to secure the freedom of humanity. However, Martí did not articulate the need for one Latin American or world government, yet he did believe in the world's nations operating together in concert. In a report on the Pan-American Monetary Conference that Martí wrote on 30 March 1891, the Cuban leader expressed that "the nations of the world should meet together in friendship and as often as possible in order to begin replacing with a system of global rapprochement, over . . . isthmuses and across seas, the system, forever extinct, of dynasties and parties".[53] Martí articulated what Bolívar had envisioned decades earlier with his Congress of Panamá. The Cuban leader foresaw and preceded US president Woodrow Wilson's project of a League of Nations. Martí's system of international relations, however, would be more democratic than Wilson's, for Martí envisioned a new system of nations replacing long-standing dynasties and elitist groups that dominated international relations.

Certain aspects of Martí's nationalist ideas were not original, finding inspiration in major European and North American secular thinkers like Henry David Thoreau and other North American Transcendentalists. Martí's originality lies, however, in his distilling European and North American nationalist ideas and developing a new nationalist doctrine free of racial demarcations for the consumption of Cuban and Latin American heterogeneous audiences, in the line of Simón Bolívar and Toussaint Louverture before him – yet unlike these intellectual predecessors, Martí wrote children's stories about the world's past to promote civic, nation-building values, as well as to develop a new way of thinking for youngsters. To build a nation and to edify an individual were two of the Cuban leader's prime objectives.

"The Story of Humanity, Told through Its Houses": Origins and Context

"The Story of Humanity" is modelled after the French essays on the 1889 Paris World's Fair pavilions that showcased the development of human dwellings. Although Martí did not visit the Paris World's Fair, he based his narrative on a thorough reading of French essays on the 1889 exposition. Specifically, the issues of *L'Exposition de Paris de 1889, Journal Hebdomadaire* that ran stories by P. Legrand, entitled "L'Habitation humaine: Histoire de la maison à travers les siècles", in instalments from 25 May to 27 June 1889, and other stories that appeared in *Revue de L'Exposition Universelle de 1889* form the basis of Martí's narrative.[54] With an interest in how technological innovations of the modern industrial age he lived in could benefit Latin American and Caribbean societies, Martí also wrote other stories in *Golden Years* and opinion pieces for Latin American newspapers, such as on New York City's Brooklyn Bridge, for example. All illustrate a fascination and an idealist stance regarding the technological feats of his time.

Martí's narrative in "The Story of Humanity" also reflects a tradition of historical writing that may be traced to the methodologies developed by scholars such as Giambattista Vico (1668–1744) and Cesare Cantù (1804–95), who pioneered the use of architecture as a reliable historical source for understanding past societies.[55] Martí bridges the past and present by writing on a thoroughly modern event of his time, the World's Fair, while simultaneously highlighting the past of global societies. Scholar of Martí studies Marlene Vázquez Pérez affirms that "more remarkable is the comparison and contrast between distant realities and the familiar reference points of a child's own world. For that reason, Martí's narrative depends from its beginning on comparisons between the past and present, between the way of life in the nineteenth century compared to the one of centuries past."[56]

In *Golden Years*, Martí contradicted traditional late nineteenth-century notions, earning the ire of conservatives, by showcasing cultures commonly considered inferior to European ones. In this respect, Martí preceded anti-colonial writers of the early twentieth century who also undermined European cultural hegemony by highlighting the value of non-Western history. In this sense, Martí's views were original for their time. Nevertheless, he did not completely abandon European models. His narratives also echo leading European thinkers, such as Niccolò Machiavelli's "civic republicanism" and other defenders of Italian city-states in the fourteenth and fifteenth centuries who viewed "the survival of the republic, and of the freedoms which it represented, dependent upon the civic virtue of its citizens".[57]

In Martí's global history narratives, the reader also confronts G.W.F. Hegel's notions of history – for Hegel, however, only Europe's was valid – as the progression of human consciousness and freedom. Martí, as Cuban scholar Medardo Vitier affirmed, "sets his beliefs in a teleological framework. His system of belief is founded on this precept. Examining the precepts underlining Martí's philosophical ideas, the first is a belief in a design, not always clear or concrete, but noticeable in the general development of an individual's behaviour and sense of being."[58] Therefore, Martí's narratives reflect an idealism, possibly a teleological spirit, in that human beings improve through the passing of time. Martí, like Hegel, believed that cultures could be assessed in terms of their degree of development and complexity. Nevertheless, Martí and

Hegel diverged in that the latter viewed non-Western history as "outside of the world's history, not part of the overall process of [global] development",[59] whereas the former, remarkably for a child of Europeans, considered and portrayed non-European cultures equally, if not as more exemplary, therefore affirming the non-superiority of European civilization and undermining the European civilizing mission. In the words of Cuban historian Pedro Pablo Rodríguez,

> Martí avoided oppositional extremes, almost as a cognitive method that prioritized the understanding of the "whole". The particular element, the genuine [component], the indigenous [aspects] of our [Latin American and Caribbean] cultures were to him as valuable and beneficial to the universal human spirit, as much as the indigenous elements of other nations and cultures [of the world]. He was an advocate of cultural exchange [and believed] one culture should have full respect for another, since to him, no culture was better or worse. The indigenous was, then, to [Martí] an expression of the universal, and the universal [spirit] manifested itself through the diversity of indigeneities. Dominating and conquering cultures and civilizations [of the world] were not justifiable nor morally valid to him.[60]

These notions support the first theme in the globalism of Martí's nationalism, his belief in a nation's right to self-determination. To Martí, societies were not superior to others, but were superior to their own pasts. Fighting for Cuban independence and promoting Latin American and Caribbean regional pride and awareness, Martí would not accept or promote European thinkers' notions of the superiority of Europe or of European culture over non-Western ones – even though he avidly admired European cultural expressions through encounters with French art and Italian cuisine[61] while he lived in New York City.[62]

The Right to Self-Determination at the National Level

In "The Story of Humanity" Martí undermines notions of European civilizational superiority by favourably comparing the Mayans of Mesoamerica to the Gauls of Europe. As Cuban scholar Roberto Fernández Retamar remarked in a study on Martí, "[the Cuban leader] belongs, by chance or by conscious choice making, *to another world*. That is where he needs to be situated in order to truly understand his work, its objectives and nature. It is not with the men of the capitalist nations [that create underdeveloped ones] which we need compare him to, but rather with those from the colonial and semi-colonial world that would [later] be called 'underdeveloped'."⁶³ Therefore, following the above assessment, one may better understand why Martí highlights the indigenous civilizations of America by comparing them to European ones, for he knew well why colonized or semi-colonized peoples suffered.

In "The Story of Humanity", Martí writes that the *menhir*, a prehistoric upright stone created by the Gauls in Europe to commemorate major past events, is comparable to Mayan structures in Mexico, referred to by the Mayans as the *katún*. The Mayans and Europeans had similar traditions, according to Martí, despite the Mayans being unaware of the Gauls' existence "on the other side of the ocean".⁶⁴ The Mayans, Martí affirms, created similar architectural objects like the distant Gauls and Germanic tribes of Europe. By providing examples of how diverse cultures created different objects for similar purposes, Martí leads the reader to reflect on the underlying commonality of humanity; different cultures through time and space indeed have points in common.

In the narrative, the Cuban leader eschews presenting the Mayans as less technologically advanced than the Europeans. Rather, through depictions of architectural structures, Martí persuades the reader to view European and American indigenous cultures as equally significant to human history, for they had comparable structures that achieved similar cultural objectives. Even though the Mayans were unaware of the existence of the Gauls, they created similar architectural structures. Implying that the Mayans did not replicate European culture, Martí undermines prevailing notions of Europeans bringing "civilization" to the indigenous Americans.

In "The Story of Humanity" Martí expresses to the child reader that "when European men lived in the Bronze Age, they built better houses, although not as detailed or perfected as the Mexicans and the Peruvians of the Americas who lived simultaneously in two ages", because, as Martí explains, the Mexicans and the Peruvians "continued working with flints when they had already developed their gold mines, and their temples with golden suns like the ones in the sky, and their *huacas*, which were Peruvian cemeteries, where they placed their dead with the [potted] jars and jewels they used while living".⁶⁵ By not specifically referring to indigenous American societies in the narrative as Inca or Aztec when describing their homes as more perfect and detailed than the

Europeans', and identifying them instead in nationalist terms as "Mexicans" and "Peruvians", Martí implies that the Mexicans and Peruvians of his time owe their cultural legacy not only to the conquering Europeans, but equally to the indigenous peoples. Referring to the pre-Columbian indigenous peoples as "Mexican" or "Peruvian" affirms that Martí's presentation of history had political implications. By not differentiating between those contemporaries identified as "Mexican" or "Peruvian" and the precolonial indigenous peoples, Martí persuades the child reader to embrace the indigenous past and not to reject it – a thread of nativism indeed emerges throughout Martí's narrative.

By referring to people in Mexico and Peru as "Mexicans" and "Peruvians" before European invasion and after decolonization, Martí de-emphasizes the European elements in Mexican and Peruvian societies. By continuing to refer to indigenous peoples in "The Story of Humanity" as "Mexicans" and "Peruvians" and not as "Spanish-Americans", Martí implies that indigenous American culture within Spanish-American society had successfully overcome the four centuries of European political and cultural suppression.

Martí also rebalances notions of the Spanish or European conquest of the Americas as a positive event. He teaches the child reader that the Spaniards destroyed indigenous architecture, "everything the Indians had built", except the structures the Spanish depended on and could not replace. Spaniards and Europeans are not presented as saviours or harbingers of civilization and progress. Rather, Martí portrays Europeans as "barbarians", uncivilized people who tore everything down because of their ignorance – and with detrimental effects, for they were unable to effectively substitute much of the indigenous technology.[66] Indigenous American technology surpassed European technology in many ways by providing indispensable water and creating a system of paved roads that, according to Martí, allowed for communication and commerce that were essential for the survival and dominance of transplanted European societies in the Americas.

Martí challenged children to think that "civilized" societies need not develop according to European patterns. The pre-Columbian Mexicans and Peruvians lived simultaneously in the Stone and Bronze Ages, since they continued using flints while mining precious metals and constructing beautiful buildings of gold. A deeper reading of Martí's narrative reveals that his descriptions of indigenous American societies, employing techniques of both ages and living simultaneously in two developmental periods, are a moral commentary on the value of maintaining older traditions, particularly indigenous American ones, even while modernizing society.

He echoed this sentiment of treasuring what is home-grown and genuine in a separate fictional story in *Golden Years* where a young girl chooses for sentimental reasons an old, black-coloured, ragged doll over a more expensive one made of fine white porcelain. By demonstrating that indigenous Americans maintained older techniques and simultaneously embraced new technologies, Martí implies that technology is not necessarily incompatible with long-standing traditions. In this context, Martí's statements emerge as a critique of the wholesale adoption of European cultural norms, driven by the pursuit of the latest fashions, material consumption and waste, which he particularly critiqued in separate newspaper articles on North American life. Although it would be difficult to imagine a young child understanding this point, an adult reading this story would certainly grasp it.

In "The Story of Humanity", Martí further implies that for societies to be considered worthy of admiration, patterns of European development need not be projected onto them, in this case pointing to indigenous American societies. One should not assume, according to Martí, that societies must develop along European linear patterns in order to reach significant levels of complexity. Martí teaches the child reader that societies developed in different ways and that different types of development are not inherently or morally inferior or superior, only divergent. These points are particularly remarkable considering Martí lived in a time of rising racism when Europeans employed judgements of "technological and civilizational development" along with racial notions to craft colonial policies towards non-Europeans.[67] Martí injects in the narrative the assumption that if Europeans (for example, the Spanish) are not the sole purveyors of civilization, then Cuba and Latin America need not be controlled by these outsiders. The narrative serves to decouple the history of the Americas from Europe in much the same way he envisioned Cuba detaching itself from the Spanish empire.

Teaching children to view the indigenous peoples of the Americas, long portrayed as inferior, as more perfect, more beautiful, equally valuable and in many ways technologically superior complicates traditional late nineteenth-century presentations of non-European societies as backward. This lesson was also meant to undermine the ongoing Latin American debate at the time of "civilization vs. barbarism", notions articulated by the highly acclaimed

Argentine author and later president Domingo Sarmiento. With "The Story of Humanity, Told through Its Houses", Martí introduces notions that he will later fully develop in his seminal essay "Nuestra América" ("Our America", 1891), for as Fernández Retamar has shown, already by 1877 the Cuban leader rejected the opposing dichotomy of "civilization" vs. "barbarism" and saw in Latin America a harmony of "natural" and "civilized" elements.[68] Martí diverged from the social expectations of his late nineteenth-century Western environment by promoting the idea that indigenous cultures should not be dismissed in order to strengthen Spanish-American consciousness.[69] Martí edified Cuban nationalism and, in a larger sense, pan-Spanish-American pride by teaching children to embrace the local past, regardless of how the "civilized" Europeans and their descendants perceived it.

Martí further complicates notions of European superiority in "The Story of Humanity" by promoting the environment as a critical factor that determined levels of societal complexity. He teaches that indigenous American and European societies emerged and developed in similar ways, for instance, when

> man began living where it was less cold and at a higher elevation ... it was where he lived longest, [and] soon came to learn and discover metals and to produce [objects]. It is in the most fertile and elevated parts of the continent that transatlantic man first civilized himself. In our America, the same occurs: in the highlands of Mexico and Peru, in the high valleys of good soil, the indigenous Americans had their best cities.[70]

By describing how "civilized man" appeared in the Americas in similar environmental and topographical conditions as in Europe, Martí undermines notions of European exceptionalism or of inherent biological superiority. Indigenous American societies urbanized like the European ones when facing similar environmental conditions.

Separately, Martí also rejected the North American historian George Bancroft's notions of US or Anglo-Saxon exceptionalism, writing about Bancroft that "his image does not appeal [for] in a mere soldier, pillaging may be normal; but any strike against [the natural] rights [of men] in their own land or in a foreign one, is a crime in an intellectual man".[71] As I will later present in chapter 6, regarding Martí's biographical essay on Ulysses S. Grant, the Cuban leader admired Bancroft's history writing – like he admired Grant as general – but not Bancroft's politics or public postures, just as he did not approve of Grant as president.

In addition to the environment, Martí promoted the idea that cross-cultural exchanges also shaped societal conditions in "The Story of Humanity". Martí believed that societal development was not a product of a linear progression of unique and innate intellectual qualities. Societal development, in Martí's mind, was not related to the time needed for developing inherent qualities, but to the willingness and the ability to acquire knowledge of the world and of other cultures.

In this sense, Martí believed that cross-cultural interactions facilitated growth and development. He expressed that sophisticated, "civilized" societies were a product of effective responses to the environment and to cross-cultural interactions. Martí's views that societies grew by exchanging knowledge and technology do not diverge from those of later global historians such as William McNeill, who highlighted the role of cultural diffusion in societal development.[72]

Martí's belief in the role of cross-cultural interactions underscores the globalism of his nationalism – a fresh understanding of global history, as he presented, complicates notions of the European civilizing mission. He undermines the belief in accepting foreigners as superiors, detonating the power of late nineteenth-century imperialist messages. His environmentally based conception of societal development also unpacks racially exclusionary nationalist notions, shifting the reasons for development from race to environment, thus allowing individuals of all backgrounds to engage in civil society and ultimately promoting wide democratic self-rule.

In his other global history narrative, "Journey through the Land of the Annamese", which appeared in the final October 1889 issue of *Golden Years*, the theme of a nation's right to self-determination appears again in Martí's challenge of the superiority of European civilization. While in "The Story of Humanity" Martí depicted diverse societies of the world through architectural structures, particularly praising indigenous societies in order to undermine the European civilizing mission, in "Journey" Martí presents the history of a Southeast Asian country (modern-day Vietnam) in order to critique colonial abuses in Cuba. No evidence has been found that Martí was aware of Spanish participation in the initial 1850s–60s French aggression against Vietnam from the Philippines, for he would have lambasted the Spanish for spending resources in the French colonial empire that could have been more aptly employed in the administration and welfare of its own colonies.[73] One of Martí's constant justifications for Cuban independence was that Spain did not have the resources to ensure the welfare of Cuba. Martí was nonetheless well informed of major events in Asia, such as the French consolidation of Indochina in 1887 and the nationalist uprisings there, through his extensive reading of domestic and foreign newspapers and magazines while living in New York City from 1880 to 1895.

Employing the history of Annam, an ancient state now part of Vietnam, to promote democratic values, Martí conveys throughout "Journey" how the people of Annam suffered at the hands of outsiders. Martí engages European cultural stereotypes of the time and overturns them in order to defend the Annamese viewpoint. By presenting how Europeans perceived these Southeast Asians, and rebutting their prejudicial notions in a dialogue with a fictional Annamese character, Martí teaches children that conceptions of beauty are relative and, significantly, that European perceptions are not necessarily better than Asian ones.

Martí describes the Annamese as follows: "they don't appear with beautiful-like bodies, nor do we appear handsome to them: [the Annamese] say that it is a sin to cut one's hair, since nature [has given] us long hair, and he who believes himself wiser than nature is presumptuous".[74] Martí continues to undermine the ideology legitimizing European rule over others by describing how the Annamese say that "men do not need to have stronger, wider backs because the Cambodians are taller and more robust than the Annamese, yet in war, the Annamese have always defeated their Cambodian neighbours". Martí further undermines racial ideology by writing in the voice of an Annamese character who tells the young reader that

> one's gaze should not be blue, because the colour blue eludes, forsakes, and deceives, like the clouds in the sky and the water in the sea; and that white should not be one's [skin] colour, for the earth which gives all that's beautiful is not white, rather it's like the hues of bronze of the Annamese; and that men should not have beards, they are beast-like: even though the French, who are now masters of Annam, respond that, regarding the [issue of the] beard, the Annamese are only jealous.[75]

These words are quite remarkable: they show a white man himself presenting views challenging what Western culture perceived as beautiful and valuable. To the average Cuban or Latin American child who most likely never met a Southeast Asian, an Annamese or a Cambodian, Martí teaches that, when following Western cultural stereotypes, Western judgements of how the Annamese look are flawed. What the Annamese find attractive is not necessarily what Europeans may deem beautiful. Martí undermines European stereotypes of superiority and contradicts prevailing views on which attributes are attractive because of his belief in the inherent equality and commonality of all people.

Beyond critiquing European ideologies of racial superiority, the voice of the Annamese character also serves to legitimize the Annamese fight for freedom against the French. Martí writes,

> [although] we are yellow, small, sickly, and ugly; we simultaneously craft bronze and silk; and when the French came to take our Hanoi, our Hue, our wooden-palaced cities, our ports, full of bamboo houses and reed boats, our fish and rice warehouses, even then, with these almond-shaped eyes, we have known how to die, by thousands and thousands, to stop them in their paths. Today they are our masters; but tomorrow, who knows?[76]

Although they may appear inferior to Western eyes, Martí portrays the Annamese as proud, defensive and defiant. Throughout the narrative, the Annamese emerge as morally superior to the French (that is, Europeans), for they know how to defend their homeland – an allusion to Cubans who had fought for the independence of their homeland for decades. Martí also weaves a nativist thread in this story: the Annamese have demonstrated their ability to fight for their freedom from foreign powers. Conveying that French colonial rule should not be automatically deemed permanent, Martí declares in the voice of the Annamese character, "Today they are our masters; but tomorrow, who knows?"

This "who knows?" indicates that foreign rule of Annam is not assured, and if the Annamese have laid their lives to block the path of the French in the past, as Martí expresses, then in the future they will most certainly be expelled from Annam. For a late nineteenth-century children's story, these views of undermining traditional Western perceptions of non-European peoples and of empowering the colonial subject are indeed subversive.[77] The French in Annam were not on a mission of peace, invading Annamese cities and taking their wealth. In this sense, Annamese rebellion is justified, implying that individuals should rise in defence of communal and national freedoms. Martí employed the history of Annam's struggle against the French as a metaphor for Cuba's fight against Spanish domination and also for Latin Americans to resist the nineteenth-century expansionist policies of the United States and other predatory powers.

In *Golden Years*, gender roles are often polarized according to the rigid binarism of the times, where "little girls are told that they are the mothers of tomorrow, while little boys will grow up to be virtuous 'gentlemen' ".[78] Nevertheless, Martí's messages of resistance include female Annamese warriors, portrayed as fierce heroines who expelled the Chinese from their trenches and fought for Annam's freedom. Martí's masculinized-for-its-time portrayal of two Annamese females demonstrates that Martí also departed from traditional late nineteenth-century attitudes by not shying away from presenting women in the same light as men. In his global historical narrative, young girls, although expected to be raised as future mothers, could nevertheless identify with Annamese female warriors.

Questioning French rule over Annam in "Journey" and presenting Europeans in "The Story of Humanity" as not the saviours or harbingers of civilization, Martí promotes in both narratives that indigenous peoples have equal, if not superior, capacities to invaders. Promoting this in a journal for children in a time when notions of replicating European and North American norms prevailed in Latin America was not only innovative, but also audacious. The French are not portrayed in "Journey" as coming to civilize; the Annamese are already highly civilized, according to Martí's descriptions. He presents the Annamese as having had material wealth, "beautiful cities with palaces and stock-piled warehouses".[79]

Martí declares in the narrative that the Annamese appear like a "society of followers" despite having "raised three storied pagodas" and having "built gigantic porcelain and bronze lions". This is what happens, according to the Cuban nationalist, when societies "tire of defending themselves: they haul their master's carriage like beasts, while the master riding in it, [looks] tanned and fat". Martí metaphorically describes the exploitive nature of the colonial master/subject relationship, hinting at Cuba's condition by expressing that "it's a difficult life for small societies". Martí informs his reader that the Annamese have also defended themselves against the Chinese and the Siamese who "have wanted to conquer them".[80] The Annamese knew how to fight for a greater, noble cause and to sacrifice their lives while achieving a higher purpose – in this case, Annam's freedom. Martí echoed these views in an August 1889 letter to Manuel Mercado where he indicated that he wrote *Golden Years* while waiting for the greater sacrifice of redeeming Cuba from its colonial condition.

Martí underscores the importance of fostering local, indigenous culture by relating that the Annamese sought to nurture knowledge of their history in the face of French imperial indoctrination. He relates in the narrative that the Annamese increased their presence at local temples and theatres, seeking to learn of their local traditions. According to Martí, the Annamese "have been living as slaves" and they "visit their pagodas often, for there, their priests speak of the saints of their homeland who are not those of the French: they visit their theatres a lot where they are not told things to laugh about, instead the history of their generals and of their kings: they kneel to listen, quietly, [to] the history of their battles".[81] The image of the Annamese engaged in nurturing local traditions in their spaces, free from French intrusion, facilitates Martí's message of the importance of keeping indigenous customs alive. By showing Latin American children how the Annamese subverted the cultural norms imposed by the French colonial system in frequenting Annamese cultural spaces, Martí affirms the view that Cuba and Latin America should nurture their cultural heritage as well, and not indiscriminately import or adopt foreign ideas from Europe or North America.

Affirming a nation's right to self-determination, the Cuban leader teaches that "smaller societies" have significantly more difficulty in surviving as independent states vis-à-vis larger nations, yet they still have a right to exist. Having lived as a youngster during the failed 1868–78 Cuban war for independence and seeking to reignite the struggle, Martí's depictions of the Annamese's long fight reflect his belief that Cuba deserved independence, especially after having fought for it for decades, and even in the face of North American annexationist drives and of Spanish colonial loyalist sentiment in Cuba.

Martí explains in the narrative that the Annamese sought alliances with other nations who offered friendship and who presented themselves as saviours, only to later enslave those they originally claimed to help. Martí indirectly instructs the child reader to be wary of seemingly well-principled declarations of assistance that later turn duplicitous. Separately, in his last writings before dying in battle in 1895, he described the possible detrimental effects on Cuban independence if the United States were to intervene in the war against Spain. The narrative allowed Martí to indirectly transmit his views on resisting foreign oppression and on the right for Cuba to be independent. Employing the history of a distant Southeast Asian nation's struggle for freedom allowed Martí to cloak the issue of Cuba's own without directly antagonizing the Spanish, and on a practical level to avoid Spanish censorship of his children's magazine in Cuba.

The Right to Self-Determination at the Personal Level

The second theme that promotes nation building and independence emerges through Martí's challenge of constraining ideologies and demagogies, particularly since these legitimized Spanish rule over Cuba during his lifetime. In "The Story of Humanity" Martí encodes, in descriptions of Spanish and Greek dwellings, the value of eschewing religious dogma. The Cuban leader renounces a Christian bias in describing these dwellings by expressing that "in Spain the Romans had also ruled, but later the Moors came to conquer, and built those temples known as mosques, and those palaces that seem the thing of dreams".[82] He then explains that Renaissance architecture emerged when "the Christians began to not believe as much in heaven as before". When people in Europe began to think about "how great Rome had been: they celebrated Greek art for its simplicity: they said that there were already too many churches: they looked for new ways to make palaces: and all that created a new way of constructing, like the Greeks, known as the architecture of the 'Renaissance' ".[83] Gothic architecture, according to Martí, was a product of men believing in the "heaven of the Christians",[84] and he describes the Renaissance in "The Story of Humanity" as a time of "richness and art, of great conquests; therefore, there were many nobles and merchants with palaces. Never had humans lived in such beautiful houses."[85] Martí conspicuously displays his predilection for the Renaissance as being a "glorious" period, notions surely shared by his contemporaries. Nevertheless, according to Martí, this "glorious" period was a result of men believing less in a Christian "heaven" or in religion. He therefore implies that there are benefits to abandoning constraining religious dogma and focusing on simplicity and rationality, like the ancient Greeks.

The implicit lesson in the narrative of rejecting religious dogma is linked to the idea of freedom of thought and expression. Martí begins "Journey" with an adaptation of a traditional Jain folk tale of six blind men and an elephant. In Martí's version of the parable, four blind men travel to the palace of an

Indian prince to determine the size and appearance of an elephant through their sense of touch. Upon meeting the blind men, the prince declares that the "blind men are saints". The Cuban leader affirms in the narrative, through the prince's voice, that "men who seek knowledge are saints: men should learn everything on their own and not believe without questioning or speak without understanding or think like slaves who are told what to believe: go forth, four blind men to see, with your own hands, what the docile elephant is like".[86] The example of the prince and the blind men serves Martí in transmitting the importance of independent, critical thinking. Later in the narrative, by depicting stories of Buddhist monks, he condemns the use of overarching ideologies such as religion to advance ambitions of power and material gain.

Martí relates a story of a corrupt band of Buddhist disciples who employed Buddhist religion to further the earthly ambitions of a king. By chastizing the nefarious Buddhist monks of Annam, Martí reiterates his interpretation of the European conquest of the Americas. In "The Story of Humanity" and in other narratives of *Golden Years* – such as on Father Bartolomé de Las Casas, defender of indigenous Americans – Martí readjusts perceptions of the conquest and colonization of the Americas as a positive event. Martí's critiques of the corrupt Buddhist monks allow him to indirectly censure the role of Christianity in the conquest and colonization of Spanish America without directly injuring the sensibilities of his Latin American Roman Catholic readers. Martí describes that "some [of Buddha's] disciples did what the king wanted, and went with the king's army to take away the freedom from the surrounding countries, under the pretext of teaching Buddha's truths", implying a parallel to Catholic missionaries who took the freedom of indigenous Americans in the name of the Spanish king. Martí relays that "then there were others who said that these disciples were lying and that the king was stealing, and that the freedom of a small nation is more important to the world than the power of an ambitious king" – the analogy between corrupt Buddhist and Catholic monks is undeniable. Some Roman Catholic mendicants, like Father Las Casas, chastized the use of Roman Catholic ideology to exploit indigenous Americans. There were also virtuous Buddhist monks, according to Martí, who revealed to the people "the lies of the priests that serve the king for money" and told them that "if Buddha were alive, he would have said the truth, that he did not come down from heaven, instead [he came] like all other people, with heaven within themselves"[87] – a statement no doubt expressing his own spiritual views of the inherently divine nature of human beings, which I explore in the following chapter.

Martí's depictions of dissenting Buddhist disciples admonishing the work of corrupt Buddhist monks teach children the value of having the courage to call out abuses of power as they happen and to correct wrongdoings wherever they occur, "for [the] love of humanity".[88] During the late nineteenth century, teaching children the courage to undermine authority when they deemed it illegitimate was considered subversive by those who taught children to be unquestionably obedient, such as the publishers of Spanish-language children's magazines. Throughout "Journey", Martí identifies who are the wrongdoers: the French imperialists, the Siamese, the Chinese and the corrupt Buddhist monks. All have played a role in taking the land away from the Annamese. Yet Martí's idealism emerges when he transmits throughout the story that actions of resistance should be based on love, and that the evil person should be treated with "compassion" as a "sick man who needs healing"[89] – thereby injecting his own spiritual notions, echoed elsewhere in his writings and speeches, of "loving" the enemy and even loving the Spaniard, but not the repressive Spanish government.

As Cuban scholar Fina García Marruz has indicated, "the first thing that one must remember when [attempting] to explain this reiterated rejection of hatred that is visible throughout Martí's revolutionary programme is the early identification that he [particularly] makes during his childhood and adolescence between the colony and hatred". If the colony (and colonialism) represented hatred – in this case, French colonialism in Annam and metaphorically the Spanish in Cuba – then love was the "revolutionary energy" that would liberate the nation.[90] The right to self-determination at the individual level – to make one's own conscious choices, to critique and, finally, even to love – would also free individuals of oppressive ideologies.

Humanitarianism

The third theme in the globalism of Martí's independence and nation building is the promotion of humanitarian ideals. Martí's humanitarian approach in transmitting civic values that build nation and elevate Latin American consciousness diverged from "the radical nationalism, the 'ethnicism' of late nineteenth-century Europe" that focused on who "belonged to the nation on the basis of 'race' " and that "claimed to have a 'scientific' answer to the problems of society".[91] Humanitarianism is a strong theme throughout both global history narratives in *Golden Years*, as well as a major aspect of Martí's own vision of the world.

In "The Story of Humanity", Martí describes diverse dwellings, such as the Hindu, Hebrew and Egyptian, but it is in his description of the ancient Greek dwelling that he reveals his belief in the value of friendship. Describing the Greek Parthenon, Martí encodes the significance of friendship, material modesty and embracing different cultures:

> Decorating motifs are not [on the Parthenon] just for decoration, that is what ignorant people do with their clothing and homes, rather, beauty emerges from a certain type of music that one feels and that cannot be heard because proportions and measurements have been executed in a way that fit with colour, and there is no element that does not fit precisely, nor a [decorative motif] placed where it disrupts. It seems as if the stones of Greece have souls. They are modest and humble and appear like friends to those who see them. They appeal to one's heart, like good friends, appearing as if they can speak.[92]

Martí anthropomorphizes the Parthenon, imbuing it with human qualities and depicting it as a friend of the child reader. The Parthenon personifies friendship and modesty, values Martí seeks to transmit. In affirming the human qualities of beauty and friendship, Martí teaches a moral lesson regarding the type of structure that truly is distinctive and regarding which elements ignorant people praise. This sentiment is echoed in his advice to the young María Mantilla, daughter of the family who ran the boarding house where he lived in New York City. In a letter written on 9 April 1895, a month before his demise on the Cuban battlefield, he wrote to the young María,

> Elegance, my María, is in [having and showing] good taste and not in its price. Elegance of dress – the real and impressive one – is in the elevation and strength of the soul. An honest soul, intelligent and free, makes the body more elegant, and [gives] more power to a woman, than fashions from the most expensive shops. A lot of shop, tiny soul. Whoever carries a lot inside, does not need much to show on the outside.[93]

His humanitarian-oriented idealism emerges again in the conclusion of "The Story of Humanity". Demonstrating the way his nationalism lacked the ethnocentrism of prevailing late nineteenth-century nationalist doctrines, Martí concludes the global history narrative by expressing how now all the peoples of the world know each other better and visit each other [more]: and in each society there is a way of building, according to whether it's hot or cold or whether they are of one race or another; but what appears new in cities is not the way of building houses, rather that in each city there are Moorish, Greek, Gothic, Byzantine, and Japanese houses, as if [we were] in a happy period when all humans treat each other like friends, and [finally] join together.[94]

Martí concludes "The Story of Humanity" as a story of "joining together", of unity and of friendship. Martí positively depicts modern cities, new technologies and a new era as allowing different cultural expressions, such as Moorish, Greek, Gothic, Byzantine and Japanese styles, to exist simultaneously, reflecting an idealist stance regarding cosmopolitanism and the technological feats of his time. One should not forget that the story was inspired by the Paris World's Fair, commemorating the one-hundred-year anniversary of the French Revolution, and the Eiffel Tower, a marvel of engineering at the time, built in celebration of the same anniversary.

In "Journey", Martí features Buddhist teachings by presenting to the child readers of *Golden Years* the story of the Buddha – the story is particularly striking for its promotion of Buddhist principles to Latin American children most likely educated as Roman Catholics. In his discussion of the Buddha in "Journey", Martí promotes the idea that perceptions are not always reflections of reality; they may be false illusions. He mentioned this earlier in "Journey" when describing how the Annamese appeared submissive to the French rulers, but in reality were not. Beyond equipping young readers with the moral values that make for responsible citizens of a budding republic, Martí also conveyed Buddhist principles as a way to familiarize children with global cultures. Martí's discussion of Buddhist principles that may coincide with Christian beliefs underscores his view that distant societies share commonalities in ideas and traditions, as seen earlier in his portrayal of the Mayans and Gauls who, though distant from each other, had similar commemorative architectural structures. Martí indeed conceived the freedom of the Cuban nation as "the precondition for the collective flowering of humanity in its constituent national communities".[95]

Further supporting the humanitarian orientation of Martí's nationalism, he describes in "Journey" how nirvana, according to Buddha, is reached by understanding that one should not live for vanity, nor should one covet what others have, nor should one harbour remorse, nor should one doubt the harmony of the world or disregard nothing in it or be hurt by the insults and envy of others, nor should one rest until one's soul becomes like the light of an aurora that fills the world with beauty and clarity, and cries and suffers for all that's sad in it, and until one sees oneself as a healer and guardian to all who have reason to suffer.[96]

By improving humanity and elevating one's larger world, one achieves nirvana, according to the views expressed in "Journey". Redemption or nirvana is not limited to serving an ethnically based, exclusionary nation. Martí imbues "Journey" with Buddhist spiritual teachings that persuade Latin American children to serve others, regardless of skin colour or origin.

The Cuban leader further develops the theme of humanitarianism and selflessness by describing how well-principled Buddhist monks advised the populace that "the love of humanity and honesty" leads them to become "as if they were not of flesh and bone, but of a clear light". The Buddhist monks who were honest preached, in Martí's words, that "for the evil person, [one should] have compassion, as for sick men who need healing and to the good ones [one should] give strength, so that they won't tire of inspiring and serving the world: now that's truly heaven, and divine joy!"[97] "Journey" showcases in a vivid manner the third and final theme of the globalism of Martí's nationalism, a strong sense of the individual as a member of an interdependent global community.

Golden Years may be considered a microcosm of Martí's larger world outlook, like the radii that Fina García Marruz referred to: radii that are not detached from their centre, the core being the much larger Cuban leader's world outlook. Martí's perception of the world, or *weltaunschauung*, was nurtured by global ideas and cultures. The Cuban leader employed the history of distant nations to promote his nationalist project. The children's magazine, therefore, has the objectives of building and improving: to improve human relations, social and political surroundings – in short, to improve the world. Likewise, the magazine is a tool to transmit the civic values that would serve to equip the future citizen of the envisioned republic, and on a larger scale to strengthen Latin American and Caribbean pride and awareness. One should not forget that the two global history narratives promote ideas of national liberation and place the Cuban activist as a defender of the "Third World" – or, in more current terms, as defender of a world politically and economically dominated by hegemonic powers. These ideas, advanced by recent scholars, Roberto Fernández Retamar and Pedro Pablo Rodríguez, as seen earlier, appear in his writings for children: "The Story of Humanity, Told through Its Houses" depicts the indigenous history of the Americas as equally if not more valuable than the European, and in "A Journey through the Land of the Annamese", the indigenous people of that land fight forcefully against the European colonizers. In absorbing these lessons, the Latin American and Caribbean child will come to understand the need and viability of defending his or her own culture, and in defending it will thus promote self-determination and national liberation.

Golden Years is a magazine abundant in rhythmic poetry and metaphorical descriptions of global historical figures and events. Martí surely created narratives for Cuban and Latin American children with the memory of his former teacher and mentor Rafael Mendive in mind. Martí realized the impact that Mendive's nationalist thought had on the evolution of his own political consciousness as a child. He therefore wrote global histories to strengthen democratic values in Latin America and the Caribbean so that Cubans would cast aside the yoke of Spanish colonialism, and so that Latin Americans would reject tyrannical governments and even the threats of outside hegemonic powers, such as growing US expansionism. García Marruz also reiterates the other grave, pressing matter on Martí's mind:

> *Golden Years* [appeared] in [1889], the same year the Pan-American Conference in Washington, DC was held. Martí described this period in his *Versos sencillos* [Modest Verses] as "that winter of agony, when led by ignorance or fanatic faith or by fear or by politeness, the Spanish American nations met together in Washington under the fearsome eagle".... Perhaps there is a relationship between this "agony" that he experienced, that "horror and shamefulness" and the legitimate fear that Cuba would be sold, annexed to the United States, that explains why he would delay the work to organize and establish the [Cuban] Revolutionary Party until 1891. How can one think to organize a war against a country that was in the midst of negotiations to sell Cuba to the United States? Therefore, he perhaps placed his "hopes" in instilling in the children of the Americas the essential notion of their duty [to their lands].[98]

Martí instilled teachings for Cuban and Latin American children in stories of diverse global subjects in order to avoid the antagonisms that more direct critiques of the Spanish rule of Cuba would bring to his independence project. When considering *Golden Years* as an instrument of his independence efforts, the global historical narratives in the magazine emerge as stories that promote innovative and subversive ideas. Martí filled his children's narratives with raw language, depicting stories of death, pain, suffering, deceit, exploitation and greed, "for a young child may not yet understand cruelty in its pure state, but must [in Martí's mind] begin to become acquainted with it, even if in the form of a history, story or art form, so that later he or she will not be terrorized by it or lack the courage to confront it",[99] as Fina García Marruz succinctly expressed. "The Story of Humanity" and "Journey" do not embellish Europeans and their colonial actions. *Golden Years* is therefore not entirely set in magical, imaginary worlds, as one would expect of children's tales, yet Martí's idealism remains with the reader: the past may be sorrowful, but the present and the future are influenced by human agency. These notions most certainly echo Hegelian views of history as the march of progress and greater freedom – and, particularly, Martí's view that knowledge of history strengthens a nation. Martí's struggle to free Cuba underpinned a *weltanschauung* characterized by humanity's capacity for progress, but a progression considered impossible as long as nations deserving to be free were not.

The two global histories in *Golden Years* provide access to Martí's unique elaboration of a nationalist doctrine in the late nineteenth-century world. The young readers of *Golden Years* provided a more receptive and malleable audience for teaching the values that edified Cuban national consciousness; elevated Latin American pride; averted anti-democratic foreign threats; and improved the condition of humanity.[100] Martí's narratives in *Global Years* serve to encapsulate his nationalist ideology, his advocacy of the right for nations and individuals to self-determination, and his position that serving humanity strengthens the nation and the individual. Martí's idealism may have reflected late nineteenth-century European and North American philanthropical notions of improving society, but they challenged Eurocentric conceptions by overturning discriminatory beliefs such as European history and culture being superior to indigenous ones – whether in the Americas or in Southeast Asia. "The History of Humanity, Told through Its Houses" and "Journey through the Land of the Annamese" portray subjects of the global past as ennobling personal and social catalysts. These narratives emerge as tools in undermining imperial rule over Cuba and challenging the wholesale adoption of European and North American values in Latin America and the Caribbean at the expense of local traditions.[101]

Like nineteenth-century historians, Martí believed that history lessons made children better citizens. Yet, unlike most European and North American historians, Martí believed non-Western, indigenous archetypes could serve as models for writing histories[102] that promoted Hegelian-like notions of humanity on its march towards greater freedom. Among the first to write these types of histories for children in Latin America, and even preceding better-known nationalist global histories for children (such as the one by Indian independence leader Jawaharlal Nehru decades later), Martí subverted prevailing racial and ethnic notions and taught children to do so as well in order to foster the love of homeland in an ethnically heterogeneous Cuba and Latin America. Using global history to build nation at an early age, these narratives of *Golden Years* impart values aimed at resisting and overthrowing oppressive ruling systems, whether externally imposed (imperialism) or internally derived (tyrannies).

Through my analysis of these two global history narratives, I have demonstrated that Martí's vision of nation building had significant global origins and connections. Three main themes emerge in his use of global histories to transmit independence and civic values: first, the right to self-determination at the national level, supported by a belief in the non-superiority of European races and civilization; second, the right to self-determination at the personal level, upheld by the belief in the need for citizens to be critical of authority and to subvert restrictive ideologies that legitimize undemocratic government; and third, humanitarianism, advancing the essential unity of humanity, the importance of humanitarian actions and attitudes for sustaining a republic, and the need for citizens to be globally conscious individuals as a means to transcend the Cuban nation's geographic insularity. Promoting these three nation-building values in a magazine for children affirms the iconoclastic globalism of José Martí's ideological construction of an independent Cuba, and ultimately his hope for future generations to succeed in attaining his vision.

3. THE HINDU INSPIRATIONS OF A FREEDOM FIGHTER'S SPIRITUAL AND WORLD OUTLOOK

When I was born, without sunlight, my mother told me:
"Of me and of Creation you are, its product and reflection,
the fish that into a bird, a steed and a man transforms
Look at these two that with pain I bring you,
Emblems of life: pick and choose.
This one is a yoke: whoever consents to it, revels in life
Does like the submissive ox, and by offering
Service to his lords, sleeps on straw
... This one, that shines and kills, is a star
Since it radiates light, sinners flee from whoever carries it, and in life,
... whoever moves with light, stands alone.
... but the man who without shame imitates the ox,
... transforms into an ox, and as a feeble idiot
the scale of the Universe, he must begin again.[1]
   – *"The Yoke and the Star" in* Free Verses, *1878*

Sometime between 1880 and 1882, Martí wrote in a personal notebook that he kept,

> Human life, by way of the moral constraints to which it is condemned, is losing each day, in my eyes, its grandeur and significance. What existence is this where unique

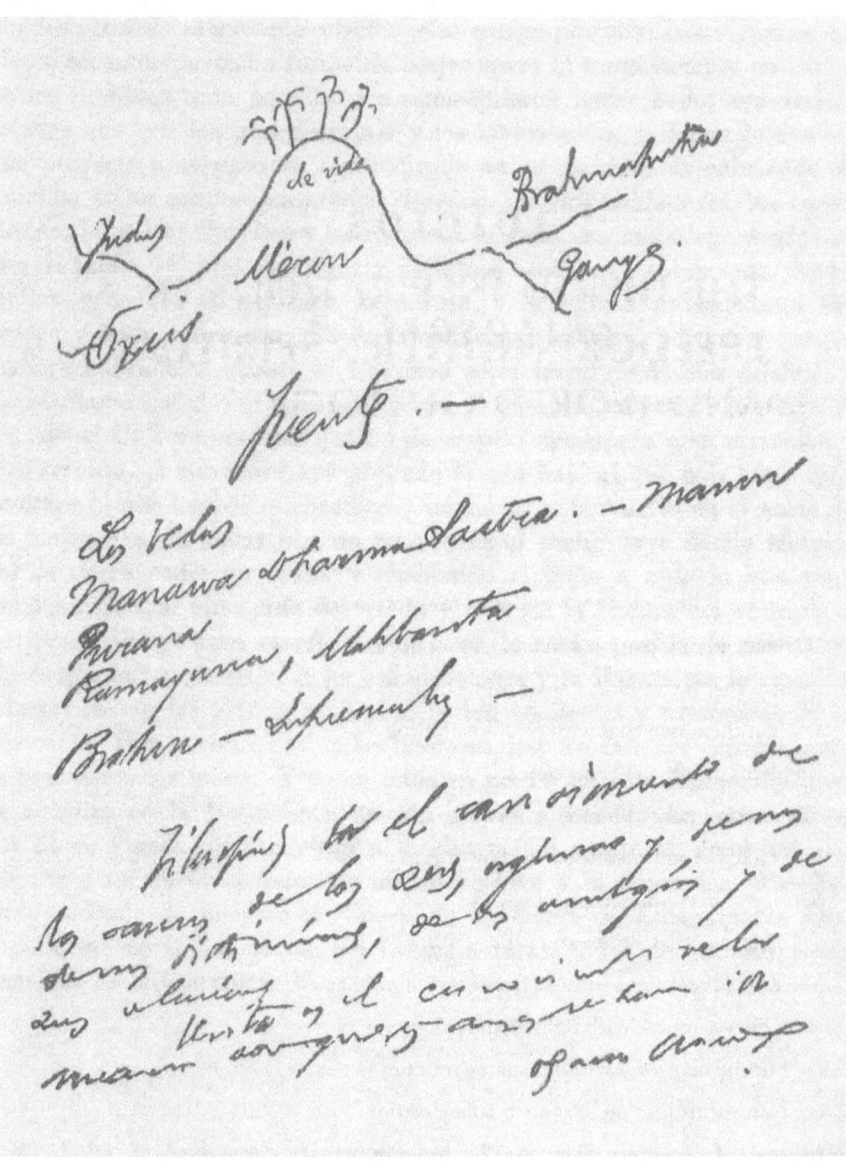

Figure 3. Notes for a lecture on Hindu philosophy during Martí's professorship in Guatemala, ca. 1877.

abilities to do good and the determined willingness to do so are not enough? Where chance conditions of colouring and atmosphere decide the transcendence and the utility of the most noble of human strengths? Where absence of all vices and a fervent love and strict practice of all virtues are insufficient to achieve peace of the soul nor enough to leave behind – for the immense pleasure of doing good – not for the soiled vanity of attaining glory, a visible and everlasting impression?[2]

These intimate notes reveal how, to Martí, his self-imposed moral constraints while leading an aesthetic life in the pursuit of Cuba's freedom caused his life to lose (in his words) "grandeur and significance". He questioned the value of his life, even though by 1880, when he wrote these reflections, he had already earned high praise for the artistic value of his literary work and the talent of his oratory. His literary productions also had significant practical value, for they largely defined, promoted or defended Cuban independence, or else they helped him to earn a living while campaigning for the Cuban cause.[3] Regardless of the praise or the worth of his speeches and writings, his life did not appear to him to convey an "everlasting impression", nor did it seem to serve as a model for the betterment of future generations. In short, it appears that his life's work did not give him a sense of inner peace.

The Hindu sacred poem the *Bhagavad-Gita*, in its gospel of selflessness and the call to duty and to action, and in its revelation of the true nature of the human soul, provides direction to Arjuna – a warrior who is confronting battle and suffering similar existential doubts. In the Hindu sacred text, Krishna, as a divine avatar, instructs Arjuna that

> Nothing of nonbeing comes to be,
> nor does being cease to exist;
> the boundary between these two
> is seen by men who see reality.[4]

Do not fear death, Krishna tells Arjuna in this Hindu holy poem, for the human soul is immortal. Krishna continues,

> No effort in this world
> is lost or wasted;
> a fragment of sacred duty
> saves you from great fear.[5]

In other words, do not agonize over leaving "a visible and everlasting impression" since "no effort in this world is lost or wasted". Indeed, a "fragment of sacred duty", as Krishna instructs and as Martí echoes in the above words, the "absence of all vices and the fervent love and strict practice of all virtues" will save "you from great fear", especially when one's life loses each day "its grandeur and its significance".

Krishna further counsels the warrior Arjuna that

> When he renounces all desires
> and acts without craving,
> possessiveness,
> or individuality he finds peace.
> This is the place of the infinite spirit;
> achieving it, one is freed from delusion;
> abiding in it even at the time of death,
> one finds the pure calm of infinity.[6]

That no effort is ever lost when desires are renounced and actions are selfless; that one ultimately achieves peace "even at the time of death"; and that "the pure calm of infinity" is attainable are words that clarify and strengthen Arjuna's mind as well as justify his actions in the war he is about to wage. Krishna's advice to Arjuna would have also resonated in Martí's mind, for he too perceived himself as a warrior fighting for Cuba's freedom and independence – a combatant, as seen in his personal annotations, who doubted the value and utility of his efforts to liberate Cuba and, on a larger scale, who doubted the value and utility of his own life. In Martí's words, his actions, after all, did not seem to leave "a visible and everlasting impression".

Martí was first exposed to Hindu thought during his first deportation to Spain in 1871. The introduction came through the burgeoning philosophical circles that followed the German thinker Karl C.F. Krause (1781–1832), who integrated Hindu philosophy into his work. Martí also often expressed his philosophical and metaphysical views in his writings. His biographical essay, a eulogy of sorts on the North American Transcendentalist, preacher and philosopher Ralph Waldo Emerson (1803–82), first published in the Venezuelan newspaper *La Opinión Nacional* of Caracas on 19 May 1882, reveals Martí's concise views on spirituality and his general outlook on life.[7] Martí wrote the Emerson essay during a particularly difficult time in his life. His wife and only son abandoned him in late 1880, while he was in New York City. Two years would pass before Martí saw them again. Also in 1880 came the failure of *La Guerra Chiquita* (the Little War), a second armed attempt at Cuban independence, with thousands of Cuban insurgents prosecuted and many imprisoned or exiled to Spanish enclaves in North Africa.

By January 1881, Martí decided to leave New York City for Venezuela, where he lectured and wrote for major newspapers, quickly gaining recognition for his literary and oratory talents. Martí stayed in Venezuela only six months, leaving abruptly, apparently due to Venezuelan strongman President Antonio Guzmán Blanco's (1829–99) disapproval of Martí not praising his government. Martí returned to New York City in July 1881, where he continued to write pieces for *La Opinión Nacional* until June 1882, when he ceased contributing to the Caracas newspaper. By March/April 1882, Martí had published his now famous short poetry volume, *Ismaelillo* (*Little Ishmael*), a father's emotional, poetic tribute to his absent and only son. Amid these dramatic life events, Martí took the opportunity of Emerson's passing to write an essay that synthesizes the preacher's life and, more importantly, presents his deepest spiritual views.

I focus on the Emerson essay in this chapter and on other reflections from Martí in his personal notebooks and diaries, writings that vividly reveal his spiritual and world outlook. By juxtaposing Hindu philosophy as presented in the *Bhagavad-Gita* with Martí's writings, I argue that Indian thought nurtured his spiritual views, further evidence of Martí's global influences. While in the next chapter I delve into how Hindu notions inspired Martí's concept of the nation-state as divine and how he promoted the struggle for independence of this divinely perceived entity, in this chapter I explore how Hindu notions, particularly by way of North American Transcendentalism, influenced Martí's personal beliefs, his sense of spirituality and his general outlook on life. Martí's spiritual beliefs are particularly important as they form the foundation of his fight against oppression, whether social, against racism (as later explored in chapter 5), or political, against corrupt government (as examined in chapter 6).

This chapter builds on previous work by scholars regarding the influence of Emerson and transcendental philosophy on Martí's work; however, I delve deeper by pointing to the major source of transcendental inspiration, Hindu philosophy. My exploration of the inner Martí highlights his views on the nature of the human soul, particularly in regards to the Hindu notion of the soul's journey through reincarnations as it seeks ultimate union with the Supreme Godhead.

Martí, in actuality, and the *Bhagavad-Gita*'s Arjuna, in the allegorical sense, were leaders of their respective military campaigns who experienced existential doubts. Parallels may therefore be drawn between Martí's writings that reflect spiritual views and the teachings of the *Bhagavad-Gita*. Proof of a direct, substantiated influence of the *Bhagavad-Gita* on Martí eludes us, since we have no way of precisely knowing if and when Martí actually read the Hindu sacred poem, just as many other details of his life are submerged in time. Nevertheless, Martí did have an understanding of Hindu notions, as demonstrated by evidence that does still remain: namely, Martí's literary production, and even a handwritten illustration and notes from a philosophy lecture he presented in Guatemala in 1877. If one considers, as scholar Anne Fountain mentions, that Martí's depictions of American literary life were based on "thorough knowledge and informed reading",[8] then Martí was substantially aware of the ideas that inspired Emerson when he wrote the essay. Furthermore, as other scholars have suggested, particularly José Ballón Aguirre, "the effort to incorporate Hindu philosophy in nineteenth-century philosophical reflections in America is a common contribution of Emerson and Martí".[9]

Martí appreciated Transcendentalism and its Eastern aspects. He particularly admired Emerson, who owned rare copies of Hindu sacred texts; Henry David Thoreau, who had an edition of the *Bhagavad-Gita* at Walden Pond; Annie Besant, who worked on a translation of the *Bhagavad-Gita*; as well as Amos Bronson Alcott and Walt Whitman, who also found inspiration in Indian works. Martí's admiration for these "Boston Brahmins" and for Sir Edwin Arnold, among the first to translate the *Bhagavad-Gita* from Sanskrit to English, is evident in his quotations from and adaptations of their work. In what critics consider Martí's literary testament – a letter written to his disciple Gonzalo de Quesada one month before he fell in battle at Dos Ríos, Cuba, in May 1895, at the launch of the final Cuban independence war – he instructed de Quesada that his prose works were to be collected in six volumes, three on North America and two volumes specifically on "North Americans".[10] Among these he specifically identified the Emerson article, signalling his admiration for the Transcendentalists.

Emerson owned one of the few copies in the United States of the English translation of the Hindu epic the *Mahabharata*. In his essay on Emerson, Martí praises how the New England preacher

> at times, in the blinding glow of those brilliant Hindu books, where human beings after purified by virtue, fly like butterflies from fire, from their earthly dregs to the core of Brahma, he sits himself to gauge, since he has found others' eyes as his own, and he sees starkly and tones down his own visions. And it [must be] that Indian philosophy captivates, like a forest of blossoms, and like watching birds soar, it sparks the yearning to take flight.[11]

Someone who had not read Hindu sacred works for himself would not have described them so vividly. With such high admiration for Ralph Waldo Emerson, Henry David Thoreau, Walt Whitman, Annie Besant and Sir Edwin Arnold, among others, it would have been irresponsible to ignore the *Bhagavad-Gita*, a work that inspired these women and men, particularly since "he consciously sought to depict American literary life for his Spanish-American readers, and did so based on *thorough* knowledge and informed reading".[12]

Sacrifice as a Purifying Agent of the Soul

According to the Hindu sacred poem, the path to salvation lies in sacrificial acts and in behaviour dedicated to the welfare of others. In an 1894 speech honouring his friend Fermín Valdés Domínguez, Martí expressed similar views: "selfishness is the blot of the world, selflessness its sun. In this world there is not but one inferior race of people: those who consider above all, their own personal interest, be it their vanity or their arrogance – nor is there but one superior race: those who consider above all, the human interest."[13] These words, referring to his friend Domínguez, also point to how Martí valued those who considered human or humanitarian interests over personal ones. One may infer by Martí's statement that thinking and acting selflessly were important in the physical and material world of humans, but altruism in Hindu philosophy was a means to purify the soul and thus facilitate union with the divine.

In Hindu thought, acting selflessly and sacrificing for others are ways to outwardly realize the inner *Atman*, the divine spark within humans. Martí also adopted and conveyed transcendental views of how humankind held a divine spark within each individual. Throughout his writings Martí reiterated notions of humanity's divine spark, which he did not refer to as *"Atman"*, for the term would have been considered distant and foreign, unintelligible to ordinary Cubans. Nevertheless, Martí echoed in other instances his belief of a divine spark or *Atman* within people. In the global history narratives Martí wrote for children, as examined in the previous chapter, the Cuban nationalist imparts Eastern philosophy through lessons of Buddhist principles. In "Journey to the Land of the Annamese", Martí tells his young readers that "women and men do not come from Heaven, but with Heaven within them"[14] – an allusion to the inner, divine *Atman*.

To the late Martí scholar Manuel Pedro González, Martí's life was one of perpetual renunciation of worldly goods and material benefits. In 1892, he resigned his posts in New York City as consul general of Argentina, Uruguay and Paraguay when Spanish authorities cast doubt on his commitment to the Cuban cause due to his representation of other Latin American nations. Also in 1892, Martí sacrificed recognition as a writer and relinquished his salary as a correspondent for several of the most influential Latin American newspapers of the time, among them *La Nación* of Buenos Aires and *El Partido Liberal* of Mexico City. He later ceased contributing to the *New York Sun* in order to dedicate all of his energies to the liberation of Cuba. Martí unexpectedly lost his beloved son and wife when both left New York City for Cuba, finding safe passage from the Spanish consul in the city – a betrayal to Martí, because his wife "refused to share his idealism and spirit of sacrifice".[15] Indeed, Martí sacrificed money and status as well as the love of family for noble ideals. He aimed to personally fulfil much of his rhetoric on sacrifice and altruism, so mentioned in the *Gita*. In a May 1894 letter to his mother in Cuba, Martí quite emotionally expresses,

> My destiny is like the light of a white charcoal that burns itself to shine its surroundings. I feel as if my struggles will never end. The private man is already dead and beyond all resurrection . . . but the vigilant and compassionate one is still alive in me, like a skeleton that would have come out of his grave; and I know that nothing else awaits him but suffering and confrontations in the contest of men, who one must enter in order to comfort and improve them. . . . Death or isolation will be my only reward.[16]

Yet in an 1880 entry in his personal notebook, Martí reveals how his concepts of salvation and redemption were linked to personal sacrifice or the letting go of self-aggrandizing objectives, a major tenet of the *Gita*. Sacrifice is also a notion present in Krishna's advice to Arjuna, and particularly expressed when Martí writes in his 1880 entry, "On this earth, there is but one salvation: sacrifice. There is no other assured good deed than that of sacrificing one's self: peace of the soul. All misfortunes begin the instant when, disguised as human reason, desire forces men to deviate – even if the departure is unnoticeable – from fulfilling a heroic duty. Sacrificing one's self: here lies [my] serenity."[17] Like Krishna's counsel to Arjuna, Martí considered the fulfilment of heroic duty and sacrifice as a prerequisite for redemption. Martí also expressed in his private notebook how peace of the soul came through sacrifice. Sacrifice and, if necessary, giving one's life while fulfilling a heroic duty redeemed and brought genuine serenity to the soul, according to Martí. The *Gita* displays similar views when Krishna advises Arjuna to "always perform with detachment any action you must do; performing action with detachment one achieves supreme good".[18] Renouncing the fruits of one's actions is a principal tenet of the *Gita*. Ultimate salvation, or *moksha* (union with the Divine), according to the *Gita*, requires the individual to perform all actions without regard for personal ambitions.

In Martí's mind, each life is either purified or further polluted by man's actions on earth, a view he expresses in the Emerson essay when he writes that presumptuous, unvirtuous men had placed "hurdles accumulated through centuries before the cradle [or birth] of Emerson".[19] Virtue, to Martí, redeemed the soul, as seen in an 1881 notebook annotation where he writes, "my heart has no strength but for virtue".[20] In the Emerson essay, Martí presents virtue as a means of purifying and of attaining peace of the soul: "virtue, with which all nature conspires, gives men and women peace, as if they have completed their task or like a curve that re-enters into its own self and needs no longer to advance and completes the circle".[21] The "circle" that Martí refers to is the unity of all beings, considered as an aspect of the Supreme Being, the source of all life. To the Cuban leader, virtue, specifically in actions, refines individuals and accelerates ultimate union with the one Great Soul of the Universe.

Midway into two hectic political fundraising trips, Martí arrived in New York City on 30 November 1891 from Tampa and departed on 22 December to Key West, Florida. In his 7 December 1891 article to the *El Partido Liberal* newspaper of Mexico City, relating recent happenings, he prominently features Annie Besant's visit to New York City. His article to the Mexican periodical describes and defends Annie Besant's views on poverty, population control and religion, and he encodes his own views on virtue and duty by praising those of Besant. Martí writes, "everything crystallizes through the exercise of goodness, and transforms itself into a spiritual essence, present, albeit invisible".[22] He further expresses that "may the highest in individuals be cultivated, in order that with eyes of greater light, he or she could join in the comfort (peace); advance in the mystery; and may explore the highest within the spiritual sphere".[23] The value of education in Hindu philosophy (the right knowledge of spiritual matters, for instance) leads humanity to a more elevated and peaceful level of existence. Martí's attitudes regarding the value of education and the cultivation of the spirit compare favourably with a fundamental principle of the *Bhagavad-Gita*, the significance of knowing the true, everlasting nature of the human soul in order to avoid fear and doubt and to gain ultimate inner peace.

Martí further writes in his 7 December 1891 letter to *El Partido Liberal* that "this is why Annie Besant came from England: to pour her sparkling and merciful word over our hearts, to feel her way in good faith with her sensible yet mystical oratory, [onto] the paths of the future [forthcoming] religion".[24] By praising Besant, and later in an article on Sir Edwin Arnold, Martí reiterates the critical role of virtue, education and the dissemination of knowledge in order to purify the human soul. Besant, according to Martí, advanced knowledge in a logical yet "mystical" form; knowledge was essential in elevating one's material condition, but importantly, it also elevated one's spiritual condition. Martí states in the article that Besant explores and feels her way through the path of a new (*venidera*) forthcoming religion, a modern one unlike Roman Catholicism or traditional Western Christianity. This new religion may have echoes in a mystical form of Christianity, but it is clearly an elaboration of Hindu-inspired elements, since Besant lived in India for a prolonged period and adopted Hindu ideas to formulate her own *weltanschauung*. Martí's 7 December 1891 letter to the Mexican newspaper visibly conveys the above-mentioned themes of virtue and purification as essential in the soul's journey to ultimate union with the Godhead. In describing Annie Besant and Sir Edwin Arnold in his editorial pieces, Martí relates his personal views on spirituality. Indeed, the Cuban leader, as scholar Oscar Montero mentioned, often "rewrote current events, transforming the grinding work of the journalist into a medium for recasting himself".[25]

The True Nature of the Soul

To Martí, all misfortunes emerged when an individual identified with personal desires. These desires may have appeared real; they manifested themselves as the *prakriti* of Hindu cosmology, the Indian term for the lower aspect of the universal Brahman (the Supreme Being) and the world of nature or visible reality, which creates the setting of the *Bhagavad-Gita*. Desires may disguise themselves as human logic or reasoning, leading men to a sense of separation from others and from the divine essence of the universe. This separation is an illusion to Martí as it was to Krishna in the *Gita*, who tells Arjuna, "when he perceives the unity existing in separate creatures and how they expand from unity, he attains the infinite spirit".[26] Martí emphasized how personal ambitions caused men to deviate from their sense of inner peace and their ultimate redemption. Martí's views echo the *Gita*'s, which states, "as the mountainous depths of the ocean are unmoved when waters rush into it, so [also] the man unmoved when desires enter him attains a peace that eludes the man of many desires".[27]

In a separate personal annotation, Martí wrote, "God Consciousness, the child of the God of creation, which is the only unanimously worshipped visible link that unites a driven human race with the divine creative and guiding force. Worshipped, and let this not appear as reminiscent of a Catholic education. This God, and God *patria* [nation], are in our society and in our lives the only elements worthy of reverence."[28] To Martí, only two forces are thus worthy of devotion, God Consciousness and the God *patria* (nation/homeland). Yet Martí wrote, "let this not be reminiscent of a [Roman] Catholic education". Martí's criticisms of the Roman Catholic Church, and his own spiritual views, may be considered in line with nineteenth-century Spanish-American liberalism. Nevertheless, his critiques of Roman Catholicism were particularly informed by his experiences in Spain where he was exposed to ultra-Catholic reactionaries such as the Spanish *Carlistas*, who sought to revive the Inquisition. Notwithstanding his critiques of the Roman Catholic Church, the Cuban patriot had no objections to marrying in it and christening his son while also engaging in Freemasonry and sharing Hindu-derived spiritual views.

In the above excerpt, where Martí states that "God [Consciousness], and God *patria*, are in our society and in our lives the only elements worthy of reverence", he suggests that human consciousness is divine and that it is also the child of the God of creation. To Martí, God Consciousness was also a bond that linked the human race, one driven by a divine creative and guiding force, the "God of creation". The *Gita* offers a comparable view of these beliefs. "Know that my brilliance, flaming in the sun, in the moon, and in fire, illumines this whole universe. I am the universal fire within the body of living beings; I dwell deep in the heart of everyone." Krishna's message to Arjuna reminds us of the divine creative and guiding force of Martí's conception.[29] Krishna continues advising Arjuna in the *Gita* that,

> Nothing is higher than I am
> Arjuna, all that exists
> is woven on me,
> like a web of pearls on a thread
> Know me, Arjuna,
> as every creature's timeless seed,
> the understanding of intelligent men,
> the brilliance of fiery heroes
> All this universe, deluded
> by the qualities inherent in nature,
> fails to know that I am
> beyond them and unchanging.[30]

Krishna explains to Arjuna the pitfalls of a deluded universe, and by deduction, of humans as well. Human beings, according to Krishna, easily succumb to personal desires when they fail to recognize the true reality, the actual nature of the human soul. Krishna continues,

> Deluded men despise me
> in the human form I have assumed,
> ignorant of my higher existence
> as the great lord of creatures.
> Reason warped, hope, action,
> and knowledge wasted,
> they fall prey to a seductive
> fiendish, demonic nature.
> In single-minded dedication, great souls
> devote themselves to my divine nature,
> knowing me as unchanging,
> the origin of creatures.[32]

Martí's reference to the concept of a God of creation, the Supreme Being that created the God Consciousness, shares the same spirit of Arjuna's response to Krishna:

> Original Creator,
> Boundless Lord of Gods,
> Shelter of All That Is,
> you are eternity,
> being, nonbeing, and beyond.
> You are the original god,
> the primordial spirit of man,
> the deepest treasure of all that is,
> knower and what is to be known,
> the supreme abode;
> you pervade the universe,
> Lord of Boundless Form.[32]

The Supreme Being (according to the *Gita*), or the Great Soul of the Universe (to the Transcendentalists), and the God of creation or "the divine creative or driving force" (to Martí) are all omnipresent and unchanging. Both the *Gita*'s Supreme Being and Martí's God of creation infiltrate and stimulate what Martí describes as "the driven human race" as well as his conception of "God Consciousness". According to the *Gita*, "the Original Creator pervades the universe"; it is a "Lord of Boundless Form". Both Martí and the *Gita* hold these notions of an ultimate divine essence that equally and thoroughly permeates the universe and even its individual inhabitants.

According to Martí, "the God of creation", the ultimate supreme deity, created "God Consciousness". God Consciousness unites the essence, "the divine guiding or creative force", with the body or form, "the driven human race". As displayed in the above excerpts of the *Gita*, humanity, and therefore all human beings, are divinely driven and inherently divine – a view shared with the Transcendentalists, but originating in Hindu thought. These views on spirituality also appear in Martí's personal diary entries and in his historical narratives for children, such as "Journey through the Land of the Annamese". They even inspired Martí to not only fight for a free Cuba, as seen in the next chapter, but also to fight racism, as explored in chapter 5.

During his first deportation to Spain for anti-colonial activities in 1871, where he stayed until 1875 and completed his university studies, seventeen-year-old Martí wrote in a personal notebook, "what abounds is the synthesis of diversity, and to the ultimate One are to go [all] the syntheses of all commonalities, everything simplifies as it *ascends*".[33] These comments provide further proof that Martí viewed humanity as inherently divine, but they also reveal how humanity, to the Cuban leader, was on an ascending journey that led to ultimate union with the Divine. Significantly, Martí mentioned that everything simplified as it rose. One may infer by this that a complex material world sheds its outward self and the underlying spirit emerges on a journey to union with the ultimate divinity. The *Gita* also presents these conceptions, particularly in Krishna's statement that "when he perceives the unity existing in separate creatures and how they expand from unity, he attains the infinite spirit".[34] In an 1887 article published in Buenos Aires's *La Nación* newspaper, Martí writes, "basic human elements can never be suppressed. Stars travel along their orbits, and among stars travels humanity. Just as eclipses are measured, so too life itself may be gauged."[35] To the Cuban nation builder, the human spirit is a part of the spirit of the universe; human life follows, metaphorically, the same trajectory as stars. The paths of humans and stars, in this sense, are comparable. Since all humans are inherently the same, physical differences are inconsequential to Martí. This view, echoed in the *Gita*, is further magnified by Martí's real-world application of it. Martí fought against racism and the social oppression of African descendants, as explored in chapter 5, not only to promote Cuban unity during the struggle for independence, but because it was a major element of his spiritual beliefs.

In his essay on Emerson, Martí relates his views on the role of virtue and of the essential unity of all living beings. Martí intersperses direct translations from Emerson with his own beliefs. For instance, Martí expresses in the essay how

> [Emerson] holds that everything and everyone [are essentially the same], that everything has the same objective, that it all rests in humanity, which beautifies everything with the mind, that the currents of nature flow through each creature, that every creature has something of the Creator in itself, and that everyone will end at the source of the creative Spirit. That there is a central unity in all deeds – in thoughts, and actions; that the human soul, in travelling through all of nature, finds itself within all of it; that the beauty of the Universe was created to inspire wishes and dreams, and to find comfort from the pains and sufferings of virtue, and to stimulate humanity to search and to find itself; that "within humanity is the soul of the whole united, of the wise silence, the universal beauty, that each part and particle is equally related to: the Eternal One".[36]

In describing the New England Transcendentalist's views, Martí depicts his own conceptions that are also basic tenets of the *Bhagavad-Gita*. For instance, "there is a central unity in all deeds – in thoughts, and in actions" is directly related to the *Gita's* idea of the cause-and-effect, or rather karmic, relationship between intentions and deeds, actions and their consequences.

The Journey of the Soul: Martí's Belief in Reincarnation

Martí believed in the essential oneness, in the interconnectedness of all, and that this unity corresponded to the everlasting true nature of the human soul and its relationship with the divine. Life on earth, being merely one incarnation of many, is a mere sojourn in the long journey of the soul to its ultimate home, the Supreme Being, according to Hindu thought. In a personal notebook, Martí wrote that "there cannot be any contradictions in Nature; the human hope of finding in love, during this existence, and in what is commonly ignored after death, that perfect type of grace and beauty, reveals that, in the totality of life, *we must joyfully reconcile, in this present life segment that we travel through, the elements that are seemingly hostile and separated*".[37]

To Martí, nature held no contradictions. By describing "this present segment of life we travel through", Martí most certainly referred to a segment of one's larger, eternal life, an incarnation, perhaps, and not necessarily to a segment of one earthly lifespan. In other entries of his personal diaries, as well as in essays on Walt Whitman, Ralph Waldo Emerson and Henry Ward Beecher, Martí provided ample evidence that revealed his beliefs regarding the true nature of the soul during and after earthly existence. Although Martí shared many of Emerson's spiritual views,[38] these did not originate with Emerson. They may be viewed as Emersonian adaptations of Hindu thought, as Emerson most likely would have taken them from the *Gita* or other Hindu texts. In turn, these concepts were embraced by Martí, reformulated and diffused by the Cuban leader to find intellectual and spiritual support.

Martí's essay on Emerson also displays much of the philosophy of the *Gita*, enveloped in Martí's own Spanish-language adaptation of Emerson's prose. Referring to Emerson, Martí writes in his essay eulogizing the New England thinker that "men placed before him all those hurdles accumulated by centuries, [that were] inhabited by presumptuous men, before the cradle [or birth] of new men".[39] Emerson, in Martí's view, strove to overcome the *hurdles* produced by centuries of presumptuous men – blemishes that impeded and lengthened the human soul's journey to the ultimate divinity. Martí further writes in the essay, "to die is to return the finite to the infinite",[40] however not in a traditional Christian sense of life after death. Instead, Martí's statement may be interpreted in connection with another statement he made in the Emerson essay: "man when facing nature that changes and passes, feels, within him or her self, something stable. He or she feels both eternally young and forgetfully old. He or she knows that what one knows well was not learned here: which reveals a previous life, in which he or she acquired the wisdom brought to this one."[41]

The concept of reincarnation, therefore, emerges as a key, yet largely ignored element in Martí's spiritual beliefs and outlook on life. Believing that an earthly life is one of many, and that humans must undergo many incarnations to purify the spirit and become one with the Great Soul of the Universe, are also convictions that Martí reveals in his writings. A Hindu reading of the Cuban leader's literary output, particularly his works on the Transcendentalists, with the *Gita* as an accessible and synthetic elaboration of Hindu thought, discloses Martí's frequent references to reincarnation. For instance, Martí's 1887 essay on Walt Whitman also expresses how "no longer do willow trees keen over tombs: death is the harvest, the opener and usher to the heavenly mansion, the great revealer; *what is, was, and shall be once more.* All apparent oppositions and grieves are commingled in a grave and celestial spring [or season]; a bone is a flower."[42] As well, in the Emerson essay, Martí explicitly states, "he or she who gave all of him or herself and did well for others will repose. He or she who wrongly did his or her task in this life will work again."[43] One more inscription in his personal diary further corroborates how the Cuban leader believed in reincarnation: "the soul post-exists. And if it post-exists, and we are not born as equals, then it pre-exists, the soul has gone through various forms – over here or there? [It may seem] useless to wonder, but it has occurred."[44] In the piece on Emerson, Martí comments on the role of reincarnation in the soul's journey to its final destination of union with the Divine, and he adopts and transmits many of Emerson's ideas on the nature of the human soul and the universe.[45] Martí writes in the Emerson essay, "and [Emerson] asks himself whether nature is not [just] fantasy, and man the one who fantasizes, and all the Universe an idea, and God the pure one, and the human being [as] the aspiring idea, that will finalize like a pearl in its shell, [or like] an arrow at the trunk of a tree, at the core of God".[46]

Analysing Martí's words on Emerson sheds light on the Cuban poet's views on the nature of the soul and facilitates a Hindu, if not more global, reading of Martí's works – particularly if one considers the large extent that Emerson, Thoreau and others employed Hinduism, and specifically the *Bhagavad-Gita*, in transcendental thought. Nowhere else among the writings that have survived are Martí's views regarding his spiritual beliefs as candid as in his piece on Emerson, where his ideas diverge from traditional Christian canon.

Among his final letters, specifically in the literary testament that Martí addressed to his secretary Gonzalo de Quesada, Martí expressed his high regard for the Emerson essay by providing specific instructions for its publication if he were not to return from the Cuban War of Independence. Separately, Martí also indicated in an 1894 personal diary annotation that one of his most glorious life moments was "the afternoon of Emerson", referring to when he wrote the composition.[47] Regarding Emerson, Martí wrote, "I have already gone through much of life, and tried its delights. But the greatest pleasure, the only pure and absolute pleasure I have enjoyed until now, was that afternoon, when half-undressed in my room, I saw the weary city, and glimpsed into the future thinking of Emerson."[48] Martí continues his praise of Emerson in a separate entry in a personal diary: "Emerson. The afternoon of Emerson: When one loses his or her sense of self and transfuses with the world."[49] According to literary scholar José Ballón Aguirre, Martí identified with Emerson; "his intellectual encounter with Emerson, upon arriving in the US in 1880, is indelible and permanent and forms an essential part of his [world outlook]".[50]

Martí's essay on Emerson is therefore revelatory, significant and essential to our understanding of his spiritual ideas as well as his concept of the world and his place in it. As entries in his personal notebooks show, Martí nurtured his ideas with Hindu thought, perhaps first acquired from texts he read while at the University of Zaragoza, in philosophy courses or while meeting in Spain with enthusiasts of the German thinker Krause's work. He also acquired Hindu-derived notions throughout his adult life, particularly in the context of his interest in metaphysics. During his stay in Mexico, he participated in spiritual and philosophical debates. Indeed, he wrote in a personal diary that "metaphysics is the combination of absolute truths that serve as explanatory and fundamental laws to all of human knowledge".[51]

To conclude this chapter, employing a perspective that goes beyond a Eurocentric framework enhances our understanding of the global origins of Martí's independence programme. Modern Martí scholars have studied the Cuban patriot extensively as a literary figure and political leader, yet his spiritual views, when studied, have often been limited to Western or Judaeo-Christian contexts. As the ideological architect of the renewed 1895 Cuban independence effort, Martí's contribution to that movement was significant, and his role throughout twentieth-century Cuban history has been substantial. Martí's ideas and actions – for instance, his formulations of Cuban independence and nationhood and his fight against racial oppression – are better understood if placed alongside the same sources that nourished his personal beliefs. Among these, Martí's distillations of Hindu beliefs are ever-present throughout his writings. Now I turn to how Martí employed this Hindu ideological influence in his epistemological construction of nation and in motivating and justifying Cuba's final confrontation against the Spanish empire.

4. MARTÍ AND THE DIVINE NATION-STATE

La revolución de independencia, iniciada en Yara, después de preparación gloriosa y cruenta, ha entrado en Cuba en nuevo periodo de guerra.

The revolution for independence, begun in Yara, after glorious and bloody preparation, has entered Cuba in a new period of war.[1]
– Manifiesto de Montecristi, *25 March 1895*

On 25 March 1895, Generals Antonio Maceo and Flor Crombet sailed for Cuba from Costa Rica to serve in the recently ignited war for independence. History would have it that on that same day, in the humble village of Montecristi near the Dominican-Haitian border, in a zinc-clad attic of a wooden-planked Caribbean home overlooking the same vast tropical Atlantic Ocean that would carry Máximo Gómez and José Martí to that same war, a document of supreme significance would be drafted. The *Manifiesto de Montecristi* is the textual embodiment of decades-long political campaigning and war preparation. It is also a document of historical transcendence for the nation-state of Cuba – it is Cuba's declaration of independence to the world. The *Manifiesto* encapsulated Martí's views of the impending revolution to topple the Spanish colonial regime and it mapped the character of the republic to come. It declared to the Cuban nation and to the world that "Cuba returned to war with a democratic and enlightened nation" and with "a warm-hearted grouping of Cubans from the most diverse origins" who "faced their nation free of all hatred".[2] It extolled the mission in profoundly spiritual terms, revealing in a public way

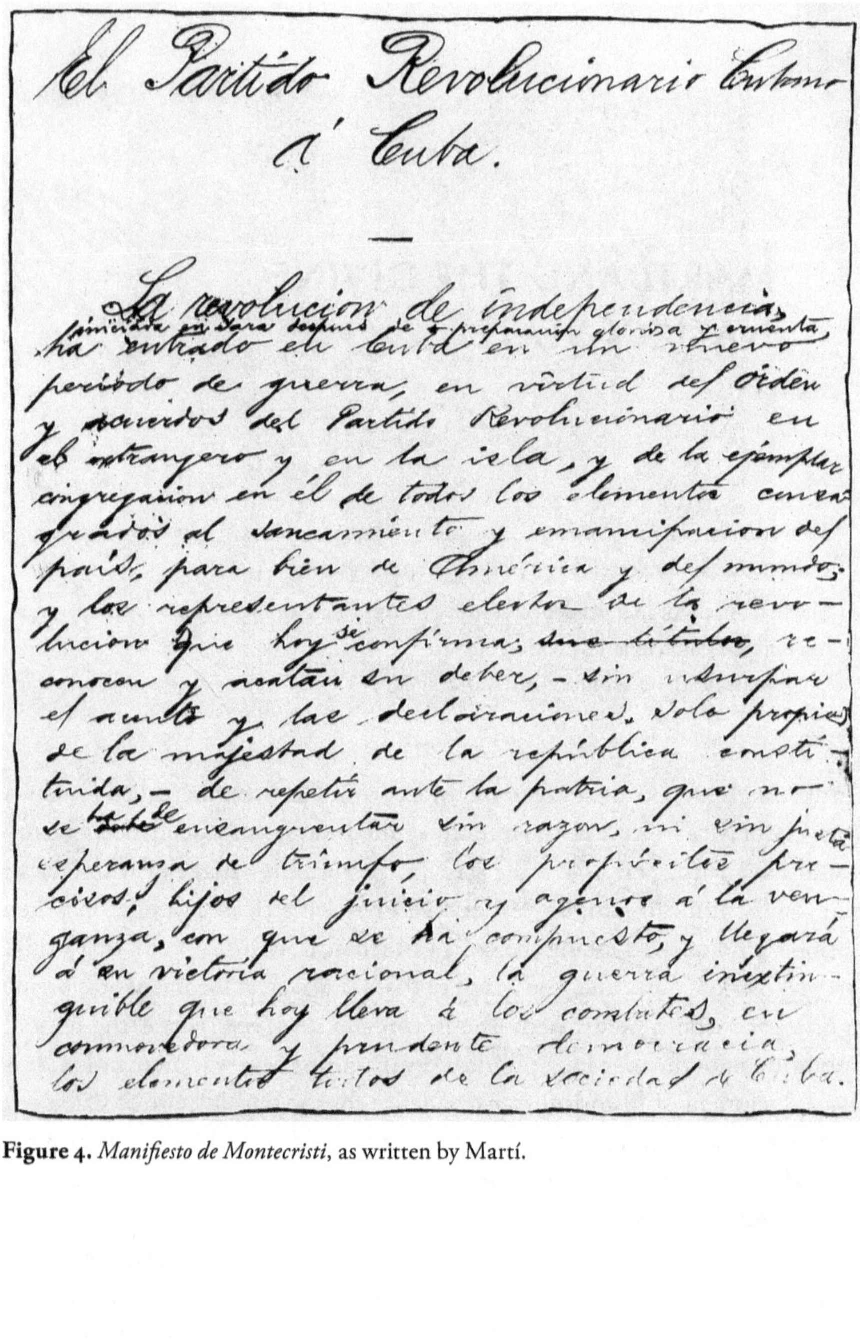

El Partido Revolucionario Cubano
á Cuba.

—

La revolucion de independencia,
iniciada en Yara despues de preparacion gloriosa y cruenta
ha entrado en Cuba en un nuevo
periodo de guerra, en virtud del órden
y acuerdos del Partido Revolucionario en
el extranjero y en la isla, y de la ejemplar
congregacion en él de todos los elementos consa-
grados al saneamiento y emancipacion del
país, para bien de América y del mundo;
y los representantes electos de la revolucion que hoy se confirma, sus títulos, re-
conocen y acatan su deber, — sin usurpar
el acento y las declaraciones solo propias
de la majestad de la república consti-
tuida, — de repetir ante la patria, que no
se ha de ensangrentar sin razon, ni sin justa
esperanza de triunfo, los propósitos pre-
cisos, hijos del juicio y agenos á la ven-
ganza, con que se ha compuesto, y llegará
á su victoria racional, la guerra inextin-
guible que hoy lleva á los combates, en
conmovedora y prudente democracia,
los elementos todos de la sociedad de Cuba.

Figure 4. *Manifiesto de Montecristi*, as written by Martí.

how the Cuban nation and the revolution were conceived by Martí. In this chapter, through an Eastern, specifically Hindu perspective, I seek to deepen the understanding of this document and of the global origins of Martí's search for an independent Cuba.

Sometime in December 1871, more than twenty years before signing the *Manifiesto*, and while still exiled in Spain, Martí wrote in his personal diary about a "God Consciousness, the child of the God of creation, which is the only unanimously worshipped visible link that unites the driven human race with the divine creative and guiding force. Worshipped, and let this not appear reminiscent of a Catholic education. This God, and God *patria* [the nation] are in our society and in our lives the only elements worthy of reverence."[3]

In the previous chapter, I focused on Martí's essays, annotations and letters that dealt with his notion of the "God Consciousness" of the above excerpt and how it was inspired by Hindu cosmology, as well as how his personal world outlook was inspired by Eastern thought. In this chapter, I examine the public Martí, the writings and efforts regarding Martí's conception of "God *patria*" as they related to his view of the nation as divine. To Martí, *patria* required the most selfless type of service, as the *Manifiesto* and Martí's other writings and public speeches demonstrate.

In a 26 January 1895 article in *Patria*, the official newspaper of the Cuban Revolutionary Party that Martí edited, the Cuban leader wrote, while preparing to join the soon-to-be ignited independence war, that "*patria* is humanity, it's that portion of humanity that we see closer [to us] and in which we happen to be born". He continues, "and one should not allow that, with the fraudulent use of its sacred name, useless monarchies, potbellied religions or shameless and greedy politics be defended, not even because these sins have often been given the name of *patria*, should man be denied from fulfilling his duty to humanity, in that portion he or she has nearer. This shines light, and one can never escape from the Sun. This is *Patria*."[4] To Martí, the Cuban *patria* was that "piece of land" that is nonetheless linked to larger humanity. One cannot serve its "sacred name" – echoes of a divine conception of nationhood – without serving larger humankind, according to the Cuban fighter. By expressing that "one can never escape from the Sun", Martí implies that just as our nearest star's light is inseparable from our world, so too should working for the *patria* be indistinct from improving the larger world. These ideas of the intrinsic unity between *patria* and humanity; of *patria* as a divine entity;

and *patria* as an element that requires sacrifice in fulfilling duty towards it, are concepts that emerge throughout Martí's work and that are characterized by Eastern inspirations.

Hindu thought inspired Martí's views on sacrifice, virtue and duty, as well as the knowledge regarding the nature of the soul. As seen in the previous chapter, the *Bhagavad-Gita* may serve as a tool to juxtapose and reveal the Hindu origins of Martí's personal spiritual views. I build on the previous discussion of the three principal ideas of sacrifice, duty and knowledge in the human soul's journey towards union with the divine in order to shed light on how they relate to his conception and promotion of *patria* and independence. I also explore these three tenets of the *Bhagavad-Gita*, showing how Martí addressed these ideas for practical purposes, particularly to legitimize war against Spain. Martí's main practical concern in life was how to successfully sever Cuba from the Spanish empire and to build a democratic nation on the island. With the dramatic backdrop of a grass-roots independence and abolition movement that ultimately failed after ten years of armed struggle – indeed, the *Manifiesto* begins by stating that the Cuban revolution has "entered a new period"[3] – Martí knew entirely that to successfully reignite and conclude the war against Spain, the strategy of the war required redrafting; the concept of nation, revolutionary reimagining.

As a late nineteenth-century nationalist, Martí stood firmly apart from others. His nationalism was void of the exclusionary, race-based politics of the time. When European nationalists conjured notions of nation based on common language, shared ancestry and identifiable ethnic traits, Martí's concept of nation was not ethnically based. Many may argue that this was necessary, considering that Cuba was a heterogeneous society. No independence movement in Cuba could succeed with the support of only one ethnic group. The painful experiences of the Ten Years' War (1868–78) had taught that Cuban independence needed the full backing of white and black populations. Martí thus developed and vociferously advocated the idea of a "raceless nation".

In Martí's new conception of nation, devotion to the *patria* outweighed other ethnic or class loyalties. To hold fast to ethnic or class loyalties would make a traitor of the Cuban. His ability to gain support of white and black Cubans, as well as wealthy elites and low-wage tobacco workers, for instance, made Martí somewhat exceptional. Even though historical hindsight may undermine the extent to which Martí confronted opposition, one may safely assume that no other Cuban leader before, or perhaps since, has been able to gain the support of such a diverse range of Cubans without alienating the middle and upper classes; nor has any Cuban leader been able to advocate for Afro-Cuban rights without causing fear in Cubans of European descent in the way Martí did at the time. Martí was able to do this because of his ability to navigate different worlds: he was at ease in the opera and at the theatre; he published critiques on European fine art – yet he was also at home with the most humble of Cubans while in prison, when lodging with former enslaved Africans or befriending as equals the inhabitants of the modest villages he visited throughout the Caribbean. These wide-ranging experiences allowed him to gain a broad, cosmopolitan vision of the world and to transcend class and race differences.

While campaigning for Cuban independence, Martí did not seek to speak solely to one segment of Cuban society, but rather for an entire nation composed of diverse and heterogeneous elements. Martí successfully organized these heterogeneous elements, and the Partido Revolucionario Cubano (PRC)[6] stands testament to this success. The PRC was a decentralized party of independence clubs that united Cubans of all backgrounds and social classes. The PRC spearheaded the 1895 Cuban independence war, the final confrontation against Spain, albeit one overwhelmed by the US intervention in 1898. Martí's success may have been a cumulative result of his talents; charisma surely added to his passionate oratory, his poetic writing, his active humanitarianism and his steadfast devotion to the Cuban cause. One particular aspect of his success was the tapping of ideas from the world and applying them in the context of his war for Cuba. The influence he gained from Hindu thought inspired his personal belief system and, in turn, his beliefs formed the basis of what he wrote and put into action regarding Cuban independence.

Exploring the inspiration of Indian sacred wisdom enriches our understanding of Martí's ideological construction and promotion of the nation. Such an investigation places Martí's writings in a context beyond recent hemispheric studies on the Cuban leader. This process involves applying a somewhat radical perspective to what many would argue is an over-studied and classic historical moment. One must move beyond what scholars Jeffrey Belnap and Raúl Fernández express as the "tension in Martí's work between national and transnational perspectives, a tension that makes his analysis of the Western Hemisphere's different national formations and their intrahemispheric relations extremely significant for reconfiguring the way we think about 'America'".[7] Juxtaposing Hindu notions as they relate to Martí's conception of nation places the Cuban leader, the Latin American and Caribbean historical figure, in a global if not globalized context.

The God *Patria*: The Nation as Inherently Divine

Hindu thought influenced Martí's personal beliefs, which spiritually supported him as he led a life of renouncing personal ambition and comfort for the sake of committing his resources and time to the independence movement. Conceiving of the nation as inherently divine, Martí indeed referred to the nation as a "God *patria*", one of only two elements worth revering in the world (the other being the ultimate and all-encompassing God).

I argue that Martí's promotion of a "raceless nation", and his ability to portray Cuban nationalism free of divisive, contentious and alienating devices even as he prepared for war, was heavily motivated by his conception of the nation as spiritually based and divine in nature, encompassing all Cuban human souls. Visible evidence of this is in his letter to his secretary Gonzalo de Quesada in New York, sent alongside the *Manifiesto*: in the letter, he comments to de Quesada that it was a collaborative product free of the divisiveness that wars often engender.[8]

There was no single doctrine that inspired Martí's views on *patria*. Hindu notions (hitherto largely ignored in his work), when employed as a tool in analysing Martí's writings and speeches, shed light on his ideological construction of nation and promotion of independence. Martí's views on nationhood may parallel other nineteenth-century thinkers, particularly the influential French scholar Ernest Renan (1823–92), who also conceived of the nation as having a "soul, as a spiritual principle". Renan considered that "two things, which in truth are but one, constitute this soul or spiritual principle. One lies in the past, one in the present. One is the possession in common of a rich legacy of memories; the other is present-day consent, the desire to live together, the will to perpetuate the value of the heritage that one has received in an undivided form."[9] To Renan and Martí, *patria* (nation) was a spiritual principle, yet for Martí, as we have seen, *patria* (nation) had more spiritual "power" than simply the nation as a soul or "spiritual principle". To Martí, *patria* was God. Martí was as passionately devoted to the cause of the Cuban nation as a religious ascetic may be dedicated to his or her religion.

In this sense, Martí, perhaps, preceded India's Gandhi in conceiving of the nation as a divine entity that required selfless devotion and unconditional love. The Chilean poet, educator and feminist Gabriela Mistral (1889–1957) has already identified parallels between Gandhi and Martí.[10] Indian scholar Vibha Maurya expands the parallels between Gandhi and Martí by expressing how "the value of the concept of loving [devotion] in Martí's humanism, his emphasis on reconquering one's self in order to gain greater love, which also [leads to greater] justice and motivates one to execute transformative actions, are some of the aspects that remind one of Gandhi's humanist thought".[11] Some may consider it extreme to compare Martí to Gandhi, especially since a principle of Gandhi's nationalism was *ahimsa* – the practice of non-violence through loving devotion – while Martí advocated war against Spain. However, one must consider that he promoted a fight against the Spanish government and not hatred against the Spaniard. The Cuban fighter declared in the *Manifiesto* that "the war is not against the Spaniard, who in the safety of his children and in his acceptance of the *patria* that they will win, he or she will enjoy respect and even love".[12]

If we consider Gandhi as a product of cultural and religious traditions spanning centuries and not the originator of the ideas he advocated, and if instead we consider him to be original in applying the essence of Hindu religion to a nationalist and independence project, then Gandhi's actions in this context become more understandable and less exceptional. Martí came from a society absent of significant segments or traditions embracing non-violence. In fact, one should consider that Martí perceived himself as inheriting an independence movement and continuing a war already launched in 1868 – a war that found, in the minds of independence fighters, only a truce in the armistice of 1878. Martí did not have a local non-violent tradition to tap from, like Gandhi, but rather was raised in a society surrounded by violence, particularly a society with enslaved individuals and the very visible public scaffold that colonial authorities employed to coerce the colonized. Martí witnessed the violence exerted on African descendants, as I will later examine in chapter 5.

Martí saw war as the fulfilment of a sacred duty, instead of one based on hatred. Martí would have agreed with Gandhi's conception of *swaraj*, or self-rule, particularly since for a nation to be free and autonomous, its individuals must also be both. In fact, Cuba as a free nation could therefore not have a system of slavery nor of citizens not being in control of their individual destinies – hence Martí's strong advocacy of education (the most visible example being *Golden Years*). The fact that Martí died at forty-three and Gandhi was assassinated at seventy-eight leads one to speculate whether the differences between both nationalists would have narrowed if Martí would have lived as long as Gandhi. Nevertheless, there are strong parallels between Martí and Gandhi's nationalist thought. Again, Maurya sheds light on these parallels by expressing how "Martí and Gandhi fought for the same cause, each in his own way, but their views on liberty in their spiritual sense, emerge from the same understanding. . . . Both insist on liberating one's self of the negative elements of hatred, religious fanaticism, racism, and to elevate one's self above these in order to achieve a revolutionary spiritual transformation."[13]

Regarding how Martí relates to other late nineteenth-century nationalists, particularly Renan, Martí further departs from him and other nationalists of the time by perceiving the nation as not necessarily having received a heritage in "undivided form", as Renan indicated, but rather as a nation, as expressed in the *Manifiesto*, composed of "the most diverse origins".[14]

The *patria* to the Cuban leader was not only, in Martí scholar Ivan Schulman's terms, "a hybrid construction of universal reach";[15] it was also, as argued here, a spiritually infused conception, connoting the divine. Considering the Eastern, particularly Hindu, influences of Martí's conception of *patria* expands our understanding of why *patria* to Martí was this "hybrid construction of universal reach" – it was godlike.

The Call to Serve Cuba: Duty as a Selfless and Sacred Act

Martí promoted the war against the Spanish empire as a call to sacred battle. The guiding spirit of Cuba's war for political freedom, according to him, would be pure, selfless and – in a passionate sense to the Cuban nation builder – sacred. In 1880, at one of the first meetings of the Cuban Revolutionary Committee founded by Martí to integrate and direct the Cuban independence forces, particularly those outside of the island, he declared,

> A nation is dying and needs new life. Who will guide them? Instinct. Who will rescue them? Their anguish. With which strengths will they struggle? With those of despair. The war for Cuba is not a problem of classes or political parties or of [different] groups;

it is a war for life itself, where there can only be two outcomes: either to endure a dark existence, ingrained with the approaching evils or to create a free life, [one] that paves the way to our healing of these ills.[16]

While on the surface this appeal to join the movement may appear as propaganda for the independence cause, a deeper reading reveals that Martí did not consider this call in mere political terms, but rather as a spiritual call to duty. Martí indicates in the above excerpt that "instinct" would lead and guide a nation towards the hoped-for "free life", a concept reminiscent of the need to follow the inner voice of duty to enable the evolution, and eventual freedom, of the human soul. In the *Bhagavad-Gita*, Krishna tells Arjuna that the war he is about to wage is equivalent to the fulfilment of a sacred duty.

In the *Gita*, an inner voice, according to Krishna, directs men and women in their path towards "right" action, which ultimately leads to realizing one's duty and accelerating the soul's union with the divine. Echoing these ideas, Martí extols his audience to follow their "instinct" – an inner voice – that will lead individuals to the fulfilment of a "national" duty.

Throughout his writings, Martí expresses the need to heed the call of duty in order to inspire and energize his audience and to ideologically legitimize the struggle against Spain. In this sense, the struggle against Spain and for establishing a Cuban nation was not only driven by class, race or politics, but also by a fundamental life, indeed a spiritual instinct. The war for Cuba was a contest for the survival of the living *patria*.

The Cuban people, according to Martí in the above excerpt, would be rescued by their suffering and agony. Cubans, having endured despotic government and enslavement by immoral authorities, required not only political emancipation, but moral redemption as well in the form of a war for freedom and autonomy. The Cuban people's suffering would not only rescue or redeem them, in Martí's eyes, but would legitimize the uprising against the Spanish empire. Denying or avoiding the fight for freedom and self-government would lead only to continued agony, and ultimately "a dark existence". According to Martí, to not fight for Cuban self-rule would be to deny one's, and in a larger sense, the nation's, inner call of duty and would allow one's *patria* to languish on a metaphorical deathbed. *Patria* was thus strengthened by the dutiful response to an instinctual call for pursuing the perceived moral course, the liberation of Cuba.

Martí did not describe the Cuban revolution as a class war or a conflict in a traditional sense. Instead, Martí formulated war as a struggle representing a people's ethical right to self-determination, as seen earlier in his allegorical lessons for children regarding the Annamese struggle against the imperial French. The struggle extended from an individual's right to think and act independently – hence his fervent opposition to slavery and racism – and reached, at the national level, the fight for a free and sovereign Cuban nation. Although Martí's calls to pursue "instinct" and to fulfil one's duty may be viewed as rhetorical strategies designed to depict war as the only heroic choice, his unflagging devotion to the cause of Cuban independence throughout his adult life offers testament that his appeals were not merely attempts to rally troops, but reflected deep spiritual beliefs.

Formulating how to conceive of nation in spiritual terms, Martí would also justify in spiritual terms the war to be unleashed against Spain. In 1884 the veteran generals of the failed Ten Years' War for independence, Máximo Gómez and Antonio Maceo, visited New York City where Martí lived at the time. The former commanders of that first independence conflict went to the North American metropolis to meet with Cuban exiles and to discuss preparations for a renewed independence effort. Martí became distraught as a result of those meetings. Knowing well the history of Latin American *caudillos* (strongman dictators) who emerged in the wake of Spanish-American independence, and having experienced first-hand *caudillismo* (dictatorships) while living in Mexico, Guatemala and Venezuela, he perhaps felt an eerie premonition that Cuba, under the leadership of victorious military generals promising national autonomy and order, would fall prey to this fate. Following their departure, Martí separated himself from the independence movement for a time, and he expressed these concerns in an October 1884 letter to General Gómez. In the letter, Martí attempts to correct the course of the independence struggle by making a moral appeal to General Gómez, stating that "one cannot establish a [new] nation the way one runs a military camp". The letter reflected Martí's critique of the style and management of the war. It was a call for greater democratic participation in the movement to lessen the concentration of power. Indeed, in light of the previous debacle, it seemed to Martí that not much had changed. Therefore, the strategy needed redrafting; the concept of the nation, reimagining. Martí further appealed to General Gómez in this letter, pleading that,

> If [this] war is possible, it is only because there exists a spirit that demands it and that makes it necessary; and it is this spirit that we must serve, and to this spirit we must show, in every private and public act, the most profound respect – as it is admirable for one to give his or her life for a great cause, it is abominable to serve oneself of a great cause to fulfil personal ambitions of power and glory, even when risking one's life while fulfilling these. – To give one's life constitutes a right only when given selflessly.[17]

On the surface, the letter to Gómez is a critique of the handling of the war and a request to make the movement more democratic since, in Martí's mind, the revolution's goal was not to serve the personal ambitions of its leaders. Analysing the Cuban leader's statement in the context of his spiritual views, particularly within a framework of Hindu-derived notions, reveals how much more was at stake to him than the political freedom of Cubans. The war for independence was legitimate because of its guiding spirit, a pure and selfless one. The war against Spain would not be legitimate, and ultimately not successful, if it did not honour that selfless spirit in service to the nation.

The leaders Gómez and Maceo were not only serving to politically separate Cuba from Spain. To Martí, they were serving a spiritual entity, the nation. Martí believed that a leader of the independence movement must remain ever faithful to the ideals of the Cuban revolution, notions based on altruism and a disregard for any self-elevating plans. In honouring and respecting both publicly and privately the ideals of the Cuban revolution, the leaders would set a legitimate example to others. On a larger scale, the war, according to Martí, would be the result of a moral assertion by the Cuban people. On a lesser one, the behaviour of the Cuban revolution's leaders reflected and affected the ethical development of the independence movement. To be respected and to receive admiration for sacrificing one's life in the war for Cuba's independence was legitimate only when done altruistically. In fact, just as the human soul, according to Hindu thought, would not be ultimately free of repeated incarnations if its duties were not fulfilled in a selfless manner true to its mission, so too the Cuban nation would not be free if its leaders did not serve it selflessly and democratically. Without these elements, the relaunching of the war, in his mind, would not be successful in the end, just as it had not been at the signing of the Cuban capitulation in 1878.

Returning to the scene of battle in which the *Bhagavad-Gita* takes place, Arjuna as leader of the Pandavas is forced to go to battle to uphold his family's honour. The fact that Arjuna fights alone with only the counsel of Krishna and with no formidable army like his opponents, the Kauravas, may have appeared suicidal to Arjuna on the surface, but this was meant to reinforce the notion of his fight as a selfless and legitimate one. Krishna advises Arjuna to "always perform with detachment any action you must do; [when] performing action with detachment one achieves supreme good".[18] This detachment from outcome and even from personal desires, according to the *Gita*, facilitates *moksha* (union with the Divine). Martí also echoes this sentiment when he tells General Gómez in the 1884 letter that "to give one's life constitutes a right only when given *selflessly*".[19] When performing actions without self-interest, according to Hindu thought, men and women accelerate their union with the Supreme Godhead. Selfless actions are thus the only legitimate actions that bring positive consequences. One may infer then that actions that fulfil personal desires lengthen the soul's journey to its union with the Divine. The notion underlying Martí's statement to Gómez is not distant from this idea of Hindu origin. Fighting and risking one's life for the ideal of nation and independence are legitimate only when done selflessly and by putting aside the furthering of political or military ambitions.

Others witnessed how Martí acted without regard for personal ambitions. Martí's long-time friend, the black Cuban patriot Rafael Serra, who I discuss in the next chapter, publicly stated how Martí instinctually deplored injustices and battled against them while aware that "tyrants come to power with promises of healing the masses".[20] The influence of Hindu thought, particularly the notion of the redemptive nature of selfless actions, surfaces in Martí's justifications for war and his ideological construction of the Cuban nation.

Martí also made other statements in his personal notebook in 1886 that relate to notions of risking one's life for Cuba, and of how serving the nation should be an exercise in selflessness: "this love of nation must be wholly pure, without mixing personal interest [in it], [it must be] active, active to the point of ecstasy, to the point of sacrifice, to the point of [total] allegiance, but with the labour of a priest, without ever staining it with the least guise of ambition or jealousy".[21] Martí believed that love and service to the nation had to be altruistic. Similarly, Krishna instructs Arjuna in the *Gita* that action is to be undertaken selflessly. The path to salvation lies, according to the *Gita*, in sacrificial acts and in behaviour dedicated to the well-being of others.

The nation, "the God *patria*", as Martí described, was also a divine creative and guiding force – it was, in his view, motivated by feelings that were free of hatred towards the enemy. The Cuban fighter's words demonstrate a Hindu inspiration, particularly in his notions of spirituality and Godliness, and of how he applied these notions to building and promoting the concept of a Cuban nation, a concept he knew he had to "sell" to his diverse Cuban audience. He iterated in several instances that the struggle for an independent Cuba was indeed a "battle of ideas", one against autocratic, racist and even defeatist ideologies.

Selfless Duty: A War Free of Hatred and the Unity of National Elements

The most visible and significant example of Martí "selling" his ideas on Cuban independence is the historic *Manifiesto de Montecristi*, where he publicly declared to the Cuban nation and to the nations of the world that "Cuba returned to war with a democratic and enlightened nation" and with "a warmhearted grouping of Cubans from the most diverse origins" who "faced their nation free of all hatred".[22]

In these historic statements, Martí's spiritual ideas emerge. Depicting Cuba as returning to war with a warm-hearted or heartfelt (*cordial* is the exact Spanish word he employed) union of Cubans without hatred, facing the nation and the world, results from his belief in waging a "just" war free of hatred. He states in the *Manifiesto*, "with what right will the Spaniards hate, if we Cubans do not hate them?",[23] and he describes the Cuban War of Independence as one of self-denial, and one that "loathes a futile vengeance".[24] In the *Manifiesto*, Martí writes that the Spanish living in Cuba need not fear the war, for there is no hatred for Spaniards. Formerly enslaved Africans and their descendants also hold no hatred towards their previous masters. The Cuban War of Independence is to be conducted free of vengeance since "in the Caribbean heart there is no hatred".[25] The *Manifiesto*, a Cuban declaration of independence and also a Caribbean document, signed near the Haitian-Dominican border with references to the Antilles throughout, therefore reads more like a noble and spiritual justification for war. Martí depicts war in the *Manifiesto* as a natural call to duty, carried out by a loving, humble nation seeking to be free from the grips of an immoral, despotic and foreign government.

In the *Bhagavad-Gita*, a source of Hindu sacred wisdom, Krishna instructs

Arjuna to also wage his war free of hatred and without the desire for vengeance. The war to be waged in the *Gita* was the fulfilment of a solemn duty to correct the wrongs the opposing party, the Karauvas, had committed, and not one fuelled by a desire for revenge. The *Manifiesto* expresses these same sentiments – except in this case, the Spanish imperial government was the opposing party.

Martí took care in crafting how he declared the reasons for Cuba's War of Independence, not only to the Cubans within Cuba but also to all nations of Latin America and the world. This concern for disseminating the *Manifiesto* across all borders may be interpreted as a reflection of the Hindu-derived belief in the unity of all living things. For if all living entities are essentially united, and the Cuban nation is considered a godlike entity, a "God *patria*", by Martí, then the new Cuban nation to be established would also be inextricably connected to the larger global community of nations. Indeed, as he iterated: "*patria es humanidad* [*patria* is humanity]".[26] Hence, Martí saw a spiritual need to transmit this *Manifiesto* to all nations in order for them to be aware of this new phase of this life-and-death contest, apart from the practical message of informing the world's nations that Cubans had launched their independence war.

The *Manifiesto* synthesizes Martí's ideas of nation, displaying his views regarding the envisioned political, social and economic conditions of the soon-to-be-liberated Republic of Cuba. The idea of Cuba as linked to the nations of the world is also explicit throughout the *Manifiesto* in Martí's references to commerce and trade; however, a deeper reading of these allusions reveals that beyond a mere economic connection between Cuba, the Caribbean and the world, spiritual unity is an underlying foundation of the relationship. In his references to the connections between Cuba, the Caribbean and the world, particularly striking is his reference to a sense of Caribbeanness, pointing to the Antilles and the archipelago as central to the Americas, and indeed central to the world.

In the *Manifiesto*, Martí refers to Cuba as "the bind that ties the bundle of islands that in few years' time will become the crossroads of commerce between continents", and he describes the independence war as "an event of great human impact".[27] The war for Cuba was not simply a colonial rebellion or even a civil war, as the Spanish imperialists sought to portray to the world. Rather, it was a war that had a great relevance to humanity, for it advanced the cause of human freedom. On yet another parallel, Martí also admired the cause of the North during the US Civil War, as I will examine in chapter 6. He promoted the cause of human freedom embodied in the North's campaign during the US Civil War as a metaphor for Cuba's own struggle.

Martí believed that, with a free Cuba, the Caribbean would become a dynamic crossroads of the world's continents. Throughout the *Manifiesto*, Martí advances the idea of Caribbeanness, of a Caribbean community, of Cuba benefiting from and serving the Antilles. In fact, this Cuban declaration of independence, a document officially ushering in the Cuban republic, was created in a Dominican town with Haitian mountains in the distance, at the home of the commander-in-chief of the Cuban Liberation Army, the Dominican General Máximo Gómez. The birth of the Cuban nation, following a lengthy campaign for Cuban independence throughout the circum-Caribbean, was truly a Caribbean effort. In this formal declaration against the Spanish empire, Martí states that the war is a product of "the right service that the judicious heroism of the Antilles lends to the stability and just treatment of the American nations, and to the balance of a shifting world".[28] The independence war was not merely the result of Cuba acting alone; rather, it was due to the "judicious heroism" of the Caribbean islands (the Antilles), which provided a "service" to the fair and just treatment of the people of the Americas. This "judicious heroism" also contributed to righting of global wrongs, to the remedy of the world's ills.

The *Manifiesto* further states that the purpose of the war for independence was to create "a free archipelago where respectful nations would pour the wealth that, as they transit, should fall over [this] crossroads of the world".[29] As seen in the *Manifiesto*, Martí perceived Cuba as central to the Caribbean, and the Caribbean as "the world's crossroads" was a nexus of the world. The trade that Cuba and the Caribbean would have with the world would naturally enrich the nations of the region. This statement in the *Manifiesto*, regarding Cuba as open to international trade, should not merely be perceived as a declaration meant to quell the anxieties of elite business sectors on the island who wanted free trade, nor should it be viewed as a move to gain support from those who opposed Spanish imperial control of Cuba's economy. Rather, it should be considered as motivated by Martí's belief in the need for the island to engage the world in all aspects. For Cuba, as a natural and free divine entity – indeed, a God *patria* – must interact and evolve with the world's community of nations.

Beyond the *Manifiesto*'s display of Martí's economic views, it also references his social views. Significant sections of the document advocate anti-racism and anti-hatred, specifically towards Spaniards. Scholars have examined the *Manifiesto* in light of these practical dimensions of waging a successful independence war and of founding an independent republic in a socially repressive environment that is extraneously controlled economically and politically. Considering his cosmopolitan spiritual views, the *Manifiesto* is better understood as the ultimate spiritual declaration of freeing the nation of Cuba, as Martí and its leaders were about to commit the ultimate sacrifice in the name of this supreme spiritual being. In the name of this divine, uniting element of all Cubans, the *patria*, Martí would indeed lose his life.

If, according to Hindu philosophy (as seen in the *Bhagavad-Gita*), the practice of virtue and fulfilment of duty facilitated the union of the human soul with the ultimate divinity, minimizing repeated incarnations in the soul's journey and accelerating its final encounter with "God Consciousness", then surely practising virtue and complying with duty also facilitated service to "God *patria*" – for "God Consciousness and God *patria* are the only two elements worthy of reverence", according to Martí's 1871 annotation in his personal diary while exiled in Spain. Therefore, Martí served his nation, or the *patria*, as a means to fulfil the inner call of duty with the ultimate objective of accelerating his soul's union with the Divine. Duty in the course of serving the Cuban nation became a purifying agent of the human soul. In serving Cuba, Martí believed he accelerated his own spiritual evolution. Viewed in this light, Martí's statements in the *Manifiesto de Montecristi*, regarding Cuba's war for independence as having great human impact and as balancing the world, become more understandable.

In this chapter, I have expanded the discussion of the Eastern, particularly Hindu, origins of Martí's work by showing how he formulated a sacred call to war and what he considered the divine Cuban nation's future to be. The Cuban revolutionary's concept of nation was spiritually derived; he even defined it as a "God *patria*". His formulations for war and his construction of nation had significant spiritual connotations, particularly inspired by Hindu thought. The Hindu-derived notions of separation as illusion and of God Consciousness uniting humanity shaped Martí's ideological construction of the Cuban nation. Martí's God *patria* facilitated the formulation of a "raceless nation" and justified his declarations in the *Manifiesto de Montecristi*. In his words, Cuba's sacred war gained the potential to have a great impact on the fate of humanity. Cuba's destiny was to be a divine nation that interacted with and belonged to a greater global community of nations. In a real sense, Cuba's anti-imperialist fight assisted in rolling back global imperialism.

Throughout his writings, Martí pointed to the need to follow one's duty in order to inspire and energize his audience and to ideologically legitimize the struggle against Spain. The *Manifiesto* as the final declaration of Cuban independence to the world – and pinnacle of his political writings – demonstrates that the nation, according to the Cuban leader, could be formed by heterogeneous elements. In this, Martí diverged from other nineteenth-century nationalists who viewed the nation as a union of homogeneous cultural and linguistic elements. To Martí, the nation did not require a common origin or heritage; it required a common love and commitment to the welfare of all who shared the space and identified with it.

His spiritual beliefs allowed him to view the essential unity in all human beings, especially in terms of all the citizens of a future Cuba. Therefore, Martí's belief in the essential unity, a divine link, the God *patria*; his formulations of a call to duty as following an "instinct" that would liberate Cubans, just as fulfilling a solemn duty would liberate the human soul from repeated incarnations and set it free at the core of the ultimate Godhead – these notions are inspired by ideas of Hindu origin.

Martí successfully organized and reignited the final war for Cuban independence. One particular aspect of this success was his ability to tap ideas from the wider world and to apply them to Cuba's reality. The influence he received from Hindu thought inspired his personal belief system and, in turn, his beliefs formed the basis of what he wrote and promoted regarding Cuban independence.

Moreover, viewing Martí's beliefs in the context of Eastern, particularly Hindu, thought reveals that his appeals when campaigning for Cuban independence were achieved from the empowered position of someone who believed that serving the Cuban nation was fulfilling a sacred duty and submitting to a divine force. Just as the human soul would not be ultimately freed of repeated incarnations if its duties were not fulfilled in a selfless manner, true to its mission, so too the Cuban nation would not be free if its leaders did not serve it selflessly and democratically. The war for Cuba, according to Martí, was to be conducted selflessly and without hatred towards the enemy. Martí's cosmopolitan spiritual views, his speeches, writings and particularly the historic *Manifiesto de Montecristi* are better understood as spiritual declarations in the course of freeing the inherently divine nation of Cuba. Moreover, this spiritual freedom speaks to the sacred task of balancing the world.

5. MARTÍ AND THE AFRICAN DIASPORA

> *La afinidad de los caracteres es más poderosa entre los hombres que la afinidad del color.*
> The affinity of character is more powerful among men than the affinity of colour.[1]
> – *"Mi raza" ("My Race")*, Patria, *16 April 1893*

In 1941 Cuba, renowned ethnographer Fernando Ortiz gave a public lecture on the subject of Martí and race, the first one of its kind.[2] A scholar of Afro-Cuban culture, Ortiz explained why fighting racism was an inextricable component of Martí's struggle for Cuban independence. With few exceptions, not since Ortiz's lecture have studies of Martí focused in a comprehensive manner on the intersections of his life and work with the African diasporic search for social justice and equality. Beyond presenting Martí's work in an African-centric context, Ortiz, in his lecture, masterfully problematized how the Spanish kept Cubans colonized. The Spanish colonial government, according to Ortiz, often silenced or ignored sound political opposition to its oppressive rule by employing racialized arguments against a significant segment of the Cuban population, especially those of some or mostly African ancestry. According to Ortiz,

> Colonial absolutism with its lack of liberties and excessive oppression, needed racism as an ideological element [to support] its social structure. It was not enough to disqualify a human opponent, one dominated and subjected, with the adequate circumstantial adjective. They had to [infuse] a biological stigma in order to justify that their social

Figure 5. Martí with Cuban émigrés during his campaign trip to Jamaica, 1892.

demerit did not depend on indisputable evidence, rather from the prejudice of a congenital fate, supported by anatomy.[3]

In looking back at Cuban history, and in order to counteract the racialized arguments in the media climate of the Cuban republic of the late 1930s and early 1940s, Ortiz insisted that promoters of the Spanish colonial system did not need to argue convincingly against its opposition. In an era of increasingly racialized politics, the Spanish colonial government simply overpowered their political adversaries by pointing to perceived and "constructed" congenital and anatomical "defects". Employing pseudoscientific, biological determinism indeed allowed the Spanish to delegitimize opposition to their colonial policies.[4]

Given the context of a racially violent social and political atmosphere, particularly with a system of enslavement in place, it would have been logical to conclude that the ultimate opposition to the Spanish colonial regime would be the unravelling of the entire system and the establishment of the means by which the colony would pursue an independent course. In Cuba, independence was linked to abolition, and no viable vision of an independent Cuba could be drawn without the total freedom of its citizens, regardless of their ethnic origins. Martí understood this essential connection between political independence and total liberation, and therefore fought racism on every front. Although much has been written on the subject of Martí's fight against racism in order to undermine Spanish colonial authority, no systematic analysis has attempted to weave together the diverse aspects of Martí's ideas, his relationships with African descendants and his efforts in the fight against racism. Studies of Martí's fight against racism have ignored the African-derived relationships and experiences that nurtured and strengthened his anti-racism and struggle against oppression. An African diasporic-centred narrative of Martí's life and work must therefore not only place African descendants in the foreground, but also consider how their troubles and concerns, their efforts and experiences, give greater meaning to Martí's legacy, particularly as an ally of the African cause in the Americas.

In this chapter I add another dimension to Martí's fight against racism. I agree with scholar Anne Fountain's assertion that "Martí fully discovered, described and reacted to the topic of race and most completely made it a part of his writing during the last fifteen years of his life, spent largely in the United States".[5] Indeed, as Fountain affirms,

> the late 1880s and the 1890s, when Martí's focus on Cuban independence intensified, coincided with his evolving and increasingly harsh views of the United States. The racial panoramas he saw in exile affected what he planned in exile and were reflected in the speeches given in Florida and the entries in *Patria* [pro-independence newspaper founded by Martí]. The spectre of racial hatred in the US South was a call to tamp down seeds of discord and to champion brotherhood. The uneasy confluence of diverse nationalities and ethnic groups in the United States signalled a need to promote a unifying national identity, *Cubanidad*.[6]

Martí's views on race, particularly his defence of the rights of African descendants, were a critical component in his pro-independence messages and of his nation-building programme. Beyond the fact that the racial and political milieu of the US influenced his views on race, I argue in this chapter that his pro-independence programme was also heavily influenced by the relationships he maintained with the sons and daughters of the African diaspora, as well as by his personal spiritual views of the intrinsic, essential unity of all human beings, as I explored in chapters 3 and 4.

Therefore, in this chapter I employ an African diaporic-centred perspective in order to demonstrate that the Cuban leader supported Afro-Cubans and the fight against racism in the 1880s and 1890s not merely in the course of uniting all Cubans in a hoped-for final and successful confrontation against the Spanish empire, and not only as a result of his experiences and witnessing of racial oppression in the United States, but because he loved and collaborated closely with people of African descent. He empathized with those across the racial divide of his times and he felt the spiritual and intellectual need to walk in their shoes and feel their pain. Supporting the African diasporic cause would not only be politically liberating for the divinely conceived nation of Cuba, but for Martí, the individual, it also freed him from the spiritual and moral shame derived from living in a society plagued by gross injustice and violence. Working to correct the wrongs against African descendants facilitated Martí's balancing of the wrongs of the world.

Martí's views on race were avant-garde for the time; he believed that race was not a scientific construct, but a social one: *"razas de librería* [races made in bookstores]".[7] Yet he maintained – in the course of promoting Cuban social unity in the independence movement – that the black Cuban man owed his freedom from slavery in part to the Cuban whites and, as a result, there should be no racial hatred among Cuban blacks towards Cuban whites.[8] In Martí's mind, freedom from slavery in Cuba had arrived at the hands of the Revolution of 1868, when Carlos Manuel de Céspedes, a prominent white planter from Bayamo, freed his enslaved workers, incited them to join him and launched the armed struggle against Spanish colonialism. Hence, Martí argued against racial fears in the independence movement by detonating Spanish reasons why Cuba should remain a part of Spain by asserting that the black man's freedom had already been fought for at Yara, scene of de Céspedes's uprising, and need not be legislated. Freedom from slavery came as a product of the struggle of both white and black Cubans – in reality, an illusion, for slavery continued in Cuba and was not abolished until 1886 by Spanish legislation. Nevertheless, the promotion of freedom as emanating from both blacks and whites, and the notion of blacks owing their freedom to Cuban whites were part of Martí's construction of nationhood and were words meant to rally and inspire.

The spectre of the Haitian revolution loomed large in the white-dominated Caribbean plantation world. Martí diffused this phantasm in white minds by exhorting that the new Cuban revolution for independence would not take the course of the Haitian one, for the Cuban war would not be one to avenge the horrors of slavery. Martí stated that in the white Cuban heart there was no hatred for his black brother. In hindsight, this was quite naïve of Martí, for US intervention in the war he organized flamed the latent racism that already existed in Cuba and lethally unravelled in the massacre of black Cubans in 1912 by troops of the Cuban republic.

Prevailing Views of Race in Martí's Time

A look at how Latin American intellectuals considered the issue of race and the debates in Cuba at the time leads to a better understanding of the context of Martí's views.[9] Although Martí lived for most of his short adult life in the United States, he did not ignore the arguments in Cuba regarding the subject – particularly since a close collaborator of his, Juan Gualberto Gómez (1854–1933), discussed later in this chapter, was involved in several disputes regarding race at the time. In the 1880s, a significant debate emerged surrounding the *Conspiración de la Escalera* (the Ladder Conspiracy) of 1844, named for the way the Spanish colonial authorities tortured the accused and the prime subject, Gabriel de la Concepción Valdés (1809–44), known as Plácido. Plácido, a well-known poet, born to a white mother and a mixed-race father, was accused by Spanish authorities of inciting a rebellion of the enslaved and a race war to annihilate the whites. He was executed by firing squad and, immediately after his execution, Spanish authorities forbade mention of him or of the Ladder Conspiracy. Decades later, under the relative loosening of colonial censorship laws by Spanish authorities in the mid-1880s, a debate emerged regarding Plácido's legacy. Had he truly incited a race war? What were his motives and the ultimate objectives of the rebellion? The debate climaxed when coloured intellectuals began organizing commemorative events honouring Plácido and explored the possibility of erecting a statue in his honour.[10] Modern scholar Agnes Lugo-Ortiz provides an analysis of these events. According to Lugo-Ortiz, in contrast to the prevailing versions (both white Cuban and Spanish colonial) surrounding Plácido's life and involvement in the Ladder Conspiracy, Cuban coloured intellectuals informally considered Plácido "as a great popular poet, martyr and race hero".[11] In 1892, incidentally the year Martí founded the Cuban Revolutionary Party, Juan Gualberto Gómez, in the pages of his newspaper, *La Igualdad* (Equality), began downplaying Plácido's role as race hero and championing him as one of the entire Cuban nation. Gómez promoted Plácido, in the words of Lugo-Ortiz, as a "representative [and] universal figure of the unity and national liberation of all Cubans", and not one limited to defending the freedom of coloured people in Cuba.[12]

In Gómez's mind, the vilification of Plácido in the decades following his demise was another instance of colonial authorities fuelling racial hatred on the island, particularly, as Lugo-Ortiz argues, when coloured sectors were increasing their presence in the social, cultural and economic life of the colony.[13] Gómez aimed to rescue Plácido from colonial defamation and argued that the Ladder Conspiracy had been a colonial terror campaign unleashed against the coloured and Plácido, its victim. The debate regarding Plácido and the Ladder Conspiracy's legacy caused frictions in Cuban independence circles, for example, in the fragile alliance between Gómez and the white Cuban Manuel Sanguily (1848–1925), a leading veteran independence fighter and Martí associate. Sanguily argued that

> it was necessary for the white Cuban to make the Revolution; that he alone [had] defied the considerable forces of Spain. [In order to achieve it], he ruined [and] sacrificed his life and estate, the peace of his home, the future of his children. The black [man] was then a slave and whoever was not a slave was something of a pariah. One would risk everything. The other risked nothing. . . . To forget what the white [Cuban] [had] done] for the coloured man, isn't that [an act] of obvious ingratitude?[14]

Sanguily, however, would later adjust his stance regarding black Cubans, without entirely abandoning racialist overtones. He wrote articles such as "Negros y blancos" ("Blacks and Whites") in 1894, where he depicted the racism that black Cuban generals and soldiers faced and their dignified response to it.[15] Sanguily would also assert that "the Spanish villager, the ignorant Spaniard, is not superior, not even the well-to-do one, over the masses of our black Cubans".[16] He also countermanded early nineteenth-century leading Cuban intellectual and statesman José Antonio Saco, who published that "in Cuba there are 'blacks' or 'coloured people' and 'Cubans'. The blacks are not 'Cubans'."[17] Sanguily counterargued that "the black man (descendant of Africans) is a Cuban: Cuban by birth, Cuban by traditions, Cuban in his accent or speech, in the end, Cuban in [his] aspirations".[18]

Martí sought to detonate these racist attitudes within Cuba and in the Cuban exile community, yet he shared the view that the white Cubans had liberated the blacks during *La Guerra Grande*, the first independence war (1868–78). In an excerpt of his personal notebook, most likely an annotation while preparing for a speech, he jotted down, "to the blacks, so that the whites would respect them for having owed them in part their freedom, and for the blacks to respect the whites since [their] freedom came from a white [Cuban]".[19] Martí's views were not too distant from Sanguily's of black Cubans owing their freedom to whites; however, Martí also believed, at least in my interpretation of his writings and speeches, that the whites owed their freedom to the blacks, for the blacks had fought for the Cuban republic. And, in the Cuban leader's view, only the Cuban republic brought, while at war, and would bring, once sovereignty was firmly conquered, freedom to all. The Cuban republic would not be viable without the support of all Cubans, regardless of colour. Martí's views on race are discussed later in this chapter; views on race in Cuba, however, require a much more extensive discussion than can fit in these pages.[20] Martí developed his views on race in the context of the racially charged environment he lived in while in the United States for nearly fifteen years, as scholar Anne Fountain affirms.[21] Even though he wrote extensively about the United States to Cuban and Latin American audiences, he also wrote and promoted his independence messages while aware of the debates in Cuba (as discussed above) and also views on race in wider Latin America.

In the *Manifiesto de Montecristi*, Cuba's announcement to the world of Cuba's independence, signed in the Dominican-Haitian border province of the same name on 25 March 1895, Martí justifies the reasons for Cuba's war of colonial liberation and portrays the war to be unleashed as one promoting freedom in the Americas – and in a greater sense, for humanity. Among these, Martí also described in the *Manifiesto* (idealistically, in hindsight) the reasons why the Cuban republic would avoid the pitfalls that plagued the fellow Spanish-American republics at their independence in the early nineteenth century. Martí catalogues the import of foreign governing models that ignored the social, demographic and economic realities of the Latin American republics and the rise of regional strongmen dictators, *caudillos*.[22] Martí was aware of this Latin American history. This awareness of the hazards of a newly liberated republic are also reflected elsewhere, in his pivotal speech known as "Con todos y para el bien de todos" ("For All and for the Good of All"),[23] delivered on 26 November 1891 to an audience of Cubans in Tampa, Florida. He emphatically stated, "we work to amend in peacetime and in fairness the rights and interests of the loyal inhabitants of Cuba, and not to erect, at the mouth of the Continent, of the Republic, the horrific controllership of Veintimilla or the bloody estate of Rosas or the dismal Paraguay of Francia!"[24] Martí knew about the dictatorships that emerged in post-independence Latin America and made it known to his Cuban audiences that the new Cuba would be saved from them. The *Manifiesto* also displays that the Cuban leader was well aware of the literature emanating from Latin America, particularly that which dealt with issues of politics and governance.

The issue of race was inextricably linked to politics and governance in Latin America. Latin American intellectuals grappled with the issue of why Latin America lagged economically compared to its North American neighbours. Major Latin American intellectuals of the nineteenth century blamed race for the relative material disparity between North and South America. The most visible expression of the issue of race, ethnicity, and the conflict between European "civilization" and indigenous American "barbarism", for instance, is the Argentine writer, statesman and (incidentally) Martí-admirer, Domingo Sarmiento, in his *Civilisation and Barbarism* (1845). Sarmiento presented Argentina's economic and political problems, particularly the Rosas dictatorship, as based on the power given to the "barbarous" elements in society. Other Latin American intellectuals of the period would echo Sarmiento's sentiments. Even in Mexico, a group of late nineteenth-century Mexican intellectuals and bureaucrats, known as the *científicos* (scientists) – who also embraced the French scholar Auguste Comte's doctrine of positivism, whereby the "scientific" method was applied to governing theories – also employed racialized arguments in politics. Martí, having lived in Mexico and having worked among these political elites, was aware of these trends in racializing political discourse.

Martí was aware of the major Latin American literature dealing with issues of race and, although some major works appeared after his death, they still reveal the general intellectual climate of his time. Agustín Alvarez's *Transformación de razas en América* (*Race Transformation in America*, 1894), Francisco Bulnes's *El porvenir de las naciones hispanoamericanas* (*The Future of Latin American Nations*, 1899), Alcides Arguedas's *Pueblo enfermo* (*Sick Nation*, 1909) and José Ingenieros's *Sociología argentina* (*Argentine Sociology*, 1910) all reflect the broad intellectual Latin American current of turning one's back on the indigenous and African elements of Latin American society and the search to "Europeanize" nations.[25] As scholar Martin Stabb indicated in the 1950s, for many of these intellectuals "the *causa causarum* of the continent's ills – its lack of material progress, its political chaos and defencelessness in the face of the 'colossus' of the North – lay in the fact that vast areas were peopled by 'inferior' races and that miscegenation had created a weak, degenerate, 'atavistic' population".[26] Leading Latin American intellectuals of the time advocated that hope for future progress lay in imitating North America and Europe. This general Latin American position, advocated by governing European-descended elites, was not too distant from the European "civilizing" mission that colonial empires employed in running non-European societies. Indeed, as Fernando Ortiz indicated in his seminal 1940s lecture on Martí and race, the Spanish empire employed notions of European racial superiority to perpetuate control of Cuba and to delegitimize opposition to the empire's colonial policies. Independence-minded Cubans, like Martí, sought to detonate these arguments.

Martí's views were also quite innovative for his time: he departed from the positivists, the *científicos*, and even from liberal elements in Latin America. In Brazil, for instance, white elites "used a liberal rhetoric to defend slavery, the plantation system, and elite suffrage".[27] In Cuba, a strong contingent of liberals supported the *autonomista* movement that advocated Cuban self-government within the Spanish empire. Most of the Cuban *autonomistas*, however, still feared black Cuban participation in government, like their Brazilian liberal counterparts. During *La Guerra Chiquita* (the Little War, 1879–80, the second major confrontation in the series of struggles for Cuban independence), the Autonomists did not shy from describing the fighters as "outlaws", "disturbers of the peace", "rebel bags of coal" or "black bandits".[28] The Autonomists, therefore, portrayed the independence struggle as one motivated by racial factors and led by "outlaw" black men in the east of Cuba. Nevertheless, the *autonomistas* walked a fine line between depicting condemnations of independence fighters as black avengers and simultaneously seeking the support of African-descended Cubans at election time. According to Cuban historian Mildred de la Torre, "the majority of [the Autonomists] agreed that they could not declare war against the blacks for they needed them for their electoral objectives".[29]

Later, when the final confrontation (largely organized by Martí) erupted in 1895, the *autonomistas*, through their political party, the *Partido Liberal* (Liberal Party), aligned themselves with Spain and not with the independence movement. In their newspapers and speeches, they publicly depicted the new uprising as "but merely a racialist movement or war of the races".[30] The Autonomists argued that those responsible for the new strife were the "mulatto Juan Gualberto Gómez and his friends in western Cuba, as well as the black man Flor Crombet and his associates, General Maceo in the East".[31] According to the *autonomistas*, in the words of modern Cuban scholars, "most of the rebels belonged to the coloured race, as well as their reckless leaders", and they promoted the idea that "Maceo sought to create in the Eastern [part of Cuba] an independent state like Haiti's".[32] When General Antonio Maceo fell in battle, *El País* (the *Homeland*), the *autonomista* newspaper, stated in its 12 December 1896 edition "that it expressed its most enthusiastic congratulations for the victory achieved by Spanish forces in the brilliant battle unleashed by Cirujeda's column in Havana province in which the ringleader Maceo of wretched remembrance was killed".[33] Yet there were black Cubans who were active in the Autonomist Party. Martín Morúa Delgado (1856–1910), a prominent black Cuban, who later became the only non-white person to ever hold the post of President of the Cuban Senate during the early republic, belonged to the Autonomist movement. Historian Melina Pappademos provides insight into these seeming incongruities: "[Morúa Delgado] believed that blacks should acquire liberal-bourgeois values of citizenship and enter mainstream politics in order to end political isolation, a gradualist approach that he also took regarding the political freedom of Cuba itself".[34] Morúa Delgado's involvement with the Autonomists, despite the party portraying the independence fighters as backward, uncivilized, dangerous blacks, is a late nineteenth-century example of what Pappademos explores in the immediate aftermath of the Independence War of 1895, that "[it should not be] presume[d] that the experience of racial marginalisation drew blacks together into a shared (universal, global) racial consciousness or that it engendered the rise of an unproblematised 'black community' ". In her work, Pappademos reconstructs "blacks' social and political heterogeneity by showing that they were motivated by complex circumstances [in] negotiat[ing] political relationships with Cubans of all colours".[35]

Returning to Martí, he criticized any policy that alienated or disenfranchised indigenous Americans or African descendants in Latin American politics; he would not support the *autonomistas*, nor did he agree with the politics of Latin American positivists and *científicos* who promoted downplaying indigenous American culture in the name of "progress". To Martí, there would be no "gradualist" approach to acquiring democratic or civil rights for all, whether white or black. In his mind, *La Guerra Grande* (the Great War, 1868–78) had already bestowed these rights; whites and blacks had won them on the independence battlefields.

Racial oppression by Europeans and their descendants around the world was condoned through racial ideologies. From biblical formulations of the right to enslave people of dark complexion to the development of "modern" anthropology, European-descended elites sought to justify the invasion, conquest and continued oppression of African, Asian and indigenous American peoples of the world. Martí, though well read in the latest scientific literature – in fact, he quipped in an August 1890 letter to his black Cuban friend Juan Bonilla that he was reading a scientific book on insects "to better know man"[36] – rejected pseudoscientific racial arguments. According to Lourdes Martínez-Echazábal, there existed in Martí's time two antithetical positions regarding the racial situation in Latin America: (1) those who promoted the pseudoscientific Darwinism of the survival of the fittest and the deterministic discourse about the "naturally inferior" races; and (2) others who advocated miscegenation and cross-racial breeding as "the antidote to barbarism and the means" to create the modern Latin American nation-states.[37] Although both positions were in opposing camps on the question of race and miscegenation, Martinez-Echazábal rightly points out that both "still reveal to be differently nuanced variations of essentially the same ideology, an ideology philosophically and politically grounded in European liberalism and positivism, evolutionary theory, and European naturalism, whose role was to support and encourage Western racial and cultural supremacy".[38]

Martí's Views on Race and Western European Culture

Regardless of whether both were inherently variations of the same theme of accepting Western cultural supremacy, Martí did not belong to either camp. He rejected the indiscriminate adoption of Western European culture, despite a recent scholarly view that he "asserted the idea that whiteness was a matter of culture, not colour [and that] anyone might acquire that culture, if only they were willing to try".[39] There is ample evidence against this; Martí never advocated the wholesale adoption of European or Anglo-North American norms.

One needs only to refer to Martí's seminal 1891 essay "Nuestra América" ("Our America") on Latin American consciousness, or the historic *Manifiesto de Montecristi*, Cuba's announcement of its independence to the world, to find evidence of Martí's rejection of acquiring white culture for its own sake. Martí also transcended racial arguments of "civilization or barbarism", as the Argentine Sarmiento had penned and indeed represented, in Martinez-Echazábal's words, "one of the earliest attempts, if not the first, at deracializing political discourse in Latin America".[40]

In contrast to most of his Latin American contemporaries who rejected all that undermined European culture, Martí believed in adopting only the constructive traits of European culture that served the well-being of non-whites in Latin America. In Martí's mind, as European descendants in America embraced the perceived positive elements of non-European societies, a new amalgamation of cultural norms faithful to the social reality of Latin America, and of Cuba, would emerge. Cuba and Latin America, in his view, would then heal themselves of the political and social ills that plagued them. In fact, Martí believed, as he wrote in the *Manifiesto de Montecristi*, that the Cuban revolutionary movement – through the "purifying" mechanism of *La Guerra Grande* (1868–78) – had overcome racial tensions. The Cuban independence movement, already healed of these racial ills, would usher a new era in Cuba, a republic free of the race-driven ideologies that plagued the North American and, to a lesser extent, the Latin American republics. Martí was an idealist indeed. For although his rhetoric and depictions envisioned an already existing Cuban national community free of racialist constraints, on the ground this was not the case. I agree with scholar Anne Fountain's view that "Martí's insistence that the Ten Years' War had freed the slaves of his homeland allowed him to imagine that slavery had ended in Cuba when, in fact, the declaration was an illusion".[41] And I add: not only did slavery last until 1886, but the racialism and division continued well into the Republican years. Already on the eve of independence, some white Cuban insurgent leaders acted upon their fears of what the hard-won equal participation of coloured Cubans would mean for the leadership of a Republic of Cuba. Pappademos recounts "how in August 1897, for the crime of flouting the concepts and precepts of power, they stripped black general Quintín Banderas (a highly ranked and respected fellow officer) of his command. At the same time, they increasingly favoured other, mostly white officers over black ones for seniority promotion", thus setting in motion what

Pappademos argues as "the social face of post-independence political administration, providing US occupation officials and republican Cuban leaders alike with a refashioned demographic profile for leadership and a precedent for later administrative appointments that implicitly argued for who in the post-war republic should lead and who would indefinitely follow".[42] Evidently, Martí's calls for a raceless nation went unheeded after his death in battle in May 1895. During his lifetime, he perhaps intuitively imagined the disenfranchisement of black Cuban fighters and activists. His persistent emphasis on unity and on the racelessness of the Cuban nation and his promotion of national identity and loyalty to the nation as trumping racial categories reveal this concern. In the words of scholar Agnes Lugo-Ortiz, "what Martí tries to do is to erase, to curb, the differences and particularities of [specific] interests in favour of representing one transcending interest, that of nation".[43]

During his campaigning for an independent Cuba, in his writings and speeches, he did not suggest that non-whites had to Europeanize or acquire an education whereby Cubans or Latin Americans could adopt the trappings of white European or North American culture, despite his having European parents. He was well aware of the heterogeneous ethnic nature of Cuban society. Late nineteenth-century Cuban society, unlike North America's binarism of either white or "coloured", was characterized by a large population of freed and urban blacks as well as people of mixed ancestry who, even if they did not command political power, at least yielded considerable economic and cultural influence in the Spanish colony.[44] Having lived over a decade in the United States, Martí was aware of North American racial politics and the plight of African-Americans in that country. His articles in Latin American newspapers on the 1886 Charleston earthquake, and on the lynchings and mob violence against African-Americans, not only reveal his awareness of the race problem in the United States but show his attempts at undermining the racial ideology of white superiority. In the free Cuba he struggled for, he sought to avoid the racial conflicts and inequalities he witnessed in the United States and he understood that a major reason for US inequalities was the ideological assumption that European or white culture was superior to others.

Therefore, Martí criticized the indiscriminate adoption of European culture. The most public example of this is in the *Manifiesto de Montecristi* where Martí depicts the reasons for the disorder and dictatorships that had plagued nineteenth-century Latin America post-independence. The stories in his children's journal, *Golden Years*, provide further evidence of his rejecting the wholesale adoption of white culture. In *Golden Years*, Martí wrote global history narratives as a means to decentre historical knowledge from Europe and to highlight other global, cultural traditions. He wrote about the distant struggle of Buddhist monks in modern-day Vietnam and the racial struggles closer to home. In other children's parables, Martí wrote stories of the intersection of race and class. In one tale, an upper-class white girl, after having received a fine white porcelain doll, prefers to sleep with a ragged, black doll that she comes to love since "nobody loves [her]".[45] These examples show how Martí indeed stood apart from the prevailing racialized intellectual climate of the time, particularly by promoting non-European culture. He publicly promoted anti-racism in speeches and writings, and he did so pedagogically to children through the stories in *Golden Years*. He even did so in his field diaries, the *Diarios de Campaña*, which reveal Martí the soldier; these were written during the weeks he arrived in Haiti, travelled through the Dominican Republic, later the Bahamas and then landed on Cuban shores, trekking through forests and then confronting battles, and they end abruptly two days prior to his being killed by Spanish forces. The diaries read like a military journal at times and a travelogue at others. In them, he depicts and promotes African descendants in heroic light. These field diaries were not written to be kept for future military record as one would expect of field or military diaries; rather, interestingly, they were created for and dedicated to *"mis niñas"* (my girls), María and Carmen Mantilla Miyares, daughters of Carmen Miyares Peoli and Manuel Mantilla Sorzano,[46] the owners of the boarding house he lived in for years while in New York City and with whom he developed close, loving bonds.

In an intellectual climate mostly hostile to African, Asian or indigenous American cultural traits and traditions, where Latin American authors prescribed Eurocentric remedies to the problems of Latin America, Martí broke against this the only way he knew how. He attempted to develop views on race that indeed served his project for an independent Cuba, but that most importantly honoured the relationships he had with members of the African diaspora. His views on race and his fight against racism were also motivated by his spiritual beliefs in the inherently divine, unifying essence of humanity. Martí was a deeply spiritual man with a cosmopolitan spiritual outlook. Indeed, Hinduism, as seen through the *Bhagavad-Gita*, emerges as a significant inspiration in his philosophical outlook. The inherently divine nature of all humans, and the essential unity of everyone, shaped his views on nation and on race. Unfortunately, his idealistic stance regarding the perfectibility of humanity did not materialize: triumphant black generals stripped of their command and blacks being largely shut out of office or from the distribution of the (later) newly established republic's resources are testament to Martí's failure to implement his vision – or to the betrayal of many of his followers to implement that dream.

Martí's Conception of Race

Martí's views on race tend to be studied under current theoretical lenses, and at times he is perceived as not acting as a progressive activist of today. Martí must be considered in the context of his time. Although he was an idealist and often "saw" into the future – as he noted in his diary when referring to his 1882 essay on Ralph Waldo Emerson, where he writes, "I gazed into the future thinking of Emerson".[47] – Martí was still a man of his time, a product of his cultural milieu and intellectual exposure. Nevertheless, within this context, Martí attempted to transcend the racial constraints he inherited; perhaps like his intellectual mentor, Emerson, who struggled (as Martí indicated) to undo "the hurdles/obstacles accumulated through centuries that were placed at [Emerson's] cradle".[48] Martí, too, sought to undo the cultural, political and ideological obstacles that impeded the realization of his political and social hopes and dreams – a desire, as he described, to "balance the world".[49]

Martí's descriptions of blacks reveal a desire to break inherited patterns, but not having yet transcended time and not having lived in some future point when a more appropriate lexicon had been developed, Martí described African descendants in the terms he knew. In March 1877, on his way back from a brief trip to Cuba to arrange some family matters and to acquire reference letters for his planned move to Guatemala City, Martí travelled by canoe from Progreso in Yucatan, Mexico, through Belize towards Guatemala. From the Caribbean port town of Livingston, Guatemala, he described the town's inhabitants in his travel diary, comparing them to the ones of Belize City, as "one does not see a single white face [here], but the black [people] of pure race bring joy to the eyes. Not the corrupted black man, bronzed, and mixed of Belize [City], but rather this other one [who is] shaped like Venus in women and, in undressed men, like Hercules."⁵⁰ Interestingly, Martí depicted the blacks of Livingston, an impression most likely of the Garifuna population, in Greco-Roman terms, another example of how the Cuban leader subverted what was considered attractive at the time by the hegemonic white culture.⁵¹

Martí's views on race were not static. They were formed by his experiences as a child, when he witnessed a slave ship that ran aground on Cuban shores and an African man hanging from a tree for running away; then as a young man in Mexico and Guatemala, where white Mexicans and Guatemalans discriminated against the indigenous – his Spanish translation of Helen Hunt Jackson's *Ramona* speaks to his concern for the plight of indigenous American populations; and later, while living in the United States in the 1880s and early 1890s, he witnessed the racial discrimination and violence that African-Americans suffered. All of these events shaped his views on race. A particularly painful instance for Martí was when he went to the Coney Island amusement park and saw men pitching balls at the nose of an African-American, jeering when the ball hit its target. These personal experiences shaped, in a visceral way, his views on race.

Martí did not believe in "scientific" racial arguments. He did not conceive race as a biological, static condition that determined intellectual aptitude, behaviour or moral character. As a child of Europeans, that was quite remarkable and indeed as a nation builder it was even more so. In fact, Martí stated that there are no races, but, as the late Fernando Ortiz rightly assessed in his 1941 lecture regarding Martí's race conceptions,

> [Martí] has no difficulty in using at times the term "race", in its improper and vague, but very current connotation so as to transmit a better understanding to his listeners or readers. But in such cases he reduces it to the social significance of a human historical group, named typically for what he qualifies, habitually, as "accumulated characteristics". Thus he used once, perhaps only once, in 1884, writing for the Argentine press, the term race, applying it to the people of our American countries, rather, to the ensemble of peoples of analogous cultural stock, those of "Our America". But Martí is not deceived. He knows that "our America" is not "our race", in any biological sense; [instead] that it is composed of many peoples, of different colours; an amalgamation of almost all the races in the world, whatever these may be and however the most anthropometric might care to define them.⁵²

Martí rejected the notion of race as a distinct, determinant factor. He also understood that race, when employing the word *raza*, was a term that related more to a group with common cultural traits than biological ones. In this sense, he would employ the term "my race". In essence, Martí believed that "race" was more a cultural distinction and not a predisposed, static and biological category.

Martí's Anti-Racism

An important aspect of Martí's anti-racism was his view against paternalistic positions in improving the conditions of African descendants in the Americas – indeed, Martí does not even take paternalistic attitudes with children in *Golden Years*. Martí was well immersed in the racial problem, particularly as it developed in the United States, as he had lived there for most of his adult life. Martí knew that, far from eliminating racial discrimination and oppression, a paternalistic posture was inherently racist, for that attitude was based on a belief that the African-descended person could only "uplift" him or herself through the guidance of a white person. Martí believed that white individuals who deemed that African descendants required "guidance" were paternalistic, for they wrongly believed that African-Americans were not equipped to advance on their own in society.[53] On 13 August 1892, Martí published in the newspaper *Patria* a response to a racialist article regarding Cuba that had appeared in Philadelphia's *Evening Telegraph*. In his response, the Cuban leader indicates how little the author of the article, a correspondent in Havana, knew about the Cuban reality. Specifically, Martí points to the history of Africans and African descendants in Cuba, of the brave ones "who fought for their freedom and who having only recently been treated as chattel in plantations, were now shaping their own destiny with what they earned from their sweat".[54] And, in arguing against the paternalistic tone of the *Evening Telegraph*'s article, Martí further states in the *Patria* response,

> the black man in Cuba is an entity of full reason who reads books and knows his waist size without the need for a civilized manna to fall from a white heaven . . . rather [what the blacks need is] for the white Cuban to give them the example of equality that nature has already bestowed. . . . In Cuba, the black man does not need to be elevated . . . for there are many whites who are also in need of elevation.[55]

Martí rejected notions that blacks required paternalistic guidance and education, further proof that he rejected the notion that African descendants should adopt white culture in order to improve their standing in society.

One of Martí's earliest praises of African-Americans is his 1886 article on the Charleston earthquake that appeared in Latin American newspapers.⁵⁶ There are many instances, too many to mention here, in which Martí showed admiration for and positively depicted African descendants and promoted their cause, but major ones include his articles in *Patria* and in Latin American newspapers where he describes scenes of race discrimination and violence, or essays on the abolitionists Henry Garnet, Wendell Phillips and Frederick Douglas, and on the US Civil War. Martí also wrote articles in Latin American newspapers praising or explaining the conditions of African-Americans in the US to teach his Latin American audiences to undermine racial ideologies.

Martí's most eloquent exposition of his views on race appeared in *Patria* on 16 April 1893 with his essay "Mi raza" ("My Race"). In the article, Martí writes, "the word racist is now becoming a confusing term, and it must be clarified. No man has any special rights over others because he or she belongs to one race or another: call him 'man' and all rights are addressed."⁵⁷ Martí consistently promoted the notion that the sole determining category that should matter is that of *hombre* – in its widest meaning, "human". In Martí's mind, particularly considering his spiritual views of the essential unity of all humanity, driven by a divine creative and guiding force (as previously discussed in chapter 3), to be a human being renders useless any labels based on outward appearances that were a product of centuries of chance environmental conditioning.

Martí further claimed in "My Race" that "everything that divides men, everything that specifies them, sets them apart, or alienates them, is a sin against humanity".⁵⁸ Once again, the inherent spiritual dimensions of his race conceptions emerge. It is a *sin* – connoting religious significance – to separate and alienate people based on race, according to Martí. And then, he continued in his article, "if one says that in the black man there is no original flaw or virus that incapacitates him in developing his entire soul as a man, then one speaks the truth and one should articulate it and show it".⁵⁹ This idea had its practical application in an anecdote told by Cuban immigrants regarding Paulina Pedroso, a black female Cuban independence activist who had immigrated to Tampa, Florida, and who was referred to by Cubans as Martí's black mother. Those near them remarked that "for Martí she was the 'loving mother [who] held him in her arms . . . and in the first Tampa days [of campaigning] when so many people were indifferent to our revolution, a black woman helped him with her money and took care of him during his illness, dismissing others who had distanced themselves from him due to fear or envy".[60] Therefore, in the article "My Race", Martí tells his readers that "affinity of characters is more powerful between men than affinity of colour". Considering Martí's conception of race and how he conceived the Cuban independence movement, tensions within the movement were not merely a result of class differences or competing affiliations. Men, according to Martí, did not automatically sympathize with each other based on colour, but rather associated with each other based on shared views or sentiments. In a separate 10 April 1893 article honouring the death of Fernando Vázquez, entitled "Vázquez, friend of *La Liga*" – an article regarding Vázquez's support of the educational institution set up by Rafael Serra, Martí and others for teaching Caribbean people of colour – Martí stated that "men are either united by vice or by virtue. There are black and white men that are so united in virtue, that it would be impossible to separate them, without first [tearing] them apart from their innermost being. One individual or other [may be motivated] by a fake arrogance or certain impatience for justice, but in open arms, all that mountain of hate crumbles down. Love is what ultimately prevails."[61] Martí did not pronounce these words merely for political purposes; they were deep convictions.

Further evidence of Martí's position against racism is a private letter of 20 July 1882 to the Cuban general Antonio Maceo. In this letter, wherein Martí seeks the general's support for a renewed independence war, Martí confides to Maceo that "the solution to the Cuban problem is not political, but social" and that "such a solution cannot be achieved without the mutual love and forgiveness of both races".[62] Further examples of Martí's views on race and how he perceived black Cubans can be found in the *Manifiesto de Montecristi*, where he writes, "black Cubans do not have schools of wrath [in Cuba], just as the black Cuban did not have in the [previous] war, one single [case] of inappropriate anger or insubordination. The republic was always safe on his shoulders and [he] never threatened it . . . only those who hate blacks see hatred in blacks."[63]

Experiencing African-Derived Cuban Culture

Martí was born in a slave society, and even though his family were not enslavers, Martí was exposed to enslaved black Cubans in domestic scenarios through his friendships and relations with his upper-class classmates. Also, since nineteenth-century Cuba had a significant population of freed Cubans of African descent, many living throughout Havana (and most certainly in the neighbourhood where Martí lived), and since his family was of the working class, Martí had significant contact with Cubans of African descent in a variety of contexts. Martí as a young adult would have also experienced the many black spiritual and religious rituals tied to music and dance in the Old Havana neighbourhoods, thus gaining significant exposure to Cubans of African descent and to their culture. Specifically, the total population of Cuba during Martí's time, according to 1877 census figures, was 1,434,747; of this, 471,572 were listed as "coloured", which included individuals of African and mixed ancestry. By 1887, Cuba had a total population of 1,631,687, of which 1,102,889 were whites and 528,798 were "coloured". In 1887, out of the six provinces of Cuba, the eastern province of Oriente and Havana province had the largest percentages of black populations in relation to the white, with 113,668 blacks and 158,711 whites in Oriente and 117,538 blacks and 142,040 whites in Havana province. Oriente, the mountainous region of the island with its long tradition of *marronage* (escape from enslavement), was the cradle of the Cuban anti-colonial rebellions. Havana, with its large percentage of African-descended inhabitants, would attest to Martí having contact with African-derived culture and people in the Havana of his youth.

Cubans of colour were also central to the struggle for independence. Despite many African-descended Cubans also fighting for the Spanish Army, supporting Cuba's continued colonial status, black Cubans played a significant role in the leadership of the Cuban Liberation Army and composed a significant percentage of its ranks. Estimates vary, but the percentage of black soldiers in the Ten Years' War (1868–78) was "between sixty and seventy, while Cubans of African descent made up about thirty-two percent of the entire population".[64] By 1895, Dominican-born Máximo Gómez and Cuban generals of African descent, such as Antonio Maceo, Quintín Banderas and Flor Crombet, commanded a Cuban Liberation Army that was fully integrated at all ranks in a country that had only abolished slavery nine years earlier. Thus, as the decade after slave emancipation in the US South gave way to the racial reaction and violence of "redemption", in the words of historian Ada Ferrer, in post-emancipation Cuba, the island saw the consolidation of a movement supported by former slave owners and former slaves, led by white and non-white officers, and committed to a powerful vision of racial inclusion.[65]

Surely one of Martí's most significant early memories of his experiences with African descendants came when he was imprisoned for anti-colonial activities in 1869 at the age of seventeen. Living in prison with individuals of diverse social classes and of varied ethnic backgrounds, Martí as a teenager relied on fellow inmates, many of whom were of African descent. Martí was also able to place his experience of African-derived culture in Cuba within the wider diasporic experience. His travels throughout the Caribbean basin offer insight into his experiences beyond the island of Cuba. A particular instance is his 1877 visit to Livingston. He described the inhabitants of Livingston, mostly descendants of enslaved Africans, as a "moral, pure, and hard-working people", and he had indeed referred to them as beautiful, the women like Venuses and men like Hercules.[66] Within the larger African diasporic context, Martí also visited other areas in the circum-Caribbean that were largely populated by African descendants. In Jamaica, Martí campaigned for Cuban independence, and in Haiti he counted on the assistance of Haitians who gave him and his associates travel documents, money and weapons to fight the final independence war.

Living in New York City for fifteen years, Martí also moved in black Caribbean immigrant circles in North America. He witnessed the exclusion, alienation and violence exacted on the African-American population by the white ruling majority in the civic, economic and political life of the North American republic.[67] The lessons he gained would strengthen his resolve to never allow these crimes to be replicated in the envisioned Cuban republic. Martí's contact and relationships with African-descended people were extensive and his actions to improve their lives were multifaceted; hence, an African diasporic-centred narrative not only expands our understanding of Martí's role in the process of decolonizing Cuba, but also pays tribute to the actions of African-descended people in securing an independent and free Cuba for all. Today Martí is a towering figure in the Cuban political imagination. This intellectual giant could not have achieved his objectives without the help of the diasporic children of Africa, for they provided support, inspiration, shelter and sustenance to him.

Martí felt a certain responsibility in racially driven crimes committed against African descendants. The lynching in Cuba of a runaway enslaved African, the whipping of another and the mockery of an African-American at the Coney Island amusement park are a few examples of the violence Martí witnessed against African descendants. In fact, Martí believed that these acts, though committed by others, brought him shame and indignity. He once remarked that "who has seen a black man being whipped and not felt indebted to him forever? I saw it as a child and [I still carry] the shame on my face."[68] These experiences, along with his spiritual belief of the essential unity of humanity, and the relationships he maintained with African descendants, motivated him to fight racism.

Martí envisioned writing a history of the black Cubans whom he knew from oral culture. Separately, in an undated personal notebook that Martí kept, he wrote a scheme, perhaps around 1890,[69] for proposed chapters in a planned volume on African descendants in Cuba; Martí kept notes on these books he hoped to write someday. Most likely, the people in question were black Cubans whom Martí knew as a young man in Cuba before being exiled: a man named Tomás, who he describes with, "Tomás was for me Mister Tomás, his most excellent Sir Tomás, his majesty Tomás; he was everything to me; he was my friend. He was good, and had a modern and artistic spirit. He used to delight me by singing and whistling. Uneasy with others, yet calm by my side."[70] Martí follows the above description of Tomás in his notebook with "but why do you hang around Tomás?" If his notebook was a means to write his innermost thoughts, then this expression refers most likely to something he heard, perhaps from others (most likely white Cuban elders) not understanding why the young Martí would surround himself with black people.

Additional proposed chapters were to be based on other people he knew. Interestingly, in his personal notebook, he writes for chapter 1, "the one who was hung in Hanabana"; for chapter 2, "Claudio Pozo's little black kid"; for chapter 3, "Isidoro, the one from Batabanó. (Waiting for my [poetic] verses, while resting at my feet. A *compadre*'s gift to Dorotea). Me, writing against my knees, me on my knees"; a chapter 4 entitled "José (Loyalty)"; for chapter 5, "Dorotea: All of them for her: Federico, Alfredo, Pepe [most likely a reference to himself, since he was often referred to as 'Pepe']"; for chapter 6, "the old man from the penitentiary, something of a broken oak: desolate majesty [a reference to Martí's time in political prison]"; for chapter 7, "Simon (Eloquence)"; for an eighth chapter, "Isabel Diago (Homosexual)"; for a ninth, "the handsome black man of Manuel's house: (with [his] hand cut off)"; for chapter 10, "the young shackled black man"; for an eleventh chapter, "Diago's coachman (he was quite a character to see)"; and a final twelfth chapter, entitled "Shackles". All these were brief annotations describing the chapters of the book he sought to write one day. One can only speculate the form these chapters would have taken if he had actually written this book on "My Black People".[71]

Martí's concern for the racism suffered by the African diaspora was not an abstract, dispassionate or merely intellectual worry. The above scheme for Martí's would-be book reveals his interest in delving into the lives of diverse African-descended peoples, from a loving companion like Tomás, to a victim of a lynching, to a young African-descended child, to a homosexual named Isabel Diago, who most likely would be considered a transgendered person today, and his description of the "handsome black man of Manuel's house" – each underscores a way of positively perceiving and depicting Cubans of African descent. In other instances, Martí would promote the beauty of black people, as in his descriptions of his trip to Belize and Guatemala. His proposed book would end with a chapter on African descendants in "Shackles". Martí was not afraid of tackling sensitive issues and this scheme for the proposed book demonstrates an interest in portraying the lives of African descendants in their diversity, but also through the lens of his close interactions and affections.

Three Historic Relationships: Maceo, Serra and Gómez

By a young age, Martí had developed close relationships with Cubans of African descent and his feelings towards them developed in hand with his views on liberating Cuba from Spanish colonialism, particularly since the Cuban independence movement from its beginnings involved the struggle against slavery. During Martí's adult years, he would develop close, lasting relationships with many black Cubans. Three individuals especially stand out in his adult life and in his programme for independence: Antonio Maceo (1845–96), Rafael Serra (1858–1909) and Juan Gualberto Gómez (1854–1933).

Antonio Maceo

"When you deal with our great soldier, I am certain you will like him very much; he is as modest as he is brave, a quality of all who are valuable", wrote Cuban General Flor Crombet to Martí in a 29 May 1884 letter describing Antonio Maceo. This came months before Martí personally met for the first time the distinguished Generals Maceo and Máximo Gómez (the Dominican-born, later commander-in-chief of the Cuban Liberation Army) at Madame

Griffou's Hotel at 21 Ninth Street in New York City. That meeting, disappointingly, ended in a break between Martí and the two generals that lasted for several years, for Martí did not share the leaders' view of Cuban independence as to be ushered and led in a purely military framework. The rupture with both generals lasted until 1887, when on 16 December he sent a letter to them in the name of Cuban exiles in New York City who were preparing for independence. From that time to Martí's death on the Cuban battlefield in May 1895, Martí's relationship with Maceo would be complex: one of respect, admiration and disappointment, but overall of deep fraternal love. His relationships with Maceo, Juan Gualberto Gómez and Rafael Serra are examples of the bonds of affection he maintained with Cuban sons and daughters of the African diaspora. I argue that an important dimension of his reasons for fighting racism and for promoting a "raceless" nation in his ideological construction of Cuban independence was the close, personal, loving relationships he held with Cubans of African descent.

Antonio Maceo was the son of a Venezuelan farmer, Marcos Maceo, and a Cuban woman of African descent, Mariana Grajales Coello, mother to a distinguished line of Cuban fighters who all sacrificed their lives for Cuban independence. Maceo had an illustrious reputation among independence supporters as a leader of the failed *Guerra Grande* (1868–78) against Spain who had refused to capitulate. He had joined the 1868 uprising as a soldier and in a matter of weeks, through his display of keen military strategy and outright bravery, was promoted to captain. Maceo is also known for his famous "Protest of Baraguá" where in 1878, in the eastern Cuban town of Baraguá, the Cuban general challenged Spanish authorities who were offering an end to hostilities with promises of political concessions that, due to the weariness of the independence efforts (after nearly ten years of ongoing scorched-earth battles), some leaders were willing to accept. Maceo took the end of hostilities as merely a truce, a respite in a war to be continued another day and until every Cuban was free, the institution of slavery eliminated and the island an independent republic. Refusing to sign the armistice, Maceo had no choice but to go into exile. He eventually settled in Costa Rica before returning to Cuba at the start of the final independence war in 1895. He was ultimately killed in battle on 7 December 1896, another major blow to the Cuban independence movement.

Martí knew that a renewed, successful independence effort against Spain would need the support of Maceo, who came from a family of distinguished

Cuban patriots. Maceo was one of five brothers who all eventually lost their lives fighting for Cuban independence, and his mother, Mariana Grajales, by the time of Martí's most active campaigning for Cuban independence, was already considered a matriarch of the movement. Martí viewed his 1892 visit to Mariana Grajales in Kingston, Jamaica, as a patriotic pilgrimage. Upon the failure of *La Guerra Chiquita* (the Little War, 1879–80), Martí wrote from New York in July 1882 his first recorded letter to Maceo, asking whether he would participate in a renewed war against Spain.[72] Eventually, their correspondence throughout the years would reach a total of 103 missives between them.[73] This first letter visibly presents Martí's views on race and the relationship between fighting racial prejudice and promoting Cuban independence. Martí confides in the general,

> I do not have time to tell you, General, how in my eyes the Cuban problem is not in a political solution, instead in a social one, and how this cannot be achieved without that mutual love and forgiveness of one race for another, and [with] that always dignified and generous prudence that I know stimulates your high and noble heart. To me, it is a crime whoever promotes hatreds in Cuba, or whoever takes advantage of the ones that exist. And another criminal is the one who attempts to suffocate the legitimate life aspirations of a good and prudent race that has already been very unfortunate. – You cannot imagine, with what most special tenderness I think of these ills, and in what manner, neither boastfully or overtly, – rather, quietly, actively, lovingly, evangelically of remedying them.[74]

The letter succinctly reveals Martí's view of the relationship between race and the Cuban revolution he organized. It suggests Martí's awareness of certain white Cubans who promoted race hatred. Elements among white Cubans tried to limit the leadership role of blacks in the revolution for fear of it being overrun by them. Even though some white Cubans attempted to limit Maceo's role in the movement at the time, Martí's letter to the Bronze Titan, as he is known in Cuba, demonstrates that Martí could not conceive of a campaign against Spain without Maceo's participation in a commanding role.[75] Importantly, Martí tells Maceo that the revolution to be unleashed is a new one – that is, one not characterized by the same detrimental (and, in this author's view, racial) politics of the previous one. Again, Martí to Maceo: "[I] will wait impatiently [for] your response regarding these thoughts I present you, and your opinion regarding this *new* shape of our task [*nueva forma de nuestra obra*]

... in order ... to create a country that, despite having been [overworked] by hatreds, all its *diverse* elements would begin to enjoy from its foundation actual rights and real conditions for a long and quiet life."[76]

Maceo responded on 19 November 1882: "My sword and last breath are in service to Cuba." Displaying a certain watchfulness regarding this new contact from this gentleman (Martí), personally unknown to him, Maceo writes, "the doubt you have [regarding] your question, whether I am willing to fight for the independence of our homeland, question that, [if] you would have known me intimately would not have made". The renowned Cuban fighter then humbly indicates that he is not the most competent of all leaders, for there are others before him such as [Máximo] Gómez, and then tells Martí that

> the military element that can be availed of, is ready to fight; what is missing is that you all, and above all, you, who are called to make the revolution of ideas, prepare the spirit of the Cuban nation for a general [call to arms], that under conditions of a formal struggle, we will lead at the opportune moment. ... Create, then, a compact mass of all Cuban element[s] and notify me when you believe the hour has arrived, that for me the moment of all my joys should have already sounded. "The War for Cuba".[77]

According to Cuban scholar Israel Escalona Chádez, the Martí-Maceo relationship can be catergorized, through a study of their correspondence, into two distinct periods. From 1887 to 1891, their correspondence reflects the years they worked independently, yet simultaneously for the Cuban cause without displaying any significant or close bonds between them.[78] In the second period, from 1892 to 1895, Martí founded the Cuban Revolutionary Party in 1892 and as a result of the failure of Maceo's own projects, particularly the Gómez-Maceo Plan of 1884–86, they intensified their revolutionary links.[79] By 1891, Maceo was able to secure an estate, an economic agricultural venture where he could congregate the loyal, surviving Cuban independence fighters in the northwestern Costa Rican province of Nicoya, despite Spanish opposition. In April 1893, a major uprising known as the Movement of Purnio failed in Cuba. It appeared that the masses were ready to begin a new war against Spain, but what was needed was the united effort that the Cuban Revolutionary Party could offer. Hence, on the heels of the failed Purnio uprising, Martí asked Maceo whether he could visit him in Costa Rica. On 5 June 1893, Martí arrived in Cap-Haïtien, then travelled through Port-au-Prince and later Panama. He arrived in Limón, Costa Rica, on 29 June and met Maceo in San José on 1 July

1893. Martí gave several speeches and met with the president and government officials of Costa Rica. On 8 July, he left for New York City, where he wrote a glowing profile on Maceo in the 6 October 1893 issue of his Cuban independence newspaper, *Patria*. Martí visited Maceo twice in Costa Rica, in 1893 and 1894, as the delegate, the elected head, of the Cuban Revolutionary Party, in preparation for the Cuban War of Independence to be launched. Following his first visit to Maceo, Martí wrote to the general, "from my visit, I brought with me one of the purest emotions of my life".[80]

When Maceo's mother died, whom Martí had visited twice in Jamaica in 1892 and then in 1893, Maceo wrote to Martí from Costa Rica on 12 January 1894, expressing, "my dear friend: three times in my anguished life as a Cuban Revolutionary, I have suffered the strongest and most tempestuous emotions of pain and sadness . . . three things!: my father, the Pact of Zanjón [the armistice of 1878] and my mother . . . oh, my friend! . . . I hope I don't upset you with this venting of grief, your grateful friend, A. Maceo."[81] The two men developed bonds of affection between them. Nevertheless, their relationship was troublesome. The conflicts were not due to racial or ethnic discrepancies, but rather because Martí and Maceo had strong personalities and often divergent views on how the movement should be led. Maceo considered that as a veteran of the previous Ten Years' War – Martí was a boy at the time – he better understood what was needed and how to more effectively direct the movement against Spain. Although Maceo was not much older than Martí (he was only eight years his senior), Maceo considered Martí an intellectual, a lawyer with good intentions who could assist the cause, but not one on whom it would depend. But Martí's personal visits to Maceo while in Costa Rica engendered fraternal love and respect between them.

In early 1895, the plan that Martí had orchestrated with the help of the Cuban Revolutionary Party of sending several ships to Cuba loaded with arms and ammunition from the port of Fernandina Beach, Florida, was discovered by US agents through the betrayal of one of the supposed Cuban supporters. The seizure of the ships in January 1895, the failure of a plan to invade Cuba that had been the result of years of political campaigning and fundraising, nearly dealt a mortal blow to the soon-to-be launched war. The plan was for the steamship *Amadis* to take Antonio and José Maceo, along with Flor Crombet and other revolutionaries from Costa Rica, to the eastern [Oriente] part of Cuba. The steamship *Lagonda* would pick up Serafín Sánchez and

Carlos Roloff in Key West, Florida, who would be taken to the province of Villa Clara, the central part of Cuba, and the ship *Baracoa* would take, from Fernandina, Martí and others, picking up along the way Máximo Gómez in the Dominican Republic, all to be dropped off in the Camagüey region.[82] As a result of the betrayal, discovery and seizure, ships, armaments and supplies had to be repurchased. The Cuban Revolutionary Party's funds were depleted. Martí wrote to Maceo in February 1895 describing the disaster and informing him that the party could only send him two thousand pesos for his expedition from Costa Rica to Cuba. Maceo wrote back to Martí informing him that he needed thirty-five hundred pesos.[83] General Flor Crombet later notified Martí that he could arrange the expedition for less. Having no more funds to send for the Maceo-Crombet expedition from Costa Rica to Cuba, Martí, with the approval of Máximo Gómez, instructed Flor Crombet to lead the expedition instead of Antonio Maceo.[84]

Martí, Gómez and four others landed on a pebbled beach in the dark of night, at Playita de Cajobabo in the modern-day province of Guantánamo, on 11 April 1895. They had been rowing a small boat for several hours away from the German steamship *Nordstrand*, which had left them about a mile from land for fear of being apprehended by Spanish authorities. Martí, describing the longed-for moment of arrival in insurgent Cuba, wrote in his field diary, "We arrive on a beach of stones. (The Little Beach, at the foot of Cajobabo.) I am the last one to leave the boat, emptying it. I jump out. Great joy."[85] Their arrival in Cuba, a result of a long, drawn-out journey through Haiti, the Dominican Republic and the Bahamas, of upsets and fears of being discovered by Spanish forces and British ships patrolling Cuban waters against insurgents, led them to trek through Cuban mountain forests in search of insurgent troops. The journeys to and through the Cuban battlefields are described in detail in Martí's and Gómez's field diaries.[86] On 25 April, José Maceo and his troops, fresh from a Cuban victory against Spanish troops, encountered Gómez, Martí and their companions. They joined José Maceo's forces and began the journey, wrought with Spanish confrontations, to meet with Antonio Maceo and his troops. On 5 May, they met with Antonio Maceo's forces, but Antonio Maceo did not lead Martí and Gómez to his camp where his two thousand troops were stationed. Instead, Maceo took them to the ruined and abandoned sugar mill *La Mejorana*. *La Mejorana* would be the scene of one of Martí's greatest disappointments, as well as the site where one of his biggest fears was realized: a soon-to-be liberated Cuba was in danger of falling prey to *caudillismo*. To Martí, the reasons for his 1884 breach with Maceo and Gómez were alive and well, despite the years of fraternal affection through visits and correspondence. Maceo told Martí and Gómez that the war and the revolution would be directed by a council of generals; Martí and Gómez disagreed. Martí argued, with Gómez's support, that he would only lay down his authority as the elected delegate of the Cuban Revolutionary Party to a civilian government that would direct the war. Maceo left *La Mejorana* enraged, without presenting Gómez and Martí to his troops. Not only had Martí – in Maceo's mind – double-crossed him by leaving him under the command of Flor Crombet during the expedition from Costa Rica to Cuba, but now he had also polluted the thinking of Gómez, who previously, Maceo believed, had sided with his view that the war and the republic should be conducted by the military. *La Mejorana* would go down in history as the scene of the second major rupture between Maceo and Martí[87] – an unsurmountable one, perhaps, in the mind of Martí.

A few weeks later, on 19 May, Martí was shot dead by Spanish troops in Dos Ríos. His demise was a profound blow to the Cuban revolutionary movement: the loss of its architect and main inspirational leader. Maceo, Gómez and the Cuban Liberation Army continued their war against Spain. By 1896, Maceo, however, adjusted his stance and came to accept the need for a civilian government to direct the revolutionary forces, but he did not, according to Martí's friends Enrique Loynaz del Castillo and Fermín Valdés Domínguez, entirely abandon his resentment of Martí.[88]

Martí and Maceo approached the independence struggle in different ways: to Maceo it was a contest between wills, military strategies and resources; and to Martí, it was focused on winning the hearts and minds of all those who longed for an independent and prosperous Cuba, regardless of whether they were Spanish colonizers (his father, after all, was a colonial police officer), black Cuban workers or white Cuban peasants. For Martí, the war would extend beyond mere resolve and resilience. Ultimately, it would depend on succeeding in the battlefield of ideas and assumptions – Maceo indeed had expressed to Martí in his first response in 1882 that it was the Cuban revolutionary architect who had been "called to make the revolution of ideas". And one particular assumption to be combatted in the revolution of ideas was racial ideology. Beyond gaining foot soldiers for the cause, Martí's anti-racism was a result of spiritual convictions, of his experiences and of witnessing the race-based violence and oppression exerted on African descendants, particularly while in the United States – but it was also, importantly, a product of his personal relationships.

Rafael Serra

On a cold winter morning, in his small Lower East Side walk-up office at 120 Front Street, under the gaze of portraits of his father and North American abolitionist Wendell Phillips, and a large map of the Caribbean looming over his desk,[89] Martí wrote a short goodbye to his dear friend, Rafael Serra:

> My dear Serra,
> Wherever I go, I will speak of you and [as if I were] with you. I have faith in you. You are a heart against all evil, a flower of tenderness, and my brother. Whether I am here or [over] there, do as if I am always [by your side]. Do not tire of defending or of loving. [Especially] never [stop] loving.
> A kiss for [your wife] Consuelo,
> Martí[90]
> [30 January 1895]

These words are significant not only for their affectionate outpouring of sentiment, but because, out of the hundreds of people Martí knew while living in New York City for fifteen years, he took the time to write these last lines to a close black Cuban friend, revolutionary collaborator and philanthropic associate on his final day in the city. The day before, Martí had signed and sent to Cuba the call to arms. This day he was settling his final affairs before boarding the next day an Atlas Line steamship bound for Cap-Haïtien, where he would rendezvous with General Máximo Gómez in Montecristi and ultimately join the battlefields of Cuba. Martí surely felt himself engulfed by the intense energy and anticipation of living the culminating moments of decades of hard work. Amid the drama of preparing to set out to risk his life in war, Martí reminisced about Serra and his work with him – indeed, he urged Serra to "never tire of defending". This important final goodbye to Rafael Serra speaks to the love Martí had for Serra and the respect the Cuban leader had for his work.

Unlike Maceo, Rafael Serra was closer to Martí and worked with Martí in other contexts beyond Cuban independence. Written evidence suggests Martí had met Serra by 1888. In a letter dated 22 September of that same year, Martí wrote to Serra inviting him to speak at an annual Cuban patriotic commemorative event honouring 10 October 1868, the day the first Cuban republic was declared, unleashing the failed *Guerra Grande*. With Rafael Serra, in January 1890 Martí established *La Liga*, the League, an educational institution dedicated to the instruction of Cubans, Puerto Ricans, Jamaicans, and other Caribbean and Latin American people of African and mixed ancestry who lived in New York City. Martí was a founding member, an honorary president and served as inspector to ensure classes were of a high quality. He also provided free lectures and books for its library. *La Liga* educated and imparted technical skills to those African descendants who could not afford an education or did not have access to one. A letter from Martí to Serra written in 1889 before opening *La Liga* reveals that Martí considered his efforts to elevate the condition of African descendants fundamentally linked to his ideas of establishing an independent Cuba. Regarding *La Liga*, Martí wrote to Serra,

Figure 6. Rafael Serra (1858–1909), close friend and collaborator of José Martí.

> we should begin with "*La Liga*" towards where we are heading, that is, not just a political change [that we seek] as the good, healthy, just, and equal social composition, without pretentiousness or demagogues or superior attitudes, without ever forgetting that to suffer greatly is a preeminent right to justice, and that men's worries and concerns, and *fleeting social inequalities, can never impose themselves over an equality that nature has created*.[91]

Martí's strong interest in improving the lives of African descendants went beyond his immediate vicinity of New York City. He helped establish another *Liga* in Tampa, Florida, in November 1891, the *Liga de Instrucción*, and one in Key West; and within the *Liga* of New York, he helped create *La Liga Antillana* or the League of the Antilles, an organization that gave mutual assistance to Cubans, Puerto Ricans, Jamaicans and immigrants from the Virgin Islands.

Martí was committed to *La Liga*'s success, as seen in a separate September 1890 letter to Serra where he explains that even though he taught Spanish at a local school from seven to nine in the evening on Thursdays, "it does not mean – it better not mean! – that I should not have the heart or voice to begin, at 9:20 [p.m.] or around that time, my Thursday lectures".[92] His devotion to *La Liga* is revealed by Martí trying to convince Serra that he could still give lectures late in the evening, even if it appeared he could not.

A close friendship developed between Serra and Martí based on their shared objectives of promoting Cuban independence, but specifically in terms of their collaboration in eliminating racial prejudice and in improving the conditions of African descendants in their direct vicinity, New York City. Both would speak highly of each other and although recent scholarship may consider that Martí "denied openly radical black activists such as Rafael Serra from leadership in the PRC [Cuban Revolutionary Party, the pro-independence party Martí spearheaded] [and] Martí acted the part of social democrat whenever the chance presented itself",[93] evidence suggests otherwise. Martí did not deny radical black activists leadership positions in the PRC. Rather, the PRC was organized by a variety of political cells and composed of independent clubs where some held a membership that was mostly or even entirely Afro-Cuban and others mostly Spanish-Cuban, and many clubs were actually of racially mixed membership. Moreover, if Serra is considered by recent scholars as a radical black activist, then Martí must also be considered radical for he always supported and collaborated with Serra's politics and efforts.

Significantly, Serra gave a speech entitled "Martí es la Democracia" ("Martí Is Democracy") on 21 January 1892 at La Liga in New York City in support of Martí. Some Cubans doubted Martí's commitment to the independence cause (they later retracted), and as a result, Serra defended Martí at this public event. Serra stated that "Martí, *by instinct*, deplores and battles the existence of disdained classes or the exclusion of rights [by anyone], because his exercise in politics has taught him that with promises of healing suffering masses, tyrants easily come to power".[94] Analysing this statement reveals that Serra stated that it was not by a desire for political gain or favour that Martí publicly deplored inequalities; rather it was "*by instinct*". Serra believed that Martí aided Caribbean peoples of African descent at La Liga (which was not a political institution like the PRC or its pro-independence clubs) not for political advancement or the opportunity to play the social democrat. Also, knowing that Martí was the elected leader, the "delegate", representing all the various pro-independence clubs that formed the PRC, and by saying that "tyrants easily come to power" when they promise to heal the masses, Serra further underscored that Martí did not address race issues or work towards correcting social inequalities to gain political advancement.

Martí had close collaborations with Serra at La Liga, and especially in editing the newspaper *Patria*, founded by Martí in New York City in 1892 as a mouthpiece for the Cuban independence movement. These associations allowed Martí the opportunity to work closely with the black Cuban Serra, for whom Martí pronounced high praises. Martí publicly described Serra favourably, saying he "is not one to jump from one group to [another] or [one] who [pawns his] free will for a crumb of flattery".[95] In a separate article in *Patria*, referring to Serra, Martí states, "when with a heart nailed with thorns, a man loves in [this] world those same ones who deny him, that man is epic".[96] Beyond praising Serra publicly, Martí showed respect for Serra's opinions, displayed affection for him as a brother and encouraged him to defy racism. In an 1891 letter to Serra, Martí tells him that

> The world, in the end, is headed where it needs to go and not where it appears. Where facts make equality obvious, one day after another, the sermon of inequality does not succeed. [Please] do not ruminate over "the injustices of man". Value the righteous man. – And the unjust one, from top to bottom, feel pity for him and forgive him. And for the practical [aspects of life], do without him, as if he did not exist.[97]

In a previous letter, a July 1889 private missive to Serra, Martí refers to a new publishing project he was beginning to pursue. Martí was in the midst of writing the journal for Latin American children, *Golden Years*, which would transmit anti-colonial and nation-building values through histories of global cultures, fictional narratives, poetry and stories of major current events of the time. The missive refers to the children's magazine project, yet it also reveals his views on Serra. Martí wrote in the letter to the Cuban patriot, "For me – you know how it is – with these things for children [that I am writing]. [They] are a labour of love [and they] are well remunerated by men of *your frame of mind and virtue* acknowledging it."[98] Martí respected Serra's opinion regarding his endeavours, and even though his children's magazine was a "labour of love", Martí had a political and ethical purpose in publishing the children's journal. He appreciated and felt vindicated by the approval of men of Serra's stature.

Respect for his opinion as a colleague and collaborator, and a fraternal affection as a close friend, are feelings Martí held for Serra and sentiments that most surely affected the way he considered race and the place of black Cubans in his hoped-for Cuban republic.

Juan Gualberto Gómez

Martí's close relationship with Rafael Serra was facilitated by Serra's living in New York City during their exile. By contrast, Juan Gualberto Gómez lived in Cuba. Although Martí did not see Gómez again after his second and final deportation from Cuba in 1879, Martí had a significant and far-reaching relationship with him, particularly in political terms. Martí's pregnant wife, Carmen Zayas Bazán, returned to Havana following the general amnesty issued by colonial authorities at the conclusion of the failed first Cuban War of Independence in 1878. She also persuaded Martí to leave Guatemala where he had been exiled since April 1877 and return to Cuba. Martí arrived in Cuba in August 1878. A few months later, he met Juan Gualberto Gómez in the law offices of Nicolás de Azcárate, a passionate Cuban abolitionist who had been previously exiled in Mexico. De Azcárate was a friend of Martí who provided him work as a paralegal, since Martí, though holding a law degree, lacked the colonial approvals to work as an attorney in Cuba.

Gómez was the son of enslaved Cubans who purchased Gómez's freedom. According to baptismal records, freedom came at twenty-five pesos, a sum paid before he was born.[99] His parents sent him to be educated in Paris, and while living in the French capital, Gómez studied at technical institutions. With the advent of the Franco-Prussian war, Gómez left his studies and turned to journalism, working as a secretary for the distinguished Cuban patriot Francisco Vicente Aguilera. Gómez translated into French Aguilera's articles that defended the cause of Cuban independence against Spanish-sponsored attacks in the French press.[100]

From Nicolás de Azcárate's law office, Martí transferred to Miguel de Viondi's, where, according to Gómez, they would see each other every day. During his brief 1878–79 stay in Cuba, Martí became active in clandestine revolutionary circles. He gave speeches in favour of Cuban independence and articulated democratic ideals at several prominent events. He spoke against the politics of conciliation that the Spanish colonialists engaged in at a banquet honouring the journalist Adolfo Márquez Sterling on 21 April 1879, and at another event honouring the violinist Rafael Díaz Albertini on 27 April. At the Albertini event, the recently arrived governor of Cuba, Captain General Ramón Blanco, was present and heard Martí's words in favour of independence – treason to Spanish colonial ears, but democratically vindicating and inspiring for those who saw independence as the way to freedom and self-determination. The mood was already tense, for in 1879 *La Guerra Chiquita* (the Little War) erupted with uprisings in the eastern (Oriente) and central (Las Villas) provinces of the island. Martí's arrest and subsequent deportation from Cuba has been attributed to the words he uttered in the presence of Captain General Blanco, who described Martí as a "dangerous madman".[101] Nevertheless, a little-known dimension of Martí's activities, as related by Gómez, reveals that Martí's arrest and deportation were direct consequences of him being in possession of a particular briefcase that contained important revolutionary documents that implicated him as having an influential role in the anti-colonial insurgency.

Gómez recounted later in life that during the early years of the Cuban republic, in order to assist the uprisings of *La Guerra Chiquita*, the then-clandestine independence clubs in Havana decided to call a meeting of all club presidents and secretaries in Regla, near Havana, to discuss ways to support the rebellion. At that meeting, according to Gómez, a central committee was established with Martí as president. Unfortunately for the rebels, colonial spies were present at the meeting and a few weeks later, on 17 September 1879, Martí was arrested. Gómez described how "after one morning when we were working hard in his office on issues relating to [the uprisings in] Las Villas, Martí took me to his home for lunch". Gómez continues his account, recorded in his memoirs, and explains that

> while still at the lunch table, Martí's doorbell rang. His wife opened it and since there was a panel between where we were eating and the door, I was unable to see the visitor. I heard his wife say in a loud voice, "The gentleman that came looking for you earlier, and to whom I told at what time he could see you, has returned. He says to finish your lunch. Since he is not in a rush, he will wait for you." Martí stood up and with his table napkin still in hand, went to the living room. After a few brief moments, Martí returned to the table and with an absolute sense of calm, he told his wife: "Please bring me my coffee for I have to leave immediately" and Martí went to his room.

Gómez continues the personal account of his final encounter with Martí:

> I saw him open a drawer in his wardrobe and [then] take some coins out and he called his wife, spoke some words to her that I could not hear. After the coffee was served, Martí came back to the table, took some sips from the coffee cup and turned to me and said, "there is no need to rush in drinking your coffee; make yourself at home, but please excuse me. I must take care of something urgent." We shook hands. He took his hat and left with the visitor. That was the last time I ever saw Martí.[102]

As soon as Martí left, escorted by the police officer, his wife asked Gómez to find out where they had taken him and to let the attorney, Nicolás de Azcárate, know about Martí's arrest. Gómez followed the two through the streets of Old Havana, reaching the police station where they detained Martí. Gómez then hurried to see de Azcárate, who was well connected to government circles. Through de Azcárate's intervention and, according to Gómez, Captain General Blanco's more lenient stance, Martí was deported to Spain instead of being prosecuted. Perhaps Blanco was more motivated to deport than to prosecute Martí since Blanco had already heard Martí speak publicly (at the violinist event), and he would not want to give Martí a platform to undermine colonial authority with his passionate rhetoric. Prosecuting Martí would have led to a show trial of sorts where Martí, as a talented orator, would surely have convinced many of the irreproachable intentions of his work of bringing justice and freedom to Cuba. Martí was thus deported a second and last time on 25 September 1879. He later left Spain in December of that year and arrived in New York City on 3 January 1880, where he would live for fifteen years, until his final return to Cuba to fight in the reignited independence war. Martí would ultimately lose his life on the battlefield in May 1895.

Meanwhile, back in Cuba, when Gómez went to see de Azcárate and advise him of Martí's arrest, de Azcárate gave Gómez some keys and instructions to pick up a small briefcase in the law offices of an attorney named de Viondi. Gómez was instructed to hand the briefcase, containing important documents relating to the rebellion, to Antonio Aguilera, who would replace Martí in the position on the central committee – both had also been selected in June 1879 by the Revolutionary Cuban Committee of New York as local representatives of the movement.[103] A few weeks after Martí's detention and deportation, Gómez recounts in his memoir that Aguilera was arrested. Yet several days before the arrest, Aguilera had visited Gómez and told him that his confidential sources in the colonial government had already advised him that he could be arrested at any moment. Aguilera returned the briefcase to Gómez and advised Gómez, "not only do the authorities know about my activities, but they also know that there are important documents that belonged to Martí in the briefcase. Please find a safe place for this briefcase; if they arrest me, read the documents and send them with a trusted messenger to Las Villas [scene of the anti-colonial uprising]."[104]

Two days later, colonial authorities arrested Aguilera. Aguilera, following Martí's fate, was also deported to Spain. Gómez opened the briefcase, read the documents and sent them to Las Villas Province. Shortly thereafter, Gómez was also arrested and deported to the North African Spanish enclave of Ceuta. According to Gómez, the briefcase was cursed; whoever possessed it would end up in jail. Gómez would later be informed that one of the most prominent men of the Havana pro-independence clubs, one who had attended the meeting that established the Central Committee in Regla, a former lieutenant colonel of the Ten Years' War, had betrayed the cause and had been working as a colonial government spy. The spy knew, and therefore the colonial authorities as well, that whoever possessed the briefcase was an important figure in the rebellion; hence, Martí's, Aguilera's and Gómez's deportations to Spain. Gómez would remain in Spain for ten years, from 1880 to 1890.

When Gómez returned to Cuba in 1890, he established a newspaper that engaged in pro-separatist (pro-independence) ideas.[105] In *La Fraternidad* (*Fraternity*), Gómez penned an article, "Why We Are Separatists", which led to his prosecution by colonial authorities and to an eight-month prison sentence. The case of the pro-independence article in Gómez's newspaper went as far as the Spanish supreme court, where the magistrates decided that it was not illegal to write about pro-independence ideas in Cuba, just as it was not illegal in Spain to publish republican ideas despite its monarchical government. Martí, aware of Gómez's return to Cuba in 1890 and of his growing activism, wrote to Gómez, re-establishing their clandestine independence collaborations. Now, however, Gómez was in a more prominent role as the main representative in Cuba of the recently formed PRC, where Gómez became the leading figure that handled, in his words, "the thread of [conspiracy activities] in Cuba".[106]

Gómez's newspapers – first *La Fraternidad* (*Fraternity*), and second, founded in April 1892, *La Igualdad* (*Equality*), the mouthpiece of the Central Directorate of the Societies of the Coloured Race in Cuba – served "to undermine the ideology of white supremacy"[107] and were also committed to the "defence of the general interests of the people of colour" in Cuba. Incidentally, Gomez's newspaper, *La Igualdad*, was founded a month after Martí, together with Rafael Serra and others, founded *Patria*, the mouthpiece of the PRC, in March 1892. To Gómez, who described his newspapers as vehicles for separatist ideas, the ideas that motivated the Cuban republic were analogous to ones that supported the efforts to correct the social wrongs inflicted on Cubans of African descent at the time. Beyond securing the freedom to publish separatist ideas in the press of the Spanish colony of Cuba, Gómez successfully litigated in the Spanish colonial courts and got Spanish authorities to rescind or impede new legislation directed at isolating and oppressing black Cubans. Gómez's activism thwarted the segregation of schools and achieved the outlawing of race discrimination in public places. Therefore, although the Spanish colonial government delegitimized opposition to its policies based on racialized arguments, as Fernando Ortiz pointed out in his seminal 1941 lecture on Martí and race, Gómez nonetheless successfully combatted the system.

In many ways, Gómez's efforts in Cuba mirrored Martí's abroad and vice versa. Writing in a 5 August 1893 letter to Gómez, Martí expressed the depth of his affection for his collaborator and friend: "my heart, you know by memory, [needs] no more than to be seen in yours".[108] The Gómez-led Central Directorate of the Societies of the Coloured Race integrated PRC initiatives and *La Igualdad*, the Central Directorate's official mouthpiece, reprinted and penned many articles mirroring those in *Patria*. One particular article that articulated the ideals of *La Igualdad* and of the Central Directorate expressed that "from the instant that differences between whites and blacks [cease to exist] in the public and social spheres; [and] from the [very] moment that certain aspirations were not special and exclusive to [certain] individuals of a single race, it would not be possible to have race associations, and the man of [one] race would cease to exist to give birth to the man without adjective".[109]

Interestingly, this article appeared in *La Igualdad* on 28 January 1893, Martí's birthday. Three months later, Martí published his seminal article against racism. "My Race" would synthesize Martí's views on race and its relationship with the envisioned Cuban republic, most likely echoing Gómez's earlier article.

Gómez thus became instrumental in disseminating Martí's views and the PRC's instructions from outside Cuba to within the island, particularly as the leader of the overarching Afro-Cuban umbrella organization, the Central Directorate of the Societies of the Coloured Race, which Gómez helped found in December 1886. This Directorate united and represented all the major black Cuban civic, educational, social, fraternal and mutual assistance organizations and institutions on the island.[110] Martí and Gómez's relationship was, therefore, significant and far-reaching.

On 29 January 1895, the leading general commanders, who had been exiled after the 1878 armistice, signed an official order declaring war against Spain and calling to arms all the soldiers of the Cuban Liberation Army. This order was sent by the PRC in New York; taken to Key West, where the document was rolled into the dried, brown tobacco leaves of a cigar; and shipped to Cuba, where it was handed to Juan Gualberto Gómez on 5 February 1895.[111] Many (most likely thousands) of the members that comprised the Afro-Cuban clubs and organizations of the Central Directorate of the Societies of the Coloured Race, upon receiving the news from Gómez, turned their civilian efforts for improving the lives of other African-descended Cubans on the island into an armed struggle as soldiers of the Cuban Liberation Army. There is no doubt Martí's independence efforts were firmly linked to the project of eliminating race inequalities and improving the conditions and opportunities for African descendants. While Gómez would live to see the founding of a Cuban republic, albeit a compromised one, in 1902, Martí would not. Gómez became a senior statesman in the Cuban republic, and sadly, he would also witness how Martí's ideals of a fully independent, racially blind nation went unfulfilled.

Martí's views on race are complex and, if anything, may be classified as avant-garde and visionary for his time. These first-hand accounts of Martí's relationships are reflections of experiences that shaped Martí personally, and that also had a significant effect on his more general and public efforts on behalf of the Cuban independence movement. The above account of his relations with these three major Cuban figures of African descent, Antonio Maceo, Rafael Serra and Juan Gualberto Gómez, are but a snapshot of Martí's lifelong interactions with members of the African diaspora – among others, Paulina and Ruperto Pedroso, and the brothers Juan and Gerónimo Bonilla, for instance – that included financial support, shelter on the campaign trail and other examples of sustenance. In December 1892, during a campaign trip to Tampa, Paulina Pedroso nursed Martí after an assassination attempt through poison. She and her husband provided protection and a brief home while away. The above accounts also reveal the context in which Martí developed his anti-racism stance and the way that fighting racial ideologies became a fundamental aspect of his programme for an independent Cuba. This chapter's African-centred narrative of Martí's interactions and the analyses of his views on race and his struggle against racial oppression, in this context, magnify his legacy and situate Martí as ally of the African cause in the Americas. Moreover, an African-centred narrative demonstrates that Martí did not break away from his Latin American contemporaries in issues of race and nation building, nor was his support of African descendants and his fight against racism simply a product of rallying support to fight against Spain. Rather, his strong commitment to the African cause in the Americas was a result of his deep associations with the children of the African diaspora. Martí's support of the African diasporic cause not only facilitated the political liberation of the Cuban nation, but considering that nation to Martí was divine and sacred, as I revealed in the previous chapter, fighting against racial injustice and violence also fulfilled a spiritual sacred mandate – a struggle that, in Martí's view, would also purify his soul.

6. TRANSMITTING PROPER GOVERNMENT
Ulysses S. Grant and the US Civil War in Martí's Imagination

> *Todo me ata a Nueva York . . . todo me ata a esta copa de veneno.*
> Everything ties me to New York . . . everything ties me to this goblet of poison.[1]
> – *Letter to Manuel Mercado, 22 April 1886*

Leaning over the veranda of a commuter ferry linking Manhattan and Brooklyn in the 1880s, the haze of the city skyline as a backdrop, Martí frequently took these minutes of relative solitude, away from his busy office and hectic schedule, to write. A critical yet little-known biographical essay on former US Civil War general and president Ulysses S. Grant (1822–85) was written in this way and "with Mexico and Cuba in [Martí's] mind".[2] Martí first published the essay "General Grant: A Study of the Formation, Development, and Influence of His Character and of the United States in His Time" in *La Nación* newspaper of Buenos Aires on 27 September 1885. It later appeared in the Cuban émigré newspaper *El Avisador* of New York City during the week of 18–25 November 1885, highlighting the importance the Cuban leader gave this biographical essay within his larger independence project.[3] It spans thirty-two pages and is divided in twelve sections, most likely the instalments he wrote on his steamboat journeys.[4]

The essay belongs to the collection of writings that Martí labelled "North

Figure 7. José Martí in his office at 120 Front Street, New York City, 1891. This painting by Swedish artist Herman Norman is the only known painting that Martí sat for; all others were created after his death.

American Scenes": newspaper articles, editorials and essays on figures and on the life of the late nineteenth-century United States. These articles on the United States were sent during the course of a decade to major Latin American newspapers of the time, such as *La Opinión Nacional* of Caracas, *La Nación* of Buenos Aires, *El Partido Liberal* of Mexico City, *La República* of Tegucigalpa and *La Opinión Pública* of Montevideo.

The biographical essay on Grant is also one of the most extensive that he wrote on a variety of North Americans that included James A. Garfield, Chester A. Arthur, Ralph Waldo Emerson, Walt Whitman, Peter Cooper, Louisa May Alcott, Jesse James and others. If the Emerson and Whitman essays display Martí's views on literature, poetry and especially on spirituality and his general world outlook, then the Grant piece showcases Martí's views on politics and government by bringing to life the dead figure of the former US general and president. The portrayal is so vivid that a reader once stopped Martí on the streets and asked him, "Where did you meet [Grant]? It seems as if you sketched him from the inside [out]."[5]

Martí's detailed personal sketch of Grant was a product of extensive reading on the former Union general and US president. He first showed interest in writing an essay on Grant in 1882.[6] Later knowing that Grant was nearing death, Martí may have finally been moved to write the essay, as he expressed in a 13 November 1884 letter to his Mexican friend Manuel Mercado.[7] In an April 1885 article sent to Latin American newspapers on the latest happenings in New York City and the United States, Martí mentions Ulysses S. Grant's role in the financial scandals that rocked the North American metropolis the previous summer. In that chronicle written for Latin American readers, as well as in the more extensive biographical Grant essay, Martí articulates three key themes I identify in this chapter and which I argue served in promoting his views on how the new nation should be governed.[8] In this light, Martí's essay on Grant was a means not only to relate the details of the life of a well-known former general and public leader to Latin Americans, but also a way to transmit his views on governance and nation building. This relaying of nation-building ideas, specifically the transmitting of right government, indeed contributed to, as Martí scholar Ivan Schulman expresses, "the process of narrating the modern nation".[9] More importantly, it shows the North American influence that, along with other world regions that I have identified in previous chapters, is evidence of the global origins of Martí's independence project.

Martí looked to several sources for information in writing the Grant essay. Perhaps the most important of these were the articles in *Century Magazine*, a weekly that he admired for its modernity.[10] Other works that Martí based his biographical essay on include that of his friend Charles Dana, *The Life of Ulysses Grant* (1885); the letters written in 1868 by Jesse R. Grant, the former general's son, and reprinted in the *New York Ledger* in August 1885; as well as Grant's own memoirs.[11] Martí also witnessed Grant's solemn and grandiose funeral procession through the streets of New York City.[12] This thorough reading of materials available on Grant, such as the published biographies, personal accounts and recent newspaper pieces on the man, as well as the emotion of the moment, provided Martí with insights that allowed the Cuban leader to sketch Grant in a personal and direct manner for his Latin American readers.

The essay gained wide recognition in Latin America, particularly since Grant was possibly the best-known North American figure in the region at the time. Most likely, the sense that he was writing about a well-known man who was highly esteemed to Latin Americans led Martí to be careful in crafting the biographical essay in a way that would not injure his audience's sensibilities and would make the essay's "teachings" more readily acceptable, particularly since it was both laudatory and highly critical of the man.[13] More importantly, the biography of Grant displays how Martí employed North American history for Cuban nation-building purposes. It was written, after all, "thinking of Mexico and Cuba". Ulysses S. Grant and US Civil War history therefore emerge as models for transmitting the ideas for right government.

Particularly significant is that the essay was also written within the context of a major disagreement then occurring in Martí's life: he withdrew from the affairs of the Cuban separatist movement, as led by Máximo Gómez and Antonio Maceo, for he was against their plan of creating a military dictatorship in Cuba during the war for independence. The Grant essay was therefore written in the shadow of this rupture between Martí and the leading veterans of the previous, failed independence war.[14] The schism between competing visions for the independence movement – one civilian, the other military-driven – and his witnessing of American expansionist politics provided the context for writing the essay. His fears of a free Cuba landing in the hands of strongmen rulers or being annexed by the United States motivated Martí to depict Grant's life and the events in the Civil War as a teachable moment and as a mechanism to advise and alert his Cuban and Latin American audiences.

Indeed, the biographical essay on Grant may be considered as part of Martí's "discourse of forewarning" (*discurso de alerta*).[15]

The way Martí portrays the Civil War in the essay reveals its significance to him as a struggle analogous to Cuba's fight for freedom. In the Civil War, Martí saw a contest to free a part of humanity that was in bondage and that suffered gross injustices. Although the Civil War may be considered a war of independence or separation by the South from the North, the South's overarching objectives of (re-)establishing independent states under a Confederation in order to maintain its system of slavery lost value in the face of the North expanding freedom. To Martí, Cuba's independence movement resonated in the Civil War and in what he considered to be the North's noble struggle. Moreover, in the words of scholar Arcadio Díaz Quiñones,

> the literature, newspaper articles, and photographs of the Civil War provide[d] Martí with an archetype of a national narrative and a collection of images. The constant representation of the war and its actors contributed to the development of a new nationalist historiography and the formation of a literary and an iconographic canon. Martí could not rely on these same resources – nor did he have the experience – to write about the Spanish American wars for independence.[16]

Grant and the US Civil War thus provided a more accessible source to narrate the nation into being than Cuba's sister Latin American republics' independence struggles, particularly if Martí wished to transmit the key themes of proper government that I argue he promoted. In the biographical essay on Grant, the Cuban activist also presents the Civil War in spiritual terms, for he considered it ultimately a war that advanced the cause of liberty, much like Cuba's own would promote the freedom of the Caribbean, complete that of Latin America and secure that of the Western Hemisphere.

In this chapter, I show Martí's complex representation of Ulysses S. Grant. Martí employed Grant as both a positive and negative model, most surely with the future government of an independent Cuba in mind. In the Grant essay, Martí is complimentary of him as a Civil War general, but more critical as a president. Among his critiques of the Grant presidency were the attempts by the US to expand into the Caribbean and the general aura of corruption and ineptitude that marked Grant's administration. These critiques of President Grant were, according to US Civil War historian James Ramage, "quite phenomenal for 1885 – a time when biographers were, generally, much more approving".[17] Indeed, Martí once commented how in the Grant essay he "stripped inside-out that genre of forceful personalities, so that they can be seen without any exaggeration or ill will, all the rough and repugnant [elements] of their insides".[18]

To Martí, the Civil War was that grandiose contest to eliminate slavery and to further the freedom of humanity, and the reconciled Union government was the product of that war, where Southerners and Northerners later joined to construct a new nation. Martí was particularly interested in this history. Portraying that history allowed him to encode the nation-building values he sought to transmit, much like he did with children's historical narratives. To Martí, writing the Grant essay was an exercise in crafting a future independence history of Cuba as a nation that was also under the real shackles of slavery until 1886, and still under what Martí considered the economic, political and moral slavery of Cuba's colonial status. He envisioned that a new Republic of Cuba would emerge as a result of a noble and sacred war of independence. Therefore, his analyses and critiques of the new North American republic that emerged, particularly as run by Grant after the Civil War, were important to him as a model for the new Cuba that would also rise – one where Spaniards, white and black Cubans, and others would reconcile and jointly govern their new nation. His critiques of Grant are particularly revealing, for they help us decipher what the Cuban leader would have wished for his republic as it emerged from its own noble war of liberation.

In examining the essay on Grant, I reveal four major themes that could be interpreted as nation-building values that Martí promotes in the course of preparing for Cuban independence. They are: (1) forgiveness and reconciliation; (2) sacrifice and selflessness; (3) the value of personal freedom; and (4) the need for educated, knowledgeable governance. Martí's depictions of the Civil War and of Grant also reveal his spiritual views.

Martí lived in New York City during the time of Grant's death and funeral and witnessed the public displays honouring the late US president and Civil War general. Martí had a strong interest in Grant, who he described in the essay as a "blazing mountain" (*la montaña encendida*),[19] and specifically as an individual who rose from modest beginnings to a commanding role – Grant, like Martí, was a nation builder of sorts who presided over the reconstruction of the United States.

The Cuban leader's biography on Grant, in its twelve sections, may appear as yet another traditional "great man" narrative of the nineteenth century. Although Martí also published a separate essay on Union general Phillip Sheridan (1831–88) in *La Nación* of Buenos Aires on 26 June 1887, the Grant essay is the more extensive and informative one with detailed descriptions of the Union general's life and his role in the Civil War. The Grant biography, unlike the short Sheridan piece, provides greater insight into how the Civil War and a major figure of that conflict could serve to promote ideals that, in the Cuban leader's view, would strengthen the Latin American republics as well as promote Cuban nation building.

There is no record of Martí having met Grant. He may have seen him in public and most definitely knew of him through newspapers and other accounts of the time. In fact, to a reader who asked Martí at what point he had met Grant, Martí responded, "I have known him in all men!" When relating this incident in a letter to his close Mexican friend Manuel Mercado, he wrote that "the human spirit is divided into family categories, just as the animal kingdom",[20] implying that Grant indeed belonged to that group of "forceful personalities".

Martí believed that biographies could serve as pedagogical tools. He remarks in an 1886 newspaper article about US political leaders that "men who represent the culmination of their nation's character and elements never die without leaving [valuable] lessons; therefore, properly understood, the biography of a prominent man is a course in History".[21] Martí's biography of Grant is that history course that he sought to impart, one where he also promotes his views on society, spirituality and ethics.

In the Grant essay, Martí reveals his general view of history: "Legitimate historical events reflect more than just all of human nature; [they] especially reflect the characters [and personalities] of the time and the nation in which they [emerge]; and [they] cease [to create], and [to be] even grandiose, in as much as they diverge from their nation and their time."[22] Martí believed historical events contained a spiritual essence, something he repeatedly points to in the Grant essay when referring to the Civil War. To Martí, historical events were not disconnected from a greater sense of the unfolding of time. In this manner, Martí may be considered to have shared a Hegelian view of history, where human events unfold in a path towards greater human freedom. Martí considered the Civil War a product of North American events, one shaped by its North American character and spirit. Referring to his views on the discipline of history, Martí believed that "neither men [nor women] nor facts derive their permanent greatness if not by being incorporated into their time and nation".[23] Therefore, Martí's depictions of Grant were attempts to portray to his Latin American audiences the spirit of the North American nation of the time.

The Grant essay also allowed Martí to employ the United States as a multifaceted model to forewarn and inform those in Latin America, the Cubans and Spanish-Americans, of what the United States was capable of, particularly its imperialist, expansionist and annexationist drives to exert control over the Caribbean and Latin America. More importantly, and even though this aspect of Martí's representations of the United States has received less attention, Martí's use of the country as a subject allowed him to warn his Cuban countrymen and other Spanish-Americans of the internal dangers that threaten republics, such as militarism and *caudillismo* (strongman politics). Grant, as the military general turned leader of his nation, provided an effective example of a North American *caudillo*. Through the Grant essay, Martí could inform his Latin American readers who often idolized the northern nation that there, too, in the United States, *caudillos* were alive and well.

Martí's biography on Grant also reveals the Cuban leader's favourable depictions of US history that include an admiration for US institutions, its enshrined, "useful" and effective freedoms and rights. These depictions underscore that Martí often employed the United States as a positive model to impart the civic values he wished for citizens to share in a future free Cuba, and to show how the Cuban republic should be governed – in other words, Martí's attempts at balancing government.

The Civil War served Martí as a model for the spiritual renewal he sought for Cuba, and in the North American sectional conflict, the North's victory resonated in the ideological battles that Martí waged against Spain. The Civil War represented to Martí the model to promote the spiritual foundations of emancipatory struggles. According to Martí, individuals were not destined for greatness. Rather, ordinary men and women held a mere spark of greatness – surely a reference to his belief in the divine essence of human beings. The actions of men and women as they responded to opportunities were what made them great. Martí opens the Grant essay by not mentioning the Union leader by name. Martí intentionally avoided naming the subject of his essay throughout the introductory paragraphs and presented the man as one of many contrasts, of humble beginnings and unremarkable profession, who later led an army of over two thousand men that fought for the "freedom of man".²⁴ Nevertheless, Martí's commendations of Grant in the essay begin shifting towards the end of the introductory section. He then depicts Grant as a highly flawed man, one who presided in a "disorderly" manner over his republic.²⁵ In this way, the essay in its first paragraph presents the story of some humble individual who gains the approval of the reader, but in the end loses it.

In the second paragraph of the essay, Martí continues describing how after his presidency, "[Grant] travelled throughout the world, who made him citizen of its best cities, led by its presidents and its kings, [yet] he later fell into commercial fraud, due to [his] vulgar appetite for fortune. In the end", Martí declares, "he has died, ennobled by his suffering".²⁶ Although this towering figure presided over his government in a "disorderly" fashion and was later involved in "commercial fraud", to Martí, the pain and suffering that Grant endured at the end of his life purified and ennobled his figure.

To the Cuban nationalist, if a historical moment exemplified the spirit of a nation, then a person may also personify that spirit. He illustrated how little there was in Grant to separate him from "that great event", the Civil War. Grant, to Martí, was great inasmuch as he reflected the sentiments of his time and nation. Referring to how Grant was a product of the Civil War and his nation, Martí wrote,

> enormous, improvised, unrefined, original and generous was the North's war, like the people who made it at the time; and the [military] leader that gave it its natural, naïve [and honest] character, and expelled from it an exotic and academic spirit. [He] was born, like his people, from poverty and deprivations; [he] took, like his [nation], more time and interest in fertile and [practical] tasks than the weak and secondary ones of books; he substituted conventional and imported ideas with new [ones] that Nature, in pristine fields and local conditions, suggested; and always, like his [nation], [he] bolted with all [the strength] of his size, firm and indistinguishable like a mountain, over the object of his will.²⁷

Martí personified the character of the US nation in the figure of Grant. This personification allowed Martí to transmit the idea that individuals whose work had a more practical, direct utility were more valuable to a nation than those who were merely intellectual. Even though Martí romanticized the "men of the earth" throughout his writings, and particularly in his poetry,²⁸ he was not one of them – the Cuban leader was unlike the young Grant, for he was a writer who earned his living from his intellectual production. Martí's description of Grant substituting "conventional and imported ideas" speaks to his repudiation of the wholesale import and uncritical imitation of European culture and his belief in adopting local approaches to local problems. In a practical sense, Martí follows this line of thought of not "importing wholesale the culture of Europe" to correct "American" (in the broad, hemispheric sense of the adjective) problems by employing an "American" man (Grant) and not some European political figure.

In the Grant essay, Martí also vividly and metaphorically describes the imagery of the Civil War. He describes Chattanooga as "the desired eminence on the banks of the Tennessee, that like a fist, clasps all the railways that move the Southern forces",[29] and later writes, "Lookout Mountain and Missionary Ridge oversee Chattanooga from their peaks, like two giants watching over a child".[30] Martí follows this with "Grant arrives by night, under a massive rainfall. He limps, [is] carried in the arms of soldiers, for he [has been] crippled by a fall from his horse."[31] Martí thus imbued his narrative with imagery and metaphors uncommon in traditional historical narratives of the time; it was written more like a novel. His biographical essay is therefore a hybrid chronicle, subject to actual events, recording and imparting historical information to his Latin American audience, but also characterized a by a certain freedom of literary expression, particularly in the way he depicts and interprets Grant's state of mind, and in how he colourfully recreates the scenes of battle.[32]

This manner of narrating history, of merging the poetic and the literary with real historical events and with the intention of recording history (in this case, biography), places Martí's essay in the style of nineteenth-century European Romantic historians, and particularly shows the influences of French historian Jules Michelet (1798–1874), who Martí admired. Martí read Michelet's works and expressed how in Michelet's books, "the heart pulses; the eyes cry; hands search for weapons; lips denounce, plead, bless, and smile. In [Michelet's narrative] there is a series of pure impressions, unforgettable, emboldening. It is a scientific book that overflows with the tenderness of a female poet and beautifies with a poet's exquisite craft."[33] To Michelet, according to Hayden White, "a poetic sensibility, critically self-conscious, provided the accesses to a specifically 'realistic' apprehension of the world".[34] The connections between Michelet and Martí are evident in the way that Martí creates a poetic, literary, expressive narrative of true historical events as a way to extract the spirit of the nation (the United States) through the "great man" (Grant), but also as a means to make his story, and the teachings within, more appealing to his readership. His admiration for Michelet and his thorough knowledge of the works of other European and North American historians of the time inspire his writing of history, but not their politics. Since Martí knew the racial positions European and white North American historians used to promote white Western historical superiority, he unpacked these notions by drafting alternative histories. Nevertheless, their flair of narrative technique inspired him. As a Cuban scholar has affirmed,

> Martí's capacity to create a [factual narrative] from his imagination without diminishing the accuracy of events, faithfully respecting the fact that is useful, but enriching it as a literary author who was also trained in journalistic production, make this an example of a unique chronicle, for he is able to embrace veracity while recreating and representing a discourse with the most effective means that he knows how: a poetic language.[35]

Among the vivid descriptions of sceneries and settings of the Civil War, Martí also provides his reader with hard facts and figures. The actual numbers of casualties in battles are woven into passages describing the mood of the conflict. In the essay, Martí describes Northern victories against Southerners and provides explicit figures, such as, "in the toughest of fights in the wilderness, in which the generals, confused in the middle of an unknown forest, lose 2,261 dead and 8,758 injured, news arrives from [other] division [commanders]: the march that will lead Sherman from victory to victory, [and] to the sea, and Grant to the foot of Richmond has begun!"[36] Providing metaphoric imagery and interspersing hard numbers lent credibility to his lyrical narrative and facilitated his audience's understanding of his nation-building views. Indeed, in the line of nineteenth-century Romantic historians, Martí weaved poetics with the craft of the historian.

Forgiveness and Reconciliation

The Grant biography allowed Martí to promote to his readers forgiveness and reconciliation as values that citizens and leaders of the new Cuban nation should hold, particularly once the divisive conflict of the former colony's independence was settled. Concerned with the task of building Cuban institutions once the war against Spain was successfully concluded, Martí promoted the theme of forgiveness and reconciliation in the Grant biography as a way to facilitate post-independence-war national reconciliation. In the future independent Cuba, Martí envisioned a nation uniting despite competing political convictions, and engaging in repairing Cuban society and economy. This vision is also echoed in the *Manifiesto de Montecristi*. The Grant essay displays an admiration of post-Civil War American society, which he depicts as having been able to reconstruct itself and to do so without hatred or revenge for past wrongdoings. Though in hindsight a naïve assessment of post-Civil War society, Martí's rather jejune depiction of the post-Civil War United States nevertheless underscores the importance he gave to a society that could unite and reconcile after a devastating conflict. Having his own society in mind, Martí wrote, "men of new [design and] composition, and radiant times are these who in twenty years learn how to love, without deceit, the ones who frustrated their hopes, destroyed their feudal estates and defeated them in war. These are [true] men, the ones who do not pawn the lives of generations and [of] their nation's peace to avenge losses and tarry over transgressions!"[37]

Martí further promotes the value of forgiveness and reconciliation in a post-war nation by affirming that, "like the Confederates at Appomattox after having been defeated, soldiers part from their generals, and without holding, over their homeland, their idle weapons nor seeking payment, like dishonourable mercenaries with fixed stipends, the prize of having fulfilled their duty, they return emboldened by their own grandeur and with that of their adversaries, to the liberated daily tasks that keep men strong and majestic".[38] Martí's romanticized view of the scene at Appomattox promotes this theme of forgiveness and reconciliation in a post-war society.

In the biography, when Martí first presents Ulysses S. Grant as "one born from poor people" in "a shaggy house in some corner of Ohio", an image of a humble man comes to mind. He then contrasts this rather meek depiction of Grant the man with his description of the former president's ceremonious funeral:

> velvet and black cloth hung from marble houses and stone palaces when all of the nation's bells were ringing, his funeral was followed through the streets of New York by Johnson who was driven out of Atlanta by [Grant's] colonel Sherman; by Buckner from whom Grant took seventeen thousand prisoners at Fort Donelson; by Fitzbugh Lee, nephew and soldier of that brilliant and merciful man, that only to Grant, did he surrender. Mountains culminate in peaks, societies in individuals.[39]

The former officers who followed Grant's funeral procession, described in vivid detail by Martí, were as noble as the man they were laying to rest, for as former adversaries they came to honour Grant at the moment of his death. In this scene, Grant is not the only "great man" to be buried; the others who follow his funeral entourage are also heroic for their willingness to put aside revenge and honour their former enemy.[40]

Sacrifice and Selflessness

To sacrifice without seeking material gain is an essential aspect of Martí's metaphysical outlook, as seen earlier through the Hindu influences on his spirituality and his conception of nation as divine. To sacrifice without personal ambition is also a fundamental component of his ideological construction of nation. The Cuban revolutionary promotes this notion of sacrifice in the Grant biography by declaring how

> to be silent is a sign of honesty and modesty in a great character; to complain is to prostitute one's character. He or she who is capable of achieving something [great] and dies without having had his or her time come, dies in peace, for somewhere it will be realized. And if it is not, it is [still] well done; for he or she is great enough just by having been able to be so.[41]

Heroic figures, "great men and women", are not merely those who have the capacity, knowledge and ability to do great things; rather, a "great character" to Martí may also be someone whose "time and opportunity has not yet arrived" to be great, but who had the intentions to do so. Martí implies in the above statement that destiny, and that even a greater design, may ultimately thwart whether a good-hearted individual is able to achieve noble actions. An individual may still be great for his or her willingness and intentions, even if destiny does not provide the opportunity to achieve his or her objectives. These statements in the essay most likely reflect Martí's own fear of not one day realizing his dream of liberating Cuba. Indeed, years later in an 1895 letter, a literary testament of sorts to his secretary Gonzalo de Quesada, written on the battlefield of the independence war, Martí expressed his views regarding his writings: "What have I written without having bled it or depicting [it with] what I have seen in front of my own eyes?"[42]

Martí affirms in the Grant essay that honest "souls" are worthy of admiration. He believes that there are two types of individuals in this world: those who take from Nature and face challenges in an original and honest manner, and others who prefer to follow convention and subordinate their originality. Martí situated Grant with the former and not in the latter group, a man recognized and praised for rising to challenges in times of crisis, yet later Grant's character became "intoxicated" with too many victories, according to the Cuban revolutionary. Grant's frankness and honesty later began to dissipate and to over-affirm themselves.

The Civil War and the Value of Personal Freedom

Throughout the essay, as Martí describes how the US Civil War erupted and how the Republican Party grew, as well as the North's reaction to Southern anger, he consistently portrays the South as reactionary and the North as noble. Martí describes the cause of the North as "the most noble crusade ever seen by men. From one ocean to the other, the states of the North flared: There shall be no more slaves."[43] In describing the North's cause, Martí writes, "[led] by an appetite for heaven and a love for adventure, other crusaders battled in times of war; but these in America shook their homes, secure, in a prosperous and peaceful age, to liberate the most unfortunate people on Earth".[44] The North's cause was a just venture, according to him. It was not a fight for "heaven", implying one led by religious ideology or "for love of adventure", surely a reference to the Crusades in the Holy Land or the European conquest of the Americas.

Martí differentiated the North's war from previous ones in history, as he would also, in the *Manifiesto de Montecristi*, idealistically distinguish the development and outcome of Cuba's own war for independence from the wars that led to unstable and undemocratic republics in Latin America. The Civil War, according to Martí, was a modern war to liberate "the most unfortunate people", not a war driven by religious fanaticism or to conquer societies, at least in his view. Therefore, the North's war, like Cuba's – the one he devoted his adult life to – was noble.

Writing to his Latin American readers, Martí contrasted his positive portrayals of the North by chastising the South:

> the South, made for ruling others, saw with anger the North's resistance to its will, and challenged [and confronted] the rough people of the free states. [The South had

risen on the backs of their slaves. The North, slow like all who are strong, cautious like all [hard] workers, saw, at first with fear, and always with shame, the danger of the rupture that the [South] provoked. There had been no peace since 1831, since "The Liberator". Through all means the South persecuted Garrison's newspaper; through President Jackson's voice it asked Congress to prosecute all abolitionist propaganda.[45]

To Martí, the South not only held fellow humans in bondage, but they were strong because of it ("they raised themselves on the backs of their slaves"), and they also persecuted anyone speaking against slavery. By censoring abolitionist propaganda, through harassment and intimidation, the South persecuted a free press. The sin of enslavement and of persecuting those voicing opinions are transgressions that Martí injects into his descriptions of the South to his Latin American readers.

In the essay, Martí promotes the idea, through his descriptions of the South's persecution of abolitionist newspapers, that a nation that holds slaves and persecutes a free press cannot be free. Through depictions of the Civil War, Martí advances the notion of the value of personal freedoms in a society. A state that claims to be free and yet holds individuals in bondage and censors free speech cannot survive.

Martí promotes the notion of the Civil War as embodying a march towards human freedom. In the essay, he describes it as "one of the more spontaneous and complete of human expressions; the most complete and artistic, perhaps, with that great artistry of universally [globally] common elements, of all that to this day man knows; for in it were in perfect analogy the elements of the event with [all] its actors and methods, determinedly developing towards the warmth of an unlimited liberty".[46] The US Civil War, to Martí, was not merely a contest between Northern and Southern armies and resources, or even a war of good versus evil. Instead, Martí meditated on the nature of the war and its history, and employed the character of Grant to promote how Grant was a man of his times whose character was moulded by the war itself. Martí saw the war as a series of events that led to an "unlimited liberty" – in other words, to the freedom of humanity.

Further promoting the value of personal freedom, Martí describes how when

> Grant advanced over Lee, powerful and impenetrable like a moving mountain, federal troops were dying from May to June, a thousand per day, in a single camp of operations. Forward columns! The nation that all men have constructed, for all men shall

remain free! President Lincoln has declared four million slaves freed, [the one] who "promised God to give them their liberty if he allowed the Confederates to be expelled from Maryland", and they shall surrender, broken forever, those who are against four million men being free!⁴⁷

Martí considers the United States a nation constructed and created by "all men", a democratic nation, and "for all men", it shall be free. Freedom, in Martí's view, should not be limited to one segment of the population. Those who opposed the noble cause of giving other humans their freedom would be forever broken and defeated. Martí identified the North's struggle to free African-Americans with his own to organize and achieve Cuba's final push towards independence from Spain; indeed, he told his close friend Mercado that he had written the essay with "Cuba on [his] mind".⁴⁸ In fact, the first battle cry of independence in 1868, establishing the first Cuban republic at arms, and the wars that concluded in failure for Cubans a decade later, were abolitionist struggles. Martí considered these to be precursors to the final confrontation he was preparing against Spain. When Martí and other revolutionaries launched the final push for independence in 1895, abolition was not the guiding principle, Spain having abolished slavery on the island in 1886. Nonetheless, Martí fought to eliminate racial prejudice and inequalities and to include all segments of Cuban society in governing the future free and independent Cuba.

Martí further espouses his beliefs when he declares, "wars should be seen [from up high], from [the distance of] clouds. It is [legitimate and] appropriate that half a million human beings perish to keep secure Humanity's only free home in the Universe."⁴⁹ Just as Martí chastised the South for its reasons for war, he honoured the North for theirs. One should consider the Civil War, according to Martí, as a great movement, a glorious action that sought to "keep Humanity" safe and secure. To Martí, humanity, or a people, could only be safe and secure if men and women were free and not subject to or owned by other men and women. Martí perceived the US Civil War as a grandiose orchestration that sought to preserve and secure the freedom of humanity in "its only free home in the Universe".⁵⁰ The Civil War thus emerges as a sacred mechanism that served to physically and spiritually liberate North Americans. In much the same way, the Cuban War of Independence would achieve these ideals for the Cubans.

In a vivid description of the US to his Latin American readers, Martí reveals his views on personal freedom:

> a country of "prayer meeting", where in church halls men and women learn to speak [out loud] revealing their sins, denouncing [and accusing] his [or her] neighbours and asking the pastor to explain to them their doubts over dogma; a nation of live newspaper, where each event, [even if it] has not yet well emerged, already has its daily newspaper, and through it, all those who hold an interest or common concern have access [to it]; therefore there is no injury [or injustice] or suspicion without a voice, and a press that publishes it, and a court willing to censor it; a nation attracted to, yes, that [type of] martial, [tough], tenacious and impetuous man just like it, who has weakened his rivals and opened paths to the greatest prosperity that written history remembers in centuries; but a country that, above everything else, to whomever deprives it or threatens its rights, denounces him and knocks him over.[51]

In the above passage, Martí praises and criticizes the United States, but the overall impression left on the reader is one of admiration for the North American nation. The United States, in his description, is quite a different country from those in which Martí's readers lived; in fact he left Mexico, Guatemala and Venezuela for their lack of civic freedoms under their strongman regimes. The United States was a free country, according to Martí, "where men and women create and employ themselves without greater contact or limit than those naturally imposed by their neighbours".[52]

Inherent in the above passage, Martí indirectly promotes his appreciation for the different types of freedoms that North Americans enjoyed, for instance, freedom of religion ("a country of 'prayer meeting,' where in church halls, men and women learn to speak out loud, revealing their sins, denouncing and accusing his or her neighbours and asking the pastor to explain to them their doubts over dogma"); freedom of speech ("and what a country of questions and answers, where every man and woman can be delaminated and stripped, examined from the inside out, and their acts seen at their deepest root, and if it is not pure, it is shattered"); freedom of the press ("a nation of live newspaper, where each event, even if it hasn't yet well emerged, already has its daily newspaper, and through it, all those who hold an interest or common concern have access, therefore there is no injury or injustice or suspicion without a voice, and a press that publishes it"); and also, the freedom to defend one's self and interest ("a country that, above everything else, to whomever deprives it or threatens its rights, denounces him and knocks him over").

Nevertheless, Martí criticizes the United States by also declaring it "a country with disdain for others, with its own way of being and capricious way of thinking that it had become accustomed to by the simple and crude acts of war!"[53] This was certainly a reference to the seizing of Mexican territories as a result of the Mexican-American War and US overtures to expand in the Caribbean. The freedom of the United States itself was threatened by the nation's own hubris ("its awareness of its strength") and by its greed ("its appetite for wealth"). By its actions during the Grant presidency, according to Martí, the United States risked losing its own freedom and those of its neighbours, indeed, threatening "the independence of its neighbouring nations and perhaps even the very independence of the human spirit".[54]

The Civil War as Means to Promote Spiritual Views

Martí also presents his spiritual views in descriptions of the Civil War throughout the Grant essay. He writes,

> Up there, from high above, men must appear – streaming, building [creating], embracing [each other] body to body, even while battling – like living flower bulbs, swollen with unnoticeable worms, that in large waves struggle with constant and awkward movements to break free from the roots of trees that they indeed [later] themselves become in a more liberated and animated form of life. They are like closed fists that push forward to come out from the deepest within the earth. Who can envision, among the magnitude of woes that this rudimentary state of the human species carries, the blessed clarity that awaits, after his or her purification and painful steps through [different] worlds? What peace to balance this beginning! It is captivating to contemplate [its] supreme fortune [and providence]; to how few is given the ability to glimpse at it, satisfied in their small [human] machines, from their [egg]shells of bone![55]

The war seen from "up high", from a wider angle, is a mechanism that purifies men, elevating their spiritual condition. Martí's imagery of worms, of men as vessels driven by a life force that metaphorically become like trees in a "more liberated and animated form of life", reflects other similar expressions on spirituality throughout his writings – a reference even to his belief in reincarnation, as explored earlier. As Martí often wrote, he would not fear giving his life for his country and for a noble cause, since those who fight for noble causes, like the worms in the above passage who become part of the tree, also become a higher expression of life. Without mentioning reincarnation outright, the "purification" and "the painful steps through [different] worlds" in this passage, from an Eastern-inspired perspective, refer to the human soul's journey through many lifetimes, continually purifying itself. As the above passage indicates, Martí viewed the war fought by the North as that spiritually purifying mechanism.

The Positive and Negative Qualities of Grant's Character

The reader may notice that in this sense, Martí, as in other instances in his writing, seeks a balanced analysis of his subject; the positives and negatives are depicted. Through detailed descriptions of events in Grant's life, Martí illustrates the Union general's qualities:

> fifteen thousand prisoners turn themselves in with Buckner, and the Cumberland is Grant's, the first major victory of the war is also Grant's. One idea or another, Grant could take from others, and even an entire battle plan, if he deemed it good, like the one for Chattanooga, by General Thomas; like the one for the siege at Vicksburg, from his assistant Rawlins; but the impetuous action, the unexpected movement, the deflecting of disaster, the original play of his troops, the instantaneous perception of a great opportunity, from no one else, but from himself did Grant [take] them.[56]

And later in the essay, in expressing how Washington (the capital) intrigues affected Grant's promotions, Martí contrasts the above positive portrayal of Grant with the following one:

> with the resentment and envy that [Grant] brought from the Mexican war, those wrongs were added [to Grant's] spirit so as to loathe, in accordance with justice, the partisanship and favouritism that paralysed the [Civil] war and deprived it of its best soldiers; in this way [Grant] accumulated that hatred, caused by fear and scorn, towards Washington [the capital], that Lincoln later moderated [and abated] with his prudence and stature; but he could not nor did Grant wish to strip himself [of the hatred], which explains, if nothing else, his ways of a *conquistador*, in that his personal desires were mingled with a certain unrefined instinct of honesty [and integrity], until with the pleasure of an excessive authority that little did his own people hold badly against him, he endeared himself to Washington, DC, in such a way that in no one else with such [high] rank as his, were personified its dangers and its vices.[57]

Martí depicts the shift from brilliant military commander to cunning and ambitious politician; indeed, he implies that the same qualities that made a man a great military commander could easily make him a tyrant, views that he echoed elsewhere.

In further describing events in Grant's life, Martí speaks against fanatic dogma. He describes how in the US Civil War, after the fall of Vicksburg and after the Union troops conquered the Mississippi,

> a commission of "Christian gentlemen" approached Lincoln to inquire if it were true that Grant – oh, the immaturity of fanatics! [Martí writes] – gave himself to drinking. "I don't truly know", Lincoln responded, as he stroked his beard; "but if he does, I would well like to know where he buys his brandy, [so] to send a barrel to each one of his generals". And the Christian gentlemen left dejected [and offended], while Grant soared, already made a general of all the region, to rescue the besieged federal troops in Chattanooga.[58]

There are two major points Martí sought to impart in the above passage. First, he depicts the "Christian gentlemen" as being petty and infantile (the actual word Martí used is *puerilidad* [puerility]), since the "Christian gentlemen" were guided by their religious fanaticism. Grant's victories mattered little to these "Christian gentlemen", nor did they see how he had significantly advanced the cause of the North. The Christian gentlemen were more concerned with Grant's drinking than with his military successes. The second point conveyed is that Lincoln did not accept the Christian gentlemen's way of thinking; Lincoln did not seek to judge Grant as the religious men had done. In writing this passage, depicting the scene of Lincoln and the Christian gentlemen, Martí demonstrates to his Latin American readers that fanaticism, be it religious or of any other type, is a sign of a lack of sophistication and maturity, since these "gentlemen" were "petty and infantile".

Describing Grant's confrontations with Southern troops, and particularly with Robert E. Lee's, Martí develops the character of the Southern commander in order to counterbalance Grant's positive and negative qualities. Martí explains, "Grant does not fight against Lee like a general who launches from afar, but rather as a mammoth that advances."[59] He later writes, "whatever Grant sets out to do, he does. Once, ten times, Lee's brave and motivated forces impede it; but he twists his horse's bridle, and a little further down the river, he attempts again, without turning his eyes [back] towards the fifty thousand dead [men] that in less than a month he has left behind; and, in the end, 'he set himself to do it; and achieves it'.[60] Martí continually referred to Grant's resolve, steadfastness and tenacity in the narrative. Martí admired these qualities, the Union general's strength of purpose and his drive to push ahead. In the end, Grant was successful, according to Martí, for his principles and his sense of dedication.

In Martí's descriptions of the events leading to the Southern surrender at Appomattox, he further discloses Grant's positive character traits. "And days later, on 9 April, Lee went despondently, leading his generals, to surrender in Grant's hands, who treated him as an [honourable] friend, the sabre, of so many [of his] victories, that Grant did not wish to place his hands on."[61] Grant, according to Martí, treated Lee as an honourable friend, even though Lee had been his foremost adversary, the commander of the enemy forces. Martí again underscores the need to be free of hatred for one's enemies. The Cuban leader also emphasizes how Grant respected Lee and did not humiliate him nor savour the victory over the Confederate general, nor did Grant aggrandize himself from it. In fact, Grant, in Martí's depiction, did not wish to place his hands on Lee's sword, one that had led Lee's forces to many victories, even considering the South's victories were a result of Northern defeats and casualties. Therefore, the image of Grant not wishing to handle Lee's sabre is a powerful one. The leading general of the Union army not wishing to touch the sword of the Southern commander is truly a sign of respect, and indicative of what type of person Grant was – and what type of person Martí considered a true and outstanding military victor to be.

In the essay, Martí also presents his overall views on war by further illustrating Grant's character traits. He informs his Latin American audience that

> Artistry of war Grant did not [find appealing] nor does it truly seem that in assaults that required spectacle and design he had many; but he was not going "to make the textbook war", rather [he sought] to save lives; to conclude fast; to exterminate the South's military power. They called him a butcher because he saw tens of thousands of soldiers die without retreating his positions, to which he claimed that to prolong the campaign [in the name of] circumspection would only result in losing more men in the end.[62]

In the above passage, Martí admired Grant for how he fought and concluded the war and for not being the man of the Washington establishment. He was not one to be distracted by insignificant intrigues. Instead, Grant, in the Cuban leader's eyes, was tenacious and magnanimous when victorious, a resourceful general. Grant knew how to act in a new type of war and how to employ modern strategies in a modern war. In this sense, Grant was unconventional, for he was not going to execute that "textbook war", as Martí mentions. The Cuban revolutionary's praise of Grant in these passages stands in contrast to other instances when Grant did not possess the qualities of a "great man". Martí clearly respects and admires Grant the general; Grant the president, however, receives less favourable treatment.

When later writing the essay on General Philip Sheridan, Martí praised the fact that Sheridan abstained from pursuing a political career, something that Martí criticized in Grant. Martí had issues with military commanders leading nations, unless they relinquished their military ways. This sentiment is present in the Grant essay and also echoed in an 1884 letter the Cuban leader wrote to General Máximo Gómez, where he indicates that "one does not establish a nation, the way [one] runs a [military] camp".[63]

In Martí's descriptions of the scene of the final Southern surrender, the Cuban leader states, "it seemed, at Appomattox, that it was he and not Lee who was defeated because of his modest dress and posture and for his humble speech and expression. He arranged the peace as he had conducted the war: without enthusiasm and wrath. He envisioned what he had done; but in his arrogance, not yet developed, he only saw then that "he did what he had set out to do".[64]

Martí wrote the biographical essay on Grant not only to describe the Union general's life to a Latin American audience, but also to teach the history of Grant's nation, the United States. Throughout his life, Martí was concerned with pedagogical issues, separately writing global history narratives for children to promote nation-building values, as I discussed in chapter 2. In the biographical essay on Grant, Martí could promote his envisioned civic values to adults. Martí believed that for the Cuban republic to succeed, its future citizens required training and teaching. Therefore, in Martí's depictions, Grant as a general was magnanimous, a just commander and a respectful individual who did not berate the efforts of his adversaries; however, the essay later presents Grant as a corrupt political leader.

In the concluding sections of the biographical essay, Martí transforms his presentation of Grant from the humble to the egotistical. Martí explains how after the war, "many cities gave Grant gifts, New York one hundred thousand dollars, Philadelphia thirty thousand, his hometown of Galena gave him a beautifully furnished home. The former Union general said his only aspiration was to be mayor of his city, so he could fix the sidewalk that went from the train station to his home".[65] Martí continues explaining how "the entire town of Galena struck with enthusiasm went to welcome him at the station and took him to his new home, on the [newly] paved sidewalk".[66]

In contrast to this meek representation of Grant, Martí unwinds this characterization of a "great man" by describing Grant's corrupt rise to the US presidency. Martí describes how politics, to Grant, was no longer unpleasant, "since he had no need to go towards it, for it was not in his nature; rather, politics came to summon him at his door".[67]

Martí presents Grant as an opportunist in the latter part of the biographical essay. Grant would have voted for the Democratic Party in the elections prior to the Civil War, Martí states. And after the war, Grant would have accepted the Democratic nomination if he would have been offered it, yet in a lunch meeting, the leader of the Republicans offered him the nomination for president. Grant did not become president driven by a wish to serve the public good; rather, he was merely invited to present himself on the electoral ticket. Forces around him connived, according to Martí, to put an individual in power that they believed could exterminate any further secessionist movements from the South, especially since Grant was "the one who saved the Union with his sword".[68] In the Cuban leader's depictions, Grant emerges as an individual who comes to power driven by the greed of others who seek to use him for their own political and commercial gain.

Regarding Grant's rise to the presidency, Martí conspicuously displayed the former general's failings. Grant either directly condoned actions that benefited only a few or, as a result of his character and attitude, he allowed the conditions to emerge where others could pursue their self-serving objectives. Martí asks the reader in the essay,

> who is this strange man, unjust, [and] ignorant of the most fundamental laws of the Republic and [the] manners and graces of government; absolutely unaware of the limits drawn between the personal rights of a leader and his public authority in the presidency of a country; incapable of understanding the indispensable relationship [between] national [positions of] employment and the individuals named to execute them; [who is this] adventurous and excessive person who places in the administration

of a country, [who guards] jealously its freedom [and self-]respect, all the mean spirited displacements and fashions that are allowed and that are even demanded by its special character and purpose in the handling of wars?[69]

Martí then responds,

> Grant is that [man], [the one] who has brought his [battle]field boots to the White House, and [tags], brands, and [marks]. There is no more complicated and subtle task than that of governing, or element that requires the [greatest] exercise in this world of submission [and humility] and science [and knowledge]. Mere instinct does not suffice, rather knowledge or genius of details; genius is [the accumulation of] knowledge. To go through all [sorts of] conditions drawn by fate is useful, in order to be benign and just, in different ways, with men [and women] of any condition.[70]

The humble Grant, the Grant from the countryside who rose to fulfil a heroic duty, the natural man who did not import ideas, but rather improvised his own according to local conditions and necessities, became quite a different man in Martí's final rendering.

The Need for Knowledge in Governance

To Martí, the running of civilian, democratic governments required a fundamentally different approach than commanding military troops. In fact, war required and demanded the "mean-spirited" behaviour that Martí describes in the essay, but the administration of a peacetime government, managing a republic, required knowledge and practice. Nevertheless, one must not assume that Martí condoned any type of "mean-spirited" behaviour in war. In other descriptions of Grant at war, Martí admired him for being fair and treating his subordinates with respect.

The Grant biography provides a platform for Martí to express his views on balancing governance. He writes, "one must place one's personal rights with those of others in the highest [and] equal levels of awareness; and for the [rights of others] one must have a more enlivened and delicate sentiment than for [one's own], because with [the neglect of one's personal rights] comes only weakness, and from the [neglect of the rights of others] one falls into despotism".[71] Specifically, Martí criticizes corrupt government in expressing how

> it is unthinkable that a leading figure [should come] to the presidency to create, with national [funds], benefits for those associated with him or [for] his clients, nor to give

his nation the form [or character] that pleases him, or to put laws [into disuse] by not employing them or [applying] the wrong [and mistaken] spirit of the laws; instead, [he or she should] govern in virtue, by means of the laws that his [or her] nation has made, without taking for [him- or her]self or for his [or hers] what the nation grants in [trust] and in custody. To govern is to obey.[72]

Showing how Grant lacked a sense of selflessness that was so important to Martí, the Cuban independence leader further develops the negative traits of Grant's character to underscore the need for humility, for compliance with established laws and for knowledge in governing a nation:

[Grant then entered] the highest political position [the presidency] with these elements: a loathing for politics and an agglomerated remorse against those who represent it; an excessive pleasure with his own manners and personality, and a wish for expansion, [aggrandizement], conquest and [continued] march; [with] a flattering way of absolute control and a complete lack in the ways of obedience; a scorn for all highly detailed and progressive laws and a career [of rapid rise] made beyond the natural and organized practice of laws [and rights]; [with] a habit of considering that everything emerged from within him, and [believing] he achieved [it all] because of his will and according to it.[73]

The United States, like the figure of Grant, is portrayed throughout the essay with positive and negative qualities. According to Martí, the United States had weakened its neighbours, but brought the "greatest" prosperity to the region "that written history remembers in centuries".[74] The United States was a land of rights, one that particularly defended its own ("a peaceful nation aroused to a great war because of its consciousness of human [decency and] respectability"). Martí employed the United States, certainly, at times as a model that should be avoided and to be wary of, but significantly for his nation-building project, he also employed the United States as an example for Latin Americans, and particularly Cubans, of what they should strive for in government.

In his descriptions of the United States, Martí inserts details of Grant's presidency to promote views on proper governance. Martí considers Grant's presidency as "therefore shameful, in its start, structure and in the attempts that followed the political life that tarnished Grant's magnanimous acts during the war".[75] Although in the earlier sections on the Civil War, Martí's Grant is admirable, Martí later informs his reader how the Union general's "magnanimous" acts were tarnished by his political career.

Even though, according to Martí, corrupt men surrounded Grant during his presidency, the Cuban leader points out how Grant had one honest and trustworthy adviser, John Aaron Rawlins. Martí states that while Rawlins, who Grant named as secretary of war, was in the Cabinet, "thieves and ill advisors [were] kept [at bay]; [with an eye to get in], yes, [but were kept] even farther away". After Rawlins's death and without him, "how shall one govern in such complicated matters, he who scorns them on purpose and knows nothing of them?", Martí asks. The Cuban leader describes Grant, without Rawlins's counsel, as, "he goes, like a ship adrift, wherever the winds take him. Whoever gives him advice, he frowns at and rejects; but he searches for, despite himself, an opinion in what he [does not know] and needs to know; [Grant], therefore, becomes, without knowing it, a slave to those who give quick advice, and not like someone who gives, but rather who takes ideas."[76]

In explaining how Grant ultimately became a detrimental leader to his nation, Martí once again communicated his views on what qualities a leader of a nation should embrace. Those who worked for Cuba's independence, as well as those who lived in the Latin American republics, would find lessons in Martí's example of Grant. Martí wrote, "whoever praises him, has him. He does not worry over those who do not praise him. He gives all to the ones that appear to believe in him. What shall a man ignorant in government do, but be the natural prey to those who know how to adulate his faults?"[77]

Towards the end of the biographical essay, Martí criticizes Grant's presidency and specifically critiques US expansionism. Martí presents the former Union general as a weak figure who is the object of commercial and political interests that use him for their benefit. Grant, Martí believed, handled the presidency as if he were a general still at war. Martí writes that "stimulated by his need for expansion and [constant] march and in agreement with his unawareness of the spirit and of the way of the law", Grant sent a private secretary, under the pretext of surveying the Bay of Samaná in the Dominican Republic, to sign a treaty of annexation with the government of Santo Domingo, without involving the legitimate diplomatic authorities. Charles Sumner (1811–74), according to Martí, "protested with indignation, for the violent way in which it appears [this treaty] subordinated a weak nation to the will of a powerful [ambitious entity], and for the danger that republican institutions run with a leader who usurps a nation's legitimate capacities".[78] Criticizing Grant's duplicitous behaviour in sending envoys to seal a deal to annex the eastern part of the island of Hispaniola, Martí also condemned the way Grant and US legislators used each other's political power to advance personal or sectarian political interests.

Nevertheless, despite Martí's negative descriptions of Grant, the former Union general and president redeemed himself in death. Martí expressed how later an illness served to close "in luminous and singular fashion, that life, [whether] brilliant, [at times and at others] guilty, that was of self [strength and action], and [in light of] the magnitude of his services, undeniably and definitely, illustrious".[79]

According to Martí, Grant's final years of pain and suffering from his disease (throat cancer), and his work writing his memoirs of the Civil War, allowed for his life to be "ended luminously". Martí concludes the biographical essay on Ulysses S. Grant with

> from his deep eyes, [that were] tender in gratitude to the good nation that forgave his [steely character] and looked at him at the hour of his death, [and] contemplated [him] with the high and dignified affection for the mistaken [and misguided] heroes who one day were made to fight without repose and to subdue without wrath; [Grant's] hand of no longer flesh, extending towards the South from the rim of his tomb in good will, has been taken with loving admiration, like a national treasure, by his brave enemies. The nation of men has begun, and this dead man, in spite of his great mistakes, helped pave its way.[80]

At first glance, Martí's biography on Ulysses S. Grant may appear as another attempt at "the great man" narrative so common in the late nineteenth century. During that time, historians wrote biographies to explain the history of a nation through the lives of distinguished individuals, and in this example of a biographical narrative, influences of nineteenth-century European Romantic historians are present, particularly Jules Michelet's. Martí also believed that through the lives of individuals, one could understand the life of a nation. Yet, in this biographical essay on Grant, Martí took the traditional "great man" historical model and created a narrative that portrayed Grant in a balanced light, highlighting the US leader's virtues as well as his flaws. In the Cuban leader's narrative, the reader does not receive a lesson on individuals making history; rather, on how a simple and practical man made general by historical forces, and later made corrupt when president by the same qualities that had made him a great military commander, was ultimately redeemed at the end of his life by suffering and by writing a history for future generations. His suffering from a disease redeemed him, and since he lived to see the public unmasking of those around him who used him to gain fortune, Grant survived afterwards, but not for long, according to Martí. Due to his magnanimous acts during such an enormous and critical period in the life of the US nation, its Civil War, Grant emerges as a noble, yet flawed character in the overall portrait of his life.

Martí affirmed several key ideas throughout the Grant essay that he sought to transmit to his Latin American audience: forgiveness and reconciliation, sacrifice and selflessness, the value of freedom and the need for knowledge in governance. These four major nation-building values were promoted through characterizations of Grant and of his nation, the United States. Indeed, Martí depicted the negative and positive qualities of both Grant and the United States as a nation. Depictions of the Civil War in the Grant biography also allowed Martí to transmit his spiritual views. The concept of knowledge, that a leader must be knowledgeable, aware, prepared and respectful when governing – in fact, "to govern is to obey" – and the notion that being a natural genius was not enough, are themes of the Grant essay. Sacrifice and selflessness, in that a leader must be willing to act humbly and not use political positions to aggrandize his or her power and stature, or the power and stature of those around him or her, also emerge as principles for civic behaviour in Martí's biography of Grant.

Ultimately, Martí's "great man" narrative is an innovative one for its time, particularly new in its approach by introducing US characters, daily life and history to Latin American readers, but also by not importing a "European great man" for use in imparting remedies for bad government in the Americas. Martí's narrative is also remarkable for the way it introduces and teaches about Grant's life and the history of the nation leading to, during and after the Civil War in a lyrical fashion, allowing the reader to engage the narrative as a historical play or novel with characters that speak to one another and come alive with vivid descriptions of scenes and settings. The Grant biography is also extraordinary for two other reasons. First, it provided Martí the opportunity to write himself into the story – indeed, in his words, what had he not written without "bleeding"? Second, the essay on Grant allowed Martí to prescribe remedies to Latin American readers by presenting North American examples.

In seeking to build a new nation, to create an independent republic in Cuba from the vestiges of centuries of Spanish colonialism, Martí wrote about the

United States – because it was the society, apart from Cuba, with whose daily life and politics he was most intimately familiar. Martí spent most of his adult life in the United States and wherever he went in the world, he returned to the United States; and wherever he went in the United States, he returned to New York City. He wrote as if the United States itself should take heed of the sectarian interests and groups that threatened to corrode and undermine its perceived democratic character. By pointing to internal menaces within democracies and by warning others of external threats to their own republics, Martí demonstrated that his pre-eminent concern was the function of democracy itself.

Ultimately, Martí concludes this twelve-part biographical essay, written on the veranda of a commuter ferry steamboat between Brooklyn and Manhattan, by describing Grant simply as a *muerto*, a dead man, a corpse, a deceased being, one who in spite of his grave errors had been forgiven. Again, the themes of reconciliation and forgiveness emerge: he describes "Grant's hand of no longer flesh, extending towards the South from the rim of his tomb in good will", and writes of how this hand was "taken with loving admiration, like a national treasure, by his brave enemies". Indeed, Martí's last words in this essay are that this "*muerto*" assisted and facilitated the "*nación de hombres*" (nation of men) – not one of kings, princes, warriors or merchants, but *hombres*. Understood in its widest original Spanish meaning, *hombres* includes all types of men and women. Since this nation is of *hombres* by definition, it is, therefore, democratic. Martí presented the United States as a nation with a trajectory, and its path had been opened thanks to Grant's efforts. This is the function of the truly "great man" in Martí's view – not one whose person and ego is raised so that he or she becomes larger than the nation. Rather, a "great man", to Martí, in this case Ulysses S. Grant, is one who serves the progression of freedom.

AFTERWORD

José Martí never saw his homeland liberated and redeemed from the evils of colonialism and dependency, and the task of liberating Cuba went unfulfilled. In the previous pages I have provided the reader with a glimpse of his messages, thoughts and efforts aimed at achieving these objectives.

Above all, my aim has been to situate Martí not only as a figure of national or hemispheric significance, but one of global reach and relevance. He has been characterized as *"el más universal de los cubanos"* (the most universal of all Cubans), I believe due to the fact that his words and efforts were not merely directed to his compatriots. To Martí, as he declared, *"Patria es humanidad"*;[1] *patria* equated to humanity. I have argued that humanity also nurtured him, for different and distant global regions from his own served as fountains of ideas and inspiration. Martí's conceptions regarding *patria*, independence and government – moreover, his political ideas – cannot be fully understood without delving into his own spiritual outlook and the worlds he experienced: the violent one of colonial Cuba steeped in slavery, that of his university years in Spain, of the Mexico that raised him to the stature of renowned writer and journalist, of the United States that opened his eyes to the feats and vices of a modern technological world and, importantly, that of his relations with the people he worked with, collaborated or loved and even those who persecuted and ridiculed him.

Chapter 6 on Ulysses S. Grant and the US Civil War delved into how Martí considered the life of a "great man" as an embodiment of the spirit of a society. Through great figures, one could understand in a concise manner the forces and elements of a nation, a belief the Cuban leader held in sync with other historians of his time. In this sense, Martí has been our "great man", for one cannot think of another Cuban that better embodies the wishes and aspirations of his nation during his epoch. Little did he know that as he wrote about Grant to represent the forces coalescing in US government and society, so too would he be depicted decades later by others to reveal the forces of the Cuban revolution of 1895. Martí has become our "great man" that through him we can come to better understand the ways the 1895 revolution took ideological shape. This "great man" that he has become, without him ever knowing it, has left a body of work that reveals the tensions of the modernizing forces and currents of the world of his time. Living nearly fifteen years in the New York metropolis, the most modern city, perhaps, of his age, allowed him instant communication and to equip himself with ideas, themes and inspirations from all around the world. He did not choose to remain in London, perhaps the nineteenth-century world's wealthiest city, or in Paris, the great cultural Mecca of the West. Rather, he chose the New York of the Gilded Age, the modern city of rising magnates and monopolists that dominated the American economy and politics, side by side with the masses of working-class residents and migrants from all over the globe, many living in squalor. Martí witnessed these extremes in New York City, even observed Grant's funeral procession.

Grant as a figure appealed to Martí in writing a biographical essay. His piece on the former US general and president reveals so much of the Cuban leader's thinking regarding his imagined independent nation: the values needed for correct government, such as forgiveness and reconciliation; sacrifice and selflessness; and the need for right knowledge. The Grant essay also offers a snapshot of Martí's views regarding the positive and negative qualities of a modern *caudillo*. Not all caudillos were bad – after all, he did admire the Spanish-American liberators Simón Bolívar and José de San Martín[2] – yet he showed his Spanish-American audiences that the *caudillo* was not only a phenomenon that plagued Latin America, but one also visible in that exemplary and modern country of the United States (as many Latin American intellectuals believed at the time). As the embodiment of the North American elements and forces, the figure of Grant provided, in Martí's mind, an opportunity for his Latin American and Caribbean readers to better understand the United States in the latter half of the nineteenth century.

I have depicted in this book a global, transnational Martí. Ironically, although his life and work were devoted to a decidedly nationalist objective, and in a broader sense, a pan-regional one, in order to more fully comprehend the Cuban leader's efforts and motivations, a transnational perspective is absolutely necessary. He took much from the United States as well as from other nations and cultures of the world; he nurtured himself significantly from positive and negative events, figures and ideas.

A transnational, global perspective of Martí must also include the African diaspora. Although relatively few of his compositions deal with Africa, the continent, he did write extensively about, corresponded with, nurtured himself from, supported, fought for and loved the children and descendants of Africa. The members of the diaspora, dispersed throughout the Americas, were a profound source of inspiration and sustenance to him and his work, as seen in chapter 5. Martí's legacy cannot be fully understood without this pan-African dimension. The father of modern Cuban anthropology, Fernando Ortiz, was the first to disseminate this perspective of Martí's work. Chapter 5 built on Ortiz's arguments by demonstrating that Martí was an anti-racist, not merely for political expediency, but rather due to his sense of spirituality and love for African descendants. His struggle to eliminate racism and racial discrimination was also motivated by a sense that he was fulfilling a spiritual duty that mandated the betterment of humanity and righting of social wrongs. Martí emerges as a thoroughly modern man, ahead of his time, by speaking that races are social constructions; races are made in "bookstores". He completely rejected race as a fixed, predetermining, biological category. His fight against racism and for equality was not only based on his desire to unite all Cubans for the success of the independence war, but the fact that he taught at, established and supported benevolent associations of mutual assistance for the benefit of African descendants, be it on a personal level or through charitable organizations, without personal gain, reveals his commitment to the same cause that the children of the African diaspora fought for in the United States and across the world: the social, economic and legal equality of humanity. Martí was horrified by slavery in Cuba and in the United States, and even more to see that segregation, social exclusion, discrimination, abuse and hatred towards African descendants continued after abolition. He fought to eradicate this as much as he could through his work and oratory, for in the Cuba he dreamed of, there would be no racism. His anti-racism was not only based on political conceptions, but, moreover, was founded on his spiritual beliefs and as a consequence of his experiences and relations with the children of the African diaspora.

The same spiritual notions that led him to fight against racism and for the equality of Africans and indigenous people led him to fight for an independent Cuba. The two concepts – anti-racism and anti-colonialism – were linked to his spiritual beliefs, particularly in terms of being purifying agents of his soul. Martí's spiritual ideas cannot be identified by tracing only one source. In chapters 3 and 4, I have offered an Eastern perspective, based on Hindu philosophy, which nurtured so many distinguished figures that the Cuban leader admired. In Spain and in Mexico, he studied and acquired Krause's philosophy; in the United States, the Transcendentalism of Emerson and others, as well as the theosophy of Annie Besant, and one should similarly not ignore his involvement with Freemasonry. He searched for new means of understanding himself and new avenues for spiritual strength and guidance in the colossal task that faced him. As a fairly short and thin man, frail at times, often disabled from the physical wounds of his first political imprisonment in the rock quarries of Cuba, how would he be able to confront and expel four hundred years of monolithic Spanish colonialism? How could he face and deter a new, emerging imperialist power from annexing and controlling the land he would be willing to sacrifice his life for? I believe that in his search for the strength that could sustain him during such a gigantic task, one sole religious ideology could not satisfy his high intellect and much less the Roman Catholic one that aligned itself with Spanish colonialism in Cuba. The Cuban leader therefore searched in other directions, alternative currents that had more in common with his own way of looking at life. I have demonstrated how Hindu philosophy through the *Bhagavad-Gita*, the ancient, sacred text that inspired Emerson, Besant and others that the Cuban leader admired, certainly offered spiritual sustenance for this mission.

At a political level, I have examined how he considered and promoted the concept of "nation" as a divine entity, for it was to him a *"Dios patria"* (God nation). Therefore, he considered the nation-state as divine and requiring altruistic and sacred devotion. Hindu philosophy, through the *Gita*, informs us that altruistic and selfless acts lead to the purification of the human soul. I have shown the links between Hinduism's selfless service to others and Martí's dedication to the *patria*. Perhaps the most selfless act that the Cuban leader could achieve was to risk and lose his life in battle for a free Cuba; to sacrifice his life, if need be, to liberate the suffering, sacred *patria*. This altruistic act would be an exercise in love, free of hatred, just as he declared in the *Manifiesto de Montecristi* and in other instances regarding the war for Cuban independence.

The war was necessary in order to pave the way to freedom and happiness for the Cubans.

Even though, in this sense, he stood apart from Gandhi, India's great independence fighter, for his promotion of war, the Cuban leader nonetheless believed in sacrificing for others and practising self-denial – to have lived far from his homeland, suffering the distance from his family, away from his beloved only son and a wife that did not understand him; forgoing stable home, income and employment; being constantly watched by his enemies; added to the pains of the physical wounds he suffered as a result of his struggles – all were efforts that Martí deemed necessary and ultimately purifying, and all were devoted to this "God *patria*", the union of all who loved and identified with Cuba, especially since that island was a "portion of land" of the larger humanity in which he happened to be born. To serve Cuba was to labour for humanity, and if humanity is driven by a divine force, then all his self-denying efforts, in the end, would lead to the purification of his soul and help him to transcend the apparent pain and finality of death.

But if Hindu philosophy, as seen through the *Bhagavad-Gita*, emerges in Martí's conception of *patria* and in how he transmitted it to his audience, then it also influenced the Cuban leader on a personal level. Martí's public life was largely indistinguishable from his personal one. He expressed to his friend Rafael Serra in 1890 that "I'm not even envious of the sun, for it cannot outdo me in warmth and purity".[3] Consequently, given this conception of "*Dios patria*" of Eastern origins, and considering, as I have done in chapter 4, that this Eastern philosophy inspired his concept of nation, we cannot ignore that it also influenced the way he viewed the world and his own spirituality.

The *Bhagavad-Gita* offers a synthesis of many ideas that have inspired Hindus. India's sacred book is a guide that offers direct advice to the warrior Arjuna through his interlocutor, the divine Krishna (God incarnated), at the moment that Arjuna is set to fight alone an overwhelming army made of his kinsmen. Krishna tells Arjuna that the battle about to be waged is a just one, for it will be the fulfilment of his duty, and following Krishna's advice, Arjuna ultimately emerges triumphant. It is a book rich in symbolism and metaphors that offers spiritual inspiration and support. In the *Gita*, like in Martí's work, the concept of sacrifice as a purifying agent of the human soul emerges. Another of the *Gita*'s lessons is regarding the true nature of the soul. The physical separation that humans see is merely illusory; all souls are intrinsically connected. This concept is reflected in Martí's notion of *patria* and in his struggle against racism. Another important element of Hindu philosophy is the continual reincarnation of human souls. The eternal wheel of reincarnation ceases only once the human soul, finally purified, reaches the core of Brahma, the supreme Godhead. I have examined this notion in Martí's writings in chapters 3 and 4. Through this Eastern perspective, I hope to have revealed a more global, if not more complete, understanding of Martí's independence efforts.

In chapter 2, I delved into another dimension of the global origins of Martí's Cuban independence programme. The Cuban leader employed global history, the past of different cultures of our planet, in order to transmit the civic values that he believed citizens of democratic republics should have. He transmitted these values in an innovative and modern fashion; particularly striking is how such a high intellectual man and political leader could write for children without patronizing or speaking down to them. Two historical narratives from his children's magazine offer a synthetic view of Martí's ideas regarding civic behaviour in order to keep the peace, promote prosperity and democracy, and secure the sovereignty of a republic. Martí specifically promotes three themes in these historical narratives: the right to self-determination at the national level; the right to self-determination at the individual level; and humanitarianism, one's duty to work for the betterment of others. In order to achieve these objectives, the Cuban leader teaches youngsters to think differently from what children's magazines of his time taught: he wrote that no civilization or nation is better than others; that there are indigenous peoples throughout the world who fight for their autonomy against foreign intruders; and that they should not believe everything that they are told, but instead learn how to think critically on their own and also strengthen their love for their home cultures and origins as children of the Americas. All these ideas were innovative and revolutionary for his time. Through the narratives of *Golden Years*, I have shown that the Cuban leader employed global history to transmit these values in order to build his envisioned republic, just as he did with adults through his biography of Grant when he transmitted the values of good government.

I therefore have examined in this book two aspects of how Martí conceived his future imagined republic: on the one hand, the values that citizens should have; and on the other, the behaviour that rulers should engage in. Global history and biography, respectively, served as tools for the Cuban leader to transmit the required elements for a free, healthy and sovereign republic.

I end, then, where I began: Martí's search for balancing the world. In order to balance the world, to correct the wrongs in it, he had to eliminate the evils in his beloved homeland first, and in a larger sense, inspire and strengthen "*nuestra América*" (Latin America and the Caribbean). I have presented the arguments that major theorists on nationalism have provided in explaining its rise, and in our study, the Cuban leader does not entirely fit into these schemes. The nation to Martí was divine, and as seen, it was also heterogeneous and, above all, modern – but not modern in the sense that it should embrace bourgeois values. In the Cuban leader's construction of an independent nation, he visibly emerges as diverging from other nationalist fighters of his time, for he adopted from transnational sources and employed "global" tools within his reach in a revolutionary and innovative manner: he used history, culture, figures and events from different points of our planet in order to nurture his own personal outlook as well as his public messages. As Cuban scholar Pedro Pablo Rodríguez has rightfully indicated, "his case is notable and remarkable for its extreme exceptionalism and complexity: Martí was one of those few people that assimilated and synthesized all the culture of his time". Therefore, as Rodríguez expressed, he was "excessive in his larger objectives: 'to detach America'; 'to unyoke man'; 'to balance the world' ".[4]

If in the *Bhagavad-Gita*'s philosophy, which so influenced individuals who Martí admired, fulfilling a duty, as one identified it, facilitated the emancipation of the human soul from its perennial earthly incarnations and finally freed it to join the essence of the universe, then we arrive at a deeper understanding of Martí's words when he uttered "*la muerte no es verdad*" – death is not real – for "when the task of life has been rightly fulfilled; the thinking skull [may] turn into dust; but the thoughts that were created in it live on and flourish, perpetually".[5]

NOTES

Chapter 1

1. José Martí, *Obras completas*, 2nd ed. (Havana, Cuba: Editorial de Ciencias Sociales, 1975), 4:160. All direct references to Martí's work are my translations from the Spanish, unless otherwise noted.
2. Ibid., 22.
3. *Patria* to Martí was more than "nation". It was a combination of homeland, fatherland or motherland and went beyond a demarcated territory. It had a spiritual nature and was the spiritual union of all those who loved, cared for and identified themselves as Cubans. In later chapters, I delve into Martí's sacred, globalized formulation of *patria*.
4. Peter Stearns, "Nationalisms: An Invitation to Comparative Analysis", *Journal of World History* 8, no. 1 (Spring 1997): 58.
5. Patrick O'Brien, "Historiographical Traditions and Modern Imperatives for the Restoration of Global History", *Journal of Global History* (2006): 1–14.
6. Pedro Pablo Rodríguez, *Al sol voy: Atisbos a la política martiana* (Havana: Centro de Estudios Martianos, 2012), 17.
7. Walter Schnee, "Nationalism: A Review of the Literature", *Journal of Political and Military Sociology* 29 (Summer 2001): 3.
8. Ibid., 5.
9. Ibid., 9.
10. Ibid., 11.
11. Craig Calhoun, *Nationalism* (Minneapolis: University of Minnesota Press, 1997), 29.
12. Schnee, "Nationalism", 13.
13. Andrew Parker, "Bogeyman: Benedict Anderson's 'Derivative' Discourse", *Diacritics* 29, no. 4 (Winter 1999): 40.
14. Pheng Cheah, "Grounds of Comparison", *Diacritics* 29, no. 4 (Winter 1999): 4.
15. Ibid., 6.

16. Ibid., 6.
17. Ibid., 14.
18. Nicola Miller, "The Historiography of Nationalism and National Identity in Latin America", *Nations and Nationalism* 12, no. 2 (2006): 203.
19. Martí's positive portrayals and support of female pro-voting rights activists such as Susan B. Anthony, and of the women's voting rights movement in the US, reveal that he would have also supported the right for women to vote and hold office in the envisioned Cuban republic. He described the renowned US women's voting rights activist as the "George Washington of the cause of the suffragettes, who must be heard" (Martí, *Obras completas*, 9:249–50). Thus, Martí's nation building was based on racially blind conceptions and, one may argue, on gender-neutral ones as well.
20. Stearns, "Nationalisms", 63.
21. O'Brien, "Historiographical Traditions", 14.
22. Miller, "Historiography of Nationalism", 204.
23. Ibid., 207.
24. Ibid.
25. Ibid.
26. Ibid.
27. For more on Martí, indigeneity and the subject of First Peoples in his work, see Jorge Camacho, *Etnografía, política y poder a finales del siglo XIX: José Martí y la cuestión indígena* (Chapel Hill: University of North Carolina Press, 2013).
28. Martí, *Obras completas*, 24:204. See also Robert McKee Irwin, "*Ramona* and Postnationalist American Studies: On 'Our America' and the Mexican Borderlands", *American Quarterly* 55, no. 4 (Dec. 2003): 539–67, for more on how Martí's interest and work on *Ramona* relates to the ideas the Cuban leader later articulates in "Nuestra América" ("Our America", 1891).
29. Martí, "Nuestra América", in *Obras completas*, 6:18.
30. Roberto Fernández Retamar, "Martí en su (tercer) mundo [Fragmentos]", in *Valoración multiple: José Martí. Edición al cuidado de Luis Toledo Sande* (Havana: Fondo Editorial Casa de las Américas, 2007), 239.
31. Leopoldo Zea, introduction, in *José Martí: A cien años de Nuestra América*, ed. Jesus Serna Moreno and María Teresa Bosque Lastra (Mexico City: Universidad Nacional Autónoma de México, 1993), 10.
32. Nancy Raquel Mirabal, " 'No Country But the One We Must Fight For': The Emergence of an Antillean Nation and Community in New York City, 1860–1901", in *Mambo Montage: The Latinization of New York*, ed. Agustín Laó-Montes and Arlene Dávila (New York: Columbia University Press, 2001), 58.
33. Pedro Pablo Rodríguez, *De las dos Américas (Aproximaciones al pensamiento martiano)* (Havana, Cuba: Centro de Estudios Martianos, 2002), 221.
34. Stefan-Ludwig Hoffman, *Civil Society* (New York: Palgrave Macmillan, 2006), 76.

35. Reinaldo Suárez Suárez, *José Martí contra Alphonse Karr: ¿De qué sirven vuestras leyes?* (Santiago: Editorial Oriente, 2009), 55.
36. Marlene Vázquez Pérez, *La vigilia perpetua: Martí en Nueva York* (Havana: Centro de Estudios Martianos, 2010), 7. See also Carmen Suárez León, *Martí y Victor Hugo en el fiel de las modernidades* (Havana: Centro de Investigación y Desarrollo de la Cultura Cubana "Juan Marinello" and Editorial José Martí, 1997), 7–28.
37. C.A. Bayly, "The Age of Revolutions in Global Context: An Afterword", in *The Age of Revolutions in Global Context, c. 1760–1840*, ed. David Armitage and Sanjay Subrahmanyam (New York: Palgrave Macmillan, 2010), 216–17.
38. Martí, *Obras completas*, 4:156–57.
39. Ibid., 3:142.
40. Martí, *Obras completas*, 21:29.
41. Rafael Rojas explains how the politics of Martí and of other Latin American political activists of the time echo Montesquieu's ideas. Rojas also has an innovative analysis comparing Francisco Madero (1873–1913) of Mexico and José Martí. Rojas discusses the *Bhagavad-Gita* as an example of the mysticism of Madero and Martí. He does not, however, link Martí's ideas on nation building to the major tenets of the *Bhagavad-Gita*, as I do in chapters 3 and 4.
42. Some may find it problematic to compare Martí to Gandhi, for Martí advocated violence (war against Spain) and Gandhi's programme was based on non-violence. I consider both as products of their respective cultures. Cuba was a violent society with no non-violent traditions. Gandhi did not develop the notion of non-violence, for it was a concept present in Jainism, for instance, and other Indian traditions. Gandhi, unlike Martí, was raised in a society with elements that embraced non-violent traditions. Nevertheless, the way Martí promoted a war without hatred and revenge; his calling it necessary, implying it was not a choice; as well as his constant references to love situate his and Gandhi's nationalism closer together.
43. Martí, *Obras completas*, 3:142.
44. Rafael Rojas, *José Martí: La invención de Cuba* (Madrid: Editorial Colibrí, 2000), 131–32.
45. Ibid., 140.
46. Martí, *Obras completas*, 20:89.
47. Ibid., 23:273.
48. Ibid., 3:142.

Chapter 2

1. Martí, *Obras completas*, 20:351.
2. Fina García Marruz, *El amor como energía revolucionaria en José Martí* (Havana: Centro de Estudios Martianos, 2003), 308.

3. Many have translated *La edad de oro* as *Golden Age*; however, I prefer *Golden Years*. Even though "age" has a similar double meaning in Spanish of the length of time an individual has lived and of a period in history, translating it into English as "the golden age" more readily conjures images of a golden period in time, rather than the precious, magical years in an individual's life, one's childhood, that to Martí were "golden". In this sense, *Golden Years* favours an understanding of childhood as the actual golden years of life, better fitting as the title of a children's magazine. Regarding his work translating texts into Spanish, among them Victor Hugo's, Martí indicated that the best translations were not literal ones, but those that best transfer the sentiment of an author's expression from one language into another, remarking that *"traducir es transpensar"* (to translate is to "trans-think", perhaps better expressed in English as to "transfer thoughts").

4. Martí acquired knowledge of global history through his university education, but more significantly from his own substantial reading of classical works, of the latest books on history and science of his time, as well as newspaper and journal articles on archaeology, the arts and other disciplines that engaged the past of global societies. In Martí's letters to his close friend Manuel Mercado and in his own personal diary, Martí disclosed the latest books he was reading. Beyond *Golden Years*, which I delve into in this chapter due to its innovative way of promoting national and regional consciousness, Martí demonstrated knowledge of global history in many articles he wrote for Latin American newspapers and in references contained in his speeches.

5. Martí, *Obras completas*, 18:296.

6. Jawaharlal Nehru, *Glimpses of World History: Being Further Letters to His Daughter, Written in Prison, and Containing a Rambling Account of History for Young People* (London: Lindsay Drummond, 1939). The essay "Nuestra América" first appeared in Mexico's *El Partido Liberal* newspaper in 1891.

7. See Jeffrey Belnap and Raul Fernández, eds., *José Martí's "Our America": From National to Hemispheric Cultural Studies* (Durham, NC: Duke University Press, 1998).

8. Salvador Arias, *Un proyecto martiano esencial: "La edad de oro"* (Havana: Centro de Estudios Martianos, 2001), 68; Fryda Schultz de Mantovani, "Introduction: 'La edad de oro' de José Martí", in *José Martí: 'La edad de oro'* (San Salvador: Departamento Editorial Ministerio de Cultura, 1955), 22.

9. Martí, *Obras completas*, 4:110–12.

10. Ibid., 111.

11. Ibid., 20:149. Martí expressed in a 26 August 1889 letter to his friend Manuel Mercado, written on paper with *Golden Years* letterhead, that "another windmill that turns in my head and a spear shaking in my hands, is the October convention", referring to the monetary conference.

12. Ibid., 6:33–70.

13. Ibid., 46.
14. Ibid.
15. Ibid., 20:147.
16. Ibid., 12:305.
17. Arias, *Un proyecto martiano esencial*, 31–32.
18. Martí, *Obras completas*, vol. 12.
19. Ibrahim Hidalgo Paz, *José Martí: Cronología, 1853–1895* (Havana: Editorial de Ciencias Sociales, 1992), 65.
20. Rodolfo Sarracino, *José Martí en el Club Crepúsculo de Nueva York: En busca de nuevos equilibrios* (Guadalajara, Mexico: Editorial Universitaria and Centro de Estudios Martianos, 2010), 17.
21. Apparently the US government had no qualms about annexing Cuba, despite the "No Transfer" doctrine passed by Congress in 1811 or the Monroe Doctrine of 1823. No transfer of colonies, in light of US actions, seemingly applied only to European powers and not to the United States acquiring new colonies. For original excerpts of the US documents, see Robert H. Holden and Eric Zolov, eds., *Latin America and the United States: A Documentary History*, 2nd ed. (New York: Oxford University Press, 2011), 6–16.
22. Cintio Vitier, "Etapas en la acción política de Martí", in *Temas martianos*, ed. Cintio Vitier and Fina García Marruz (Havana: Centro de Estudios Martianos, 2011), 21.
23. Fina García Marruz, *Temas martianos: Tercera serie* (Havana: Centro de Estudios Martianos, 1995), 205.
24. Martí, *Obras completas*, 2:176–77.
25. Vitier, "Etapas", 50.
26. Martí, *Obras completas*, 20:146.
27. Ibid.
28. Ibid., 148.
29. Ibid., 146.
30. Aaron Da Costa Gómez, a wealthy Brazilian businessman in New York City who came from a prominent merchant family, underwrote the publication of *Golden Years*. The Da Costa Gómez brothers had business relationships throughout Latin America. Martí met Aaron, a New York life insurance agent, through his friend Manuel Mercado while living in Mexico City in the late 1870s and while Aaron was an agent there.
31. Martí, *Obras completas,* 20:350.
32. I thank Cuban scholar Salvador Arias for providing this information.
33. Roberto Fernández Retamar, *José Martí:* La edad de oro. *Edición crítica anotada y prologada por Roberto Fernández Retamar* (Mexico City: Fondo de Cultura Económica, 1992), 12.

34. Eduardo Lolo, *Mar de espuma: Martí y la literatura infantil* (Miami: Ediciones Universal, 1995), 40.
34. Ibid., 43.
36. Silvia A. Barros, "La literatura para niños de José Martí en su época", in *Estudios críticos sobre la prosa modernista hispanoamericana*, ed. José Olivio Jiménez (New York: Eliseo Torres, 1975), 110.
37. Barros, "La literatura para niños de José Martí en su época", 108.
38. Félix Flores Varona, *Traspasos de* La edad de oro (Havana: Centro de Investigación y Desarrollo de la Cultura Cubana "Juan Marinello", 2003), 15.
39. For more on Emerson in Martí's work, refer to José Ballón Aguirre, *Autonomía cultural americana: Emerson y Martí* (Madrid: Pliegos, 1986); Anne Fountain, *José Martí and US Writers* (Gainesville: University Press of Florida, 2003); Armando García de la Torre, "José Martí and the Global Dimensions of Late Nineteenth-Century Nation Building" (PhD diss., Washington State University, 2006).
40. Elena Jorge Viera, "Notas sobre la función de *La edad de oro*", in *Acerca de* La edad de oro, ed. Salvador Arias (Havana: Centro de Estudios Martianos, 1989), 314.
41. Arias, *Un proyecto martiano esencial*, 49. See also Herminio Almendros, *A propósito de "La edad de oro": Notas sobre literatura infantil* (Havana: Instituto Cubano del Libro, 1972).
42. Noemí Beatriz Tornadú, "Introducción y vocabulario", in *La edad de oro: Publicación de recreo e instrucción dedicada a los niños de América* (Buenos Aires: Editorial Huemil, 1966), 18–19.
43. Arias, *Un proyecto martiano esencial*, 53.
44. José Ismael Gutiérrez, "José Martí y la traducción de cuentos para niños: Tradición y originalidad", *Hispanófila* 141 (2004): 31.
45. Arias, *Un proyecto martiano esencial*, 172.
46. Martí, *Obras completas,* 20:153.
47. Ibid.
48. Fina García Marruz, "Lecciones de 'La edad de oro' ", in *Temas martianos: Tercera serie* (Havana: Centro de Estudio Martianos, 1995), 223.
49. John Lawrence Tone, *War and Genocide in Cuba, 1895–1898* (Chapel Hill: University of North Carolina Press, 2006), 37–38. Tone has an enlightening discussion on Martí's sense of nationalism. For further reading on nationalism, see Benedict Anderson's *Imagined Communities*; Eric J. Hobsbawm's *Nations and Nationalism since 1780*; George Mosse's *Nationalism and Sexuality*; Anthony Smith's *Theories of Nationalism*; and Stuart Woof's *Nationalism in Europe, 1815 to the Present*.
50. Tone, *War and Genocide*, 37–38.
51. Ibid.
52. Graciella Cruz-Taura, "El pensamiento histórico de José Martí", in *Transcendencia*

cultural de la obra de José Martí: Actas del simposio internacional celebrado en Praga, del 21 al 23 de octubre de 2002, ed. Anna Housková (Prague: Department of Philosophy and Letters, Charles University, 2003), 92.
53. Martí, *Obras completas*, 6:153.
54. José Martí, *La edad de oro: Edición crítica de Eduardo Lolo*, ed. Eduardo Lolo (Miami: Ediciones Universal, 2001), 91.
55. Cruz-Taura, "El pensamiento histórico", 99.
56. Marlene Vázquez Pérez, "Historia, recepción y literatura en *La edad de oro*", *Anuario del Centro de Estudios Martianos* 22 (1999): 124–25.
57. Virginia A. Hodgkinson and Michael W. Foley, eds., *The Civil Society Reader* (Lebanon, NH: University Press of New England, 2003), x.
58. Medardo Vitier, "Dimensión filosófica [de José Martí], sobre todo en su sentido de la vida", in *Valoración multiple: José Martí. Edición al cuidado de Luis Toledo Sande* (Havana: Fondo Editorial Casa de las Américas, 2007), 221–22.
59. Peter Singer, *Hegel* (Oxford: Oxford University Press, 1983), 10.
60. Pedro Pablo Rodríguez, "Autoctonía y universalidad en José Martí: Puntos para un debate en su contexto histórico", in *Al sol voy*, 252.
61. Incidentally, Martí celebrated his last birthday, 28 January 1895, with his close friends in New York City at his favourite Italian restaurant, Delmónico, days before setting sail on the steamship that would eventually take him to the Cuban battlefield. Carlos Ripoll, "Martí: su ultimo cumpleaños", *Diario las Américas*, Thursday, 29 January 1987.
62. Martí followed the art of the Impressionists and wrote positive critiques of the latest French styles of art for Latin American newspapers.
63. Fernández Retamar, "Martí en su (tercer) mundo", 237. Emphasis is Fernández Retamar's.
64. Martí, *Obras completas*, 18:357.
65. Ibid., 359.
66. Ibid., 371.
67. See Michael Adas, *Machines as the Measure of Men: Science, Technology and Ideologies of Western Dominance* (Ithaca: Cornell University Press, 1989).
68. Fernández Retamar, "Martí en su (tercer) mundo", 235–63.
69. Martí, *Obras completas*, 20:153.
70. Ibid.
71. Ibid., 13:312.
72. William McNeill, *The Rise of the West: A History of the Human Community* (Chicago: University of Chicago Press, 1963).
73. I thank Cuban historian Graciella Cruz-Taura for this insight.
74. Martí, *Obras completas*, 18:460–61.

75. Ibid., 461.
76. Ibid.
77. Howard M. Fraser, "*La edad de oro* and José Martí's Modernist Ideology for Children", *Revista Interamericana de Bibliografía* 42, no. 2 (1992): 223–32.
78. Oscar Montero, *José Martí: An Introduction* (New York: Palgrave Macmillan, 2004), 13–14.
79. Ibid.
80. Martí, *Obras completas*, 18:462.
81. Ibid., 464.
82. Ibid., 369.
83. Ibid., 370.
84. Ibid.
85. Ibid.
86. Ibid., 459.
87. Ibid., 467
88. Ibid.
89. Ibid.
90. García Marruz, *El amor*, 31.
91. Hoffman, *Civil Society*, 76.
92. Martí, *Obras completas*, 18:366–67.
93. Ibid., 20:219.
94. Ibid., 18:366–67.
95. Tone, *War and Genocide*, 38.
96. Martí, *Obras completas*, 18:466.
97. Ibid., 467.
98. García Marruz, "Lecciones", 217–18.
99. Ibid.
100. Marnie Hughes-Warrington, "Readers, Responses, and Popular Culture", in *World Histories* (London: Palgrave Macmillan, 2005), 222. Hughes-Warrington states how children provided a malleable audience for teaching histories of meaning.
101. Ivan A. Schulman, *José Martí: Ismaelillo, Versos Libres, Versos Sencillos* (Madrid: Ediciones Cátedra, 1999), 19.
102. Tornadú, *La edad de oro*, 17.

Chapter 3

1. Martí, *Obras completas*, 16:161–62. Excerpt of Martí's poem "Yugo y Estrella" in *Versos Libres*. My translation of the Spanish.

    Cuando nací, sin sol, mi madre dijo:
    ". . . De mí y de la Creación suma y reflejo,

>   Pez que en ave y corcel y hombre se torna,
>   Mira estas dos, que con dolor te brindo,
>   Insignias de la vida: ve y escoge.
>   Este, es un yugo: quien lo acepta, goza.
>   Hace de manso buey, y como presta
>   Servicios a los señores, duerme en paja
>   . . . Esta, que alumbra y mata, es una estrella.
>   Como riega luz, los pecadores
>   Huyen de quien la lleva, y en la vida,
>   . . . Todo el que lleva luz se queda solo.
>   . . . Pero el hombre que al buey sin pena imita,
>   Buey torna a ser, y en apagado bruto
>   La escala universal de nuevo empieza . . ."

2. Martí, *Obras completas*, 21:246.
3. While living in New York City, Martí wrote to his friend Manuel Mercado in Mexico that he was working "for a great Buenos Aires daily, but the salary goes to *mamá* [mother in Cuba]". Ibid., 20:76.
4. Barbara Stoler Miller, trans., *The Bhagavad-Gita: Krishna's Counsel in Time of War* (New York: Bantam Books, 1986), 2.15–16. The *Bhagavad-Gita* is seven hundred verses from the great Hindu epic, the *Mahabharata*. It is considered Hindu sacred scripture and believed to have been written between the fifth and second centuries BCE by the poet Vyasha. In the *Mahabharata*, prior to going to war at Kurukshetra (scene of the *Bhagavad-Gita*), the Kauravas are given a choice to fight the Pandavas with the assistance of a large army or of the avatar Krishna alone. The Kauravas select the formidable army presented, while Arjuna (the Pandavas) prefers the guidance of Krishna. In dialogue format, Krishna instructs Arjuna on the true nature of the soul, on the need to follow one's duty, to renounce the fruits of one's actions, and on how to attain eternal union with the Divine. The *Bhagavad-Gita* is further referred to as the *Gita*.
5. Miller, *Bhagavad-Gita*, 2.39–40.
6. Ibid., 2.71–72.
7. Roberto D. Agramonte, *Martí y su concepción del mundo* (San Juan: Editorial Universitaria de Puerto Rico, 1971), 56. Agramonte's is perhaps the most extensive study to date that synthesizes Martí's views on politics, economy, society, technology, philosophy and the arts.
8. Fountain, *José Martí and US Writers*, xiv.
9. José Ballón Aguirre, *Lecturas norteamericanas de José Martí: Emerson y el socialismo contemporáneo (1880–1887)* (Mexico City: Universidad Nacional Autónoma de México, 1995), 86.

10. Martí, *Obras completas*, 20:476–77.
11. Ibid., 13:27.
12. Fountain, *José Martí and US Writers*, xiii–xiv. Emphasis is mine.
13. Martí, *Obras completas*, 4:325.
14. Ibid., 18:467.
15. Manuel Pedro González, *José Martí: Epic Chronicler of the US in the Eighties* (Chapel Hill: University of North Carolina, 1953), 73.
16. Martí, *Obras completas*, 20:459.
17. Ibid., 2:138.
18. Miller, *Bhagavad-Gita*, 3.19.
19. Martí, *Obras completas*, 13:23.
20. Ibid., 21:144.
21. Ibid., 13:26.
22. Ibid., 12:504.
23. Ibid.
24. Ibid., 503–4.
25. Oscar Montero, "Review of *The American Chronicles of José Martí. Journalism and Modernity in Spanish America*, by Susana Rotker", trans. Jennifer French and Katherine Semler, *Hispanic Review* 70, no. 3 (Summer 2002): 473.
26. Miller, *Bhagavad-Gita*, 13.30.
27. Ibid., 2.70.
28. Martí, *Obras completas*, 21:29.
29. Ibid., 15:12–15.
30. Miller, *Bhagavad-Gita*, 7.7–13.
31. Ibid., 9.11–13.
32. Ibid., 11.37–38.
33. Martí, *Obras completas*, 21:47. Emphasis is mine.
34. Miller, *Bhagavad-Gita*, 13.30.
35. Martí, *Obras completas*, 11:155.
36. Ibid., 13:24.
37. Ibid., 134. Emphasis is mine.
38. For a detailed discussion on Emerson and Martí, see José Ballón Aguirre, *Lecturas norteamericanas*.
39. Martí, *Obras completas*, 13:23.
40. Ibid., 24.
41. Ibid., 26.
42. Ibid., 134; and José Martí, *Selected Writings*, ed. and trans. Esther Allen (New York: Penguin, 2002), 186. Emphasis is mine.
43. Martí, *Obras completas*, 13:17–18.

44. Ibid., 21:43.
45. Ballón Aguirre, *Lecturas norteamericanas*, 80.
46. Martí, *Obras completas*, 13:27.
47. Martí, *Selected Writings*, 116.
48. Martí, *Obras completas*, 22:323.
49. Ibid., 21:387.
50. José Ballón Aguirre, *Martí y Blaine en la dialéctica de la Guerra del Pacífico (1879–1883)* (Mexico City: Universidad Nacional Autónoma de México, 2003), 420.
51. Martí, *Obras completas*, 21:48.

Chapter 4

1. Martí, *Obras completas*, 4:93. My translation of the opening lines of the *Manifiesto de Montecristi*.
2. Ibid., 94.
3. Ibid., 21:29.
4. Ibid., 5:468.
5. Ibid., 4:93.
6. The PRC or Cuban Revolutionary Party was the political party Martí and other Cuban independence leaders founded in 1892 to coordinate and channel pro-independence efforts and resources through one organization. A conglomeration of pro-independence clubs from the localities that had a measurable amount of Cuban immigrants, such as New York City, Tampa, Key West, Chicago, Philadelphia, New Orleans and Kingston, Jamaica, among other places, formed the membership of the PRC.
7. Jeffrey Belnap and Raúl Fernández, eds., *José Martí's "Our America": From National to Hemispheric Cultural Studies* (Durham, NC: Duke University Press, 1998), 3–4.
8. Martí, *Obras completas*, 4:113.
9. Ernest Renan, "What Is a Nation?" in *Becoming National: A Reader*, ed. Geoff Eley and Ronald Grigor Suny (New York and Oxford: Oxford University Press, 1996), 52.
10. Roberto Fernández Retamar, *José Martí: Páginas escogidas*, vols 1 and 2 (Havana: Editorial de Ciencias Sociales, 1985), 27–28.
11. Vibha Maurya, "Una visión india: El humanismo de José Martí y Mahatma Gandhi", *Anuario del Centro de Estudios Martianos* 10 (1987): 241.
12. Martí, *Obras completas*, 4:94.
13. Maurya, "Una visión india", 245–46.
14. Martí, *Obras completas*, 4:100.
15. Ivan Schulman, "José Martí: Migraciones, viajes y la creación de la nación cubana", *Revista Iberoamericana* 69, no. 205 (October–December 2003): 928.

16. Martí, *Obras completas*, 1:154.
17. Ibid., 178.
18. Miller, *Bhagavad-Gita*, 3.19.
19. Emphasis is mine.
20. Rafael Serra, "Martí es la Democracia", *Anuario del Centro de Estudios Martianos* 5 (1973): 272–74.
21. Martí, *Obras completas*, 21:284.
22. Ibid., 4:94.
23. Ibid., 99.
24. Ibid., 101.
25. Ibid., 97.
26. Ibid., 5:468.
27. Ibid., 101.
28. Ibid.
29. Ibid., 100–101.

Chapter 5

1. Martí, *Obras completas*, 2:299.
2. Fernando Ortiz, "Cuba, Martí and the Race Problem", *Phylon* 3, no. 3 (1942): 253–76.
3. Fernando Ortiz, *Martí y las razas: Conferencia pronunciada el día 9 de julio de 1941 en el salón de recepciones del Palacio Municipal de La Habana* (La Habana: Publicaciones de la Comisión Nacional Organizadora de los Actos y Ediciones del Centenario y el Monumento de Martí, 1953), 7.
4. Ortiz, "Cuba, Martí", 264. Ironically, although Ortiz is known more for his later work as a seminal figure of Afro-Cuban ethnography, he began studying Afro-Cuban traditions as a way to undermine them. His *Los Negros brujos* (*The Black Sorcerers*, 1906) is, according to George Brandon, "essentially a treatise on criminology . . . a study of witchcraft and sorcery among Cuban blacks which was aimed at producing a coherent and accurate description of the sorcerers and their beliefs and practices in order to eliminate them more quickly and efficiently". George Brandon, *Santería from Africa to the New World: The Dead Sell Memories* (Bloomington: Indiana University Press, 1993), 91–92. Nevertheless, Ortiz underwent a significant intellectual evolution during the nearly forty years from when *Los Negros brujos* first appeared to when he gave the lecture on Martí. By then, Ortiz had become one of the strongest advocates of the African legacy in Cuban culture.
5. Anne Fountain, *José Martí, the United States, and Race* (Gainesville: University Press of Florida, 2014), xii.
6. Ibid., 131–32.

7. Martí, *Obras completas*, 6:22. Excerpt from "Nuestra América".
8. Ibid., 22:108. In a personal annotation, perhaps while preparing a speech or article, Martí wrote sometime between 1885 and 1895 in his notes, "Bueno. A los negros, pa que los blancos los respeten por haberles debido en parte la libertad, y pa que los negros respeten a los blancos porque la libertad les vino de un blanco [Well. To the blacks so that the whites would respect them for partly owing them their freedom, and so that the blacks respect the whites since freedom (came to them) from a white (man).]" Nevertheless, in a previous annotation among his papers, perhaps preparing for a meeting with the Haitian president or a Haitian audience, he wrote, "La libertad de la Ama. del Sur fue cierta porque a Bolívar lo protegió Pétion en un momento oportuno. Pétion era Presidente de Haití. – V. es para mi más que un Presidente." (South America's freedom was secured because Pétion protected Bolívar at the right moment. Pétion was President of Haiti. – You are more to me than a president.)
9. I focus more on the debates and views of Latin Americans and in Cuba, since Anne Fountain's *José Martí, the United States and Race* provides a thorough overview of the political and intellectual climate regarding race while Martí lived in the United States. By no means do I attempt to provide an exhaustive examination of all debates; rather, I focus on the major ones that Martí contended.
10. Agnes Lugo-Ortiz, *Identidades imaginadas: Biografía y nacionalidad en el horizonte de la guerra (Cuba 1860–1898)* (San Juan: Editorial de la Universidad de Puerto Rico, 1999), 143–44.
11. Ibid.
12. Ibid., 144.
13. Ibid.
14. Manuel Sanguily, "Los negros y su emancipación" ("Blacks and Their Emancipation") and "Hojas literarias" ("Literary Pages"), in *Brega de libertad* (*Struggle for Freedom*), prologue and selection by Ernesto Ardura (Havana: Publicaciones del Ministerio de Educación. Dirección de Cultura, 1950), 193. Also quoted by Agnes Lugo-Ortiz in *Identidades imaginadas*.
15. In 1874, Sanguily recounted how José Antonio Maceo (1846–96), Antonio Maceo's brother and also general of the Cuban Liberation Army, was "a distinguished man and loved by all; as a mulatto he achieved the highest rank in our Army of Major-General. Nevertheless, one day, in Camagüey, he was invited to a dance that the young white Cuban aides of General Gómez had spontaneously organized in a ranch belonging to a humble peasant family, I am still not sure that they did it with their boss's consent. Cajoled by the [young soldiers] to dance, [José Antonio Maceo] politely approached a young lady, asking her for a dance. The young lady rudely and arrogantly responded, 'forgive me: but I do not dance but with [men] of my class'. The distinguished general did not feel the painful shun more than his friends; but moments later no one paid attention to it, nor have I known of the blacks, who

were in the majority, to have been largely or little unsettled by it." Manuel Sanguily, "Negros y blancos", in *Brega de libertad*, 207–8. My translation of the Spanish.
16. Ibid., 210. My translation of the Spanish.
17. Agnes Lugo-Ortiz quotes Saco in footnote 36 of *Identidades imaginadas*, 149. My translation of the Spanish.
18. Ibid. My translation of the Spanish.
19. José Martí, *Obras completas*, 22:108. Martí's Spanish original reads, "a los negros, para que los blancos los respeten por haberles debido en parte la libertad, y para que los negros respeten a los blancos porque la libertad les vino de un blanco". Most likely, the "blanco" (or "white Cuban") he refers to is Carlos Manuel de Céspedes. All quotations from Martí are from this edition of his works, unless otherwise noted.
20. Aline Helg, in *Our Rightful Share: The Afro-Cuban Struggle for Equality, 1886–1912* (Chapel Hill: University of North Carolina Press, 1995), and Rebecca Scott in *Slave Emancipation in Cuba: The Transition to Free Labor* (Princeton, NJ: Princeton University Press, 1985), provide detailed discussions of the views on race in Cuba during the late nineteenth century.
21. Fountain, *José Martí, the United States, and Race*, xii.
22. Martí, *Obras completas*, 4:94–95.
23. Vitier, "Etapas". The Cuban Martí scholar charts Martí's political efforts into seven stages: (1) 1869–73; (2) 1875–79; (3) 1880–81; (4) 1882–85; (5) 1886–91; (6) November 1891–29 January 1895 [when he delivered two speeches in Tampa, Florida, to when he signed the official call to arms in New York]; (7) 31 January 1895–18 May 1895 [when he departed New York City for the Dominican Republic, with an ultimate destination of the Cuban battlefields, to the date of his final letter addressed to his Mexican friend Manuel Mercado, a day before falling in battle]. The speeches given on 26 and 27 November 1891, "Con todos y para el bien de todos" and "Los pinos nuevos" ("The New Pines"), were given at the invitation of Néstor Carbonell of the Independence Club Ignacio Agramonte of Tampa, Florida. Vitier refers to Carbonell's letter inviting Martí to speak at both fundraising events for the Cuban cause as "la llamada del destino" (the call of destiny), and they ushered in, according to Vitier, "the years of [his] most intense political campaigning and of [his] most hectic organizing endeavours", 21–22. I agree with Vitier's view of the speech as "pivotal".
24. Martí, *Obras completas*, 4:270. Martí refers to the dictatorships of Ignacio de Veintemilla y Villacís (1828–1908) in Ecuador, Juan Manuel de Rosas (1793–1877) in Argentina and José Gaspar Rodríguez de Francia (1766–1840) in Paraguay.
25. Martin S. Stabb, "Martí and the Racists", *Hispania* 40, no. 4 (December 1957): 434.
26. Ibid., 434–35.
27. Aline Helg, "Race and Black Mobilization in Colonial and Early Independent Cuba: A Comparative Perspective", *Ethnohistory* 44, no. 1 (Winter 1997): 57.

28. Elier Ramírez Cañedo and Carlos Joane Rosario Grasso, *El Autonomismo en las horas cruciales de la nación cubana* (Havana: Editorial de Ciencias Sociales, 2008), 60.
29. Mildred de la Torre, *El Autonomismo en Cuba, 1878–1898* (Havana: Editorial de Ciencias Sociales, 1997), 121.
30. Ramírez Cañedo and Rosario Grasso, *El Autonomismo*, 65–66.
31. Ibid., 76–77.
32. Ibid.
33. De la Torre, *El Autonomismo*, 205. De la Torre's excerpt of the 12 December 1896 edition of *El País*: "mostraba sus más entusiasta felicitación por el triunfo alcanzado por las armas españolas en el brillante combate librado por la columna Cirujeda en la provincia de La Habana y en el que resultó muerto el cabecilla Maceo de funesta recordación". My translation of the Spanish.
34. Melina Pappademos, *Black Political Activism and the Cuban Republic* (Chapel Hill: University of North Carolina Press, 2011), 134.
35. Ibid., 8.
36. Martí, *Obras completas*, 1:261.
37. Lourdes Martínez-Echazábal, "Martí y las razas (Martí and Race): A Re-evaluation", in *Re-reading José Martí (1853–1895): One Hundred Years Later*, ed. Julio Rodríguez-Luis (Albany: State University of New York Press, 1999), 116.
38. Ibid., 116.
39. Lillian Guerra, *The Myth of José Martí: Conflicting Nationalisms in Early Twentieth Century Cuba* (Chapel Hill: University of North Carolina Press, 2005), 34.
40. Martínez-Echazábal, "Martí y las razas", 116.
41. Fountain, *José Martí, the United States, and Race*, 76.
42. Pappademos, *Black Political Activism*, 21.
43. Lugo-Ortiz, *Identidades imaginadas*, 165–66. My translation of Lugo-Ortiz's Spanish original, which reads: "En Martí de lo que se trata es de borrar, disciplinar, las diferencias y la particularidad de los intereses en favor de la representación de un interés trascendente que es el de la nación."
44. For a discussion on racial categories in colonial and early independence Cuba, see Helg, "Race and Black Mobilization", 58.
45. Martí, *Obras completas*, 18:484.
46. José Martí, *Diarios de campaña*, ed. Mayra Beatríz Martínez (Havana: Centro de Estudios Martianos Press, 2014), 17.
47. Martí, *Obras completas*, 22:323.
48. Ibid., 13:23.
49. Ibid., 3:142.
50. Ibid., 19:37. It may appear by this statement that Martí stood against miscegenation, however in other instances he praised individuals of mixed ancestry.

51. His positive renditions of the Garifuna contrast with his depictions of the African-descended population he saw in Curaçao on the way to his stay in Venezuela in 1881. Some scholars have attributed that negative depiction to the harsh economic conditions he saw in Curaçao, where blacks had less economic agency than in Belize and Caribbean Guatemala.
52. Ortiz, "Cuba, Martí", 264.
53. Dionisio Poey Baró, "José Martí: 'Mi Raza' un siglo después", *Anuario del Centro de Estudios Martianos* 17 (1994): 87.
54. Martí, *Obras completas*, 2:108–9.
55. Ibid. See also Oscar Montero, "José Martí against Race", in *The Cuban Republic and José Marti: Reception and Use of a National Symbol*, ed. Mauricio A. Font and Alfonso W. Quiroz (Lanham, MD: Lexington Books, 2006), for further discussion of Martí's depictions of African descendants and his concept of race.
56. Martí, *Obras completas*, 11:65–76.
57. Ibid., 2:298.
58. Ibid.
59. Ibid.
60. Josefina Toledo Benedit, *La madre negra de Martí* (Havana: Casa Editorial Verde Olivo, 2009), 135.
61. Martí, *Obras completas*, 4:436–37.
62. Ibid., 1:172.
63. Martí, *Obras completas*, 4:97.
64. Montero, "José Martí against Race", 99. See also Ada Ferrer, "The Silence of Patriots: Race and Nationalism in Martí's Cuba", in *José Martí's "Our America": From National to Hemispheric Cultural Studies*, ed. Jeffrey Belnap and Raúl Fernández (Durham, NC: Duke University Press, 1998), 230.
65. Ferrer, "The Silence of Patriots", 230.
66. Dionisio Poey Baró, "Visión martiana del negro: Interiorización de una mirada", *Anuario del Centro de Estudios Martianos* 21 (1998): 146.
67. Montero, "José Martí against Race", 103.
68. Martí, *Obras completas*, 22:189.
69. The notebook where the scheme appears is undated and there is no precise way of knowing when he wrote these notes. However, in the same notebook he wrote about "María's bee" as one of his life's supreme moments, when he and his "adopted" daughter, María Mantilla, at age ten, went to the beach and a bee stung her. This event happened in 1890, so the entries in the notebook most likely date from that period.
70. Ortiz, "Cuba, Martí", 261.
71. Martí, *Obras completas*, 18:285.

72. Israel Escalona Chádez, *José Martí y Antonio Maceo: La pelea por la libertad* (Santiago: Editorial Oriente, 2004), 76.
73. Rafael Ramírez García, *Martí-Maceo: Cartas Cruzadas* (Santiago: Editorial Oriente, 2003), 157.
74. Martí, *Obras completas*, 1:172.
75. Oscar Montero quotes Philip S. Foner regarding the idea of some white Cuban apprehension against Maceo and their seeking to limit black Cuban leadership in the movement. Oscar Montero, "José Martí against Race", 110. Nevertheless, many Cuban commanders in the liberation army and local leaders of Cuban independence party organizations were of African descent, demonstrating that in the overall struggle for Cuban independence African descendants played predominant roles. This fact later allowed for Afro-Cubans to legitimately demand fulfilment of the political ideals promoted during the Cuban independence struggles, but mostly neglected by white elites after the US intervention in the final Cuban War of Independence.
76. Martí, *Obras completas*, 1:173. Emphasis is mine.
77. Letter from General Antonio Maceo to José Martí, 19 November 1882, in *Destinatario José Martí*, ed. in Luis García Pascual (Havana: Casa Editora Abril, 1999), 111–12.
78. Escalona Chádez, *José Martí*, 114.
79. Ibid., 138.
80. Martí, *Obras completas*, 2:458–60.
81. Ramírez García, *Martí-Maceo*, 57.
82. Escalona Chádez, *José Martí*, 199.
83. Letter from Maceo to Martí, 22 February 1895, San José, Costa Rica, in García Pascual, *Destinatario José Martí*, 331–32.
84. Ibrahim Hidalgo Paz, *José Martí: Cronología, 1853–1895* (Havana: Centro de Estudios Martianos Press, 2012), 148–49.
85. "Arribamos a una playa de piedras (La Playita, al pie de Cajobabo.) Me quedo en el bote el último, vaciándolo. Salto. Dicha grande." Martí, *Diarios de campaña*, 66.
86. Máximo Gómez, *Diario de campaña (1868–1899)* (Oviedo, Spain: Universidad de Oviedo, 2005); Martí, *Diarios de campaña*.
87. Ramírez García, *Martí-Maceo: Cartas Cruzadas*, 11–12.
88. Escalona Chádez, *José Martí y Antonio Maceo*, 224.
89. Guillermo de Zéndegui, *Ambito de Martí* (Madrid: Escuela Gráfica Salesiana, 1954), 127.
90. Martí, *Obras completas*, 20:473.
91. Ibid., 345. Emphasis is mine.
92. Ibid., 372.
93. Guerra, *The Myth*, 27.
94. Emphasis is mine. Serra's exact statement in Spanish was "Martí . . . deplora y combate

la existencia de clases desdeñadas o excluidas de derechos, por instinto, y porque la práctica política le advierte, que con las promesas de reparar a las masas que sufren, fácil van los tiranos al poder". Rafael Serra, "Martí es la Democracia", 272–74. Serra and others defended Martí against claims by a contemporary fellow Cuban, Enrique Collazo, who questioned Martí's commitment to the Cuban independence cause. Collazo would later adjust his stance, and Martí and Collazo would reconcile and work together for the independence cause.

95. Ortiz, "Cuba, Martí", 268.
96. Martí, *Obras completas*, 4:381.
97. Ibid., 20:385.
98. Ibid., 351. Emphasis is mine.
99. Luis Toledo Sande, "José Martí y Juan Gualberto Gómez: Toda la justicia", *Anuario del Centro de Estudios Martianos* 8 (1985): 58.
100. José Luciano Franco, "José Martí y Juan Gualberto Gómez", *Anuario del Centro de Estudios Martianos* 4 (1972): 279.
101. Jorge Mañach, *Martí, el apóstol*, 7th edition (Madrid, Spain: Espasa-Calpe, S.A., 1998), 112.
102. Juan Gualberto Gomez, "Martí y yo", *Revista Bimestre Cubana*, February 1933, reprinted in *Anuario del Centro de Estudios Martianos* 8 (1985): 279–80.
103. Rafaela Chacón Nardi, *José Martí: Cien apuntes cronológicos* (Havana: Editorial Pablo de la Torriente, 2000), 15.
104. Gualberto Gómez, "Martí y yo", 279–80.
105. Jorge Castellanos, *Encuentro en 1898: Tres pueblos y cuatro hombres, España, Cuba, Estados Unidos* (Miami: Ediciones Universal, 2006), 475.
106. Gonzalo de Quesada y Miranda, "El Directorio de Sociedades y la Guerra del 95", *Anuario del Centro de Estudios Martianos* 5 (1973): 190–99.
107. Helg, "Race and Black Mobilization", 58.
108. Martí, *Obras completas*, 20:426.
109. Luis Toledo Sande quotes Juan Gualberto Gómez in "José Martí y Juan Gualberto Gómez", 60.
110. Ibid., 70.
111. Chacón Nardi, *José Martí*, 33.

Chapter 6

1. Martí, *Obras completas*, 20:90.
2. Ibid., 89; 313.
3. Vázquez Pérez, *La vigilia perpetua*, 3. Vázquez Pérez has written an excellent and detailed study of the morphological development of the Grant essay. She compares

4. Although the essay may have been partly written during Martí's commuter steamboat journeys, the published version is not a document that was written in haste. Rather, Martí significantly revised and edited it, as shown in a second draft manuscript. Martí's original first manuscript of the Grant essay is lost. See Vázquez Pérez, *La vigilia perpetua*.
the published versions to original manuscripts held in custody by the Centro de Estudios Martianos and traces Martí's thought process throughout the documents. This type of linguistic and literary analysis remains beyond the scope of this study, but nonetheless supports the arguments set forth in this chapter.
5. Martí, *Obras completas*, 20:89. Martí relates the story of writing the Grant essay to his close Mexican friend Manuel Mercado in an 1886 letter.
6. Vázquez Pérez, *La viglia perpetua*, 40.
7. Ibid., 50.
8. Ibid., 2.
9. Ivan A. Schulman, "Narrando la nación moderna", in *Vigencias: Martí y el Modernismo* (Havana: Centro de Estudios Martianos Press, 2005), 11–44.
10. Arcadio Díaz Quiñones, "Martí: La guerra desde las nubes", *Revista del Centro de Investigaciones Históricas* 9 (Río Piedras: University of Puerto Rico, 1997), 13.
11. Vázquez Pérez, *La vigilia perpetua*, 16.
12. Blanche Z. de Baralt, *El Martí que yo conocí* (Havana: Editorial de Ciencias Sociales, 1980), 76.
13. Marlene Vázquez Pérez, introduction, in José Martí, *Norteamericanos: Apostoles, poetas, bandidos*, ed. Marlene Vázquez Pérez (Havana: Centro de Estudios Martianos Press, 2009), 18.
14. Díaz Quiñones, "Martí", 4. See Martí's letter to General Máximo Gómez where he tells Gómez, "one does not found a nation, as one commands a military camp" (Martí, *Obras completas*, 1:280–83). Martí believed in a civilian leadership of the Cuban republic and not a military one, even though he was aware that to evict Spain from Cuba, the independence movement needed the military.
15. Martí scholars have termed Martí's writings that warn Cubans and Latin Americans of impending dangers to sovereignty and democratic practice as a "discurso de alerta" (discourse of forewarning). Vázquez Pérez, *La vigilia perpetua*, 9.
16. Díaz Quiñones, "Martí", 11.
17. James Ramage, Regents Professor of History, Northern Kentucky University, United States, email message to author, 27 September 2007.
18. Martí, *Obras completas*, 20:89. In his 1886 letter to Mercado.
19. Ibid., 13:85.
20. Ibid., 20:89.
21. Ibid., 13:156.

22. Ibid., 104.
23. Ibid.
24. Ibid., 83.
25. Ibid.
26. Ibid.
27. Ibid., 104.
28. One need only see the lyrics to the famous Cuban folk song "Guantanamera", taken from Martí's poetic verses of "Yo soy un hombre sincero de donde crece la palma" (I am an honest man from where palm trees grow).
29. Martí, *Obras completas*, 13:99.
30. Ibid.
31. Ibid.
32. See Susana Rotker, *Fundación de una escritura: Las crónicas de José Martí* (Havana: Casa de las Américas, 1992); Julio Ramos, *Desencuentros de la modernidad en América Latina (Literatura y política en el Siglo XIX)* (Mexico City: Fondo de Cultura Económica, 1989); Luis Álvarez, Matilde Varela and Carlos Palacio, *Martí biógrafo* (Santiago: Editorial Oriente, 2007). All discuss Martí's use of the "chronicle" as a genre to weave different literary styles into one narrative.
33. Martí, *Obras completas*, 23:273.
34. Hayden White, *Metahistory: The Historical Imagination in Nineteenth-Century Europe* (Baltimore: Johns Hopkins University Press, 1973), 149.
35. Vázquez Pérez, "Historia", 129.
36. Martí, *Obras completas*, 13:100.
37. Ibid., 83.
38. Ibid., 84.
39. Ibid.
40. Although Martí highlights the notion of forgiveness and reconciliation in the Grant essay, considering it a key element to be transmitted to his Latin American audience and the Cuban émigré community, he was aware that the rapprochement between the North and South had been far more fluid. His articles in Latin American newspapers regarding the inauguration of Grover Cleveland (Democrat) in 1885, and later Benjamin Harrison's (Republican) election in 1888, reveals that he was aware of the fluctuating nature of North/South relations.
41. Martí, *Obras completas*, 13:88.
42. Ibid., 1:27.
43. Ibid., 13:90.
44. Ibid.
45. Ibid.
46. Ibid., 103–4.
47. Ibid., 93.

48. Ibid., 20:89.
49. Ibid., 13:93.
50. Ibid.
51. Ibid., 109–10.
52. Ibid., 109.
53. Ibid., 109.
54. Ibid.
55. Ibid., 93.
56. Ibid., 96.
57. Ibid., 97.
58. Ibid., 98–99.
59. Ibid., 101.
60. Ibid., 102.
61. Ibid.
62. Ibid., 102–3.
63. Ibid., 1:177.
64. Ibid., 13:103.
65. Ibid., 105.
66. Ibid.
67. Ibid., 105–6.
68. Ibid., 106.
69. Ibid.
70. Ibid.
71. Ibid.
72. Ibid., 106–7.
73. Ibid., 108.
74. Ibid., 110.
75. Ibid.,
76. Ibid.
77. Ibid., 111.
78. Ibid.
79. Ibid., 114.
80. Ibid., 115.

Afterword

1. Martí, *Obras completas*, 5:468.
2. Pedro Pablo Rodríguez, *Un caudillo útil: San Martín en José Martí* (Havana: Centro de Estudios Martianos Press, 2012).

3. Martí, *Obras completas*, 20:373.
4. Pedro Pablo Rodríguez, *De todas partes: Perfiles de José Martí* (Havana: Centro de Estudios Martianos Press, 2012), 91–92.
5. Martí, *Obras completas*, 6:420.

SELECTED BIBLIOGRAPHY

Abad, Diana. "El Partido Revolucionario Cubano: Organización, funcionamiento y democracia". *Anuario del Centro de Estudios Martianos* 4 (1972): 231–56.

Adas, Michael. *Machines as the Measure of Men: Science, Technology and Ideologies of Western Dominance*. Ithaca: Cornell University Press, 1989.

Agramonte, Roberto D. *Martí y su concepcion del mundo*. San Juan: Editorial Universitaria de Puerto Rico, 1971.

Alba-Buffill, Elio, ed. *José Martí ante la crítica actual (En el centenario de* Ismaelillo*)*. New York: Círculo de Cultura Panamericano, 1983.

Almendros, Herminio. *A propósito de* La edad de oro*: Notas sobre literatura infantil*. Havana: Instituto Cubano del Libro, 1972.

Álvarez, Luis, Matilde Varela and Carlos Palacio. *Martí biógrafo*. Santiago: Editorial Oriente, 2007.

Anderson, Benedict. *Imagined Communities: Reflections on the Origins and Spread of Nationalism*. London: Verso, 1983.

Andino, Alberto. *Martí y España*. Madrid: Playor, 1973.

Arce, Reinerio. *Religión, poesía del mundo venidero: Implicaciones teológicas en la obra de José Martí*. Havana: Consejo Latinoamericano de Iglesias, 1996.

Argüelles, Luis Angel. "La huella martiana en Fernando Ortiz". *Anuario del Centro de Estudios Martianos* 5 (1977): 218–33.

Arias, Salvador. *Un proyecto martiano esencial:* La edad de oro. Havana: Centro de Estudio Martianos, 2001.

———, ed. *Acerca de* La edad de oro. Havana: Centro de Estudios Martianos, 1980.

Armero, Gonzalo. *Poesía: Revista ilustrada de información poética, no. 42: José Martí, obra y vida*. Madrid: Ministerio de Cultura y Ediciones Siruela, 1995.

Armitage, David, and Sanjay Subrahmanyan, eds. *The Age of Revolutions in Global Context, c. 1760–1840*. New York: Palgrave Macmillan, 2010.

Arroyo, Jossianna. "Technologies: Transculturations of Race, Gender and Ethnicity in Arturo A. Schomburg's Masonic Writings". *Centro Journal (City University of New York. Centro de Estudios Puertorriqueños)* 17, no. 1 (Spring 2005): 4–25.

———. *Writing Secrecy in Caribbean Freemasonry*. New York: Palgrave Macmillan, 2013.
Ballón Aguirre, José C. *Autonomía cultural americana: Emerson y Martí*. Madrid: Pliegos, 1986.
———. *Lecturas norteamericanas de José Martí: Emerson y el socialismo contemporáneo (1880–1887)*. Mexico City: Universidad Nacional Autónoma de México, 1995.
———. *Martí y Blaine en la dialéctica de la Guerra del Pacífico (1879–1883)*. Mexico City: Universidad Nacional Autónoma de México, 2003.
Barros, Silvia A. "La literatura para niños de José Martí en su época". In *Estudios Críticos sobre la prosa modernista hispanoamericana*, edited by José Olivio Jiménez, 107–19. New York: Eliseo Torres, 1975.
Bayly, C.A. "The Age of Revolutions in Global Context: An Afterword". In *The Age of Revolutions in Global Context, c. 1760–1840*, edited by David Armitage and Sanjay Subrahmanyam, 209–17. New York: Palgrave Macmillan, 2010.
———. *The Birth of the Modern World, 1780–1914: Global Connections and Comparisons*. Malden, MA: Blackwell, 2004.
Bejel, Emilio. *José Martí: Images of Memory and Mourning*. New York: Palgrave Macmillan, 2012.
Belnap, Jeffrey, and Raúl Fernández, eds. *José Martí's "Our America": From National to Hemispheric Cultural Studies*. Durham, NC: Duke University Press, 1998.
Brandon, George. *Santería from Africa to the New World: The Dead Sell Memories*. Bloomington: Indiana University Press, 1993.
Cairo Ballester, Ana, ed. *Valoración multiple: José Martí. Edición al cuidado de Ana Cairo Ballester*. Havana: Fondo Editorial Casa de las Américas, 2007.
Calhoun, Craig. *Nationalism*. Minneapolis: University of Minnesota Press, 1997.
Camacho, Jorge. *Etnografía, política y poder a finales del siglo XIX: José Martí y la cuestión indígena*. Chapel Hill: University of North Carolina Press, 2013.
Castellanos, Jorge. *Encuentro en 1898: Tres pueblos y cuatro hombres, España, Cuba, Estados Unidos*. Miami: Ediciones Universal, 2006.
Chacón Nardi, Rafaela. *José Martí: Cien apuntes cronológicos*. Havana: Editorial Pablo de la Torriente, 2000.
Cheah, Pheng. "Grounds of Comparison". *Diacritics* 29, no. 4 (Winter 1999): 3–18.
Cruz-Taura, Graciella. "El pensamiento histórico de José Martí". In *Transcendencia cultural de la obra de José Martí: Actas del simposio internacional celebrado en Praga, del 21 al 23 de octubre de 2002*, edited by Anna Houskova, 91–100. Prague: Department of Philosophy and Letters, Charles University of Prague, 2003.
de Baralt, Blanche Z. *El Martí que yo conocí*. Havana: Editorial de Ciencias Sociales, 1980.
de la Fuente, Alejandro. *A Nation for All: Race, Inequality, and Politics in Twentieth-Century Cuba*. Chapel Hill: University of North Carolina Press, 2001.

———. "Race, National Discourse and Politics in Cuba: An Overview". *Latin American Perspectives* 25, no. 3 (May 1998): 43–69.
de la Torre, Mildred. *El Autonomismo en Cuba, 1878–1898*. Havana: Editorial de Ciencias Sociales, 1997.
de Onis, José. "José Martí in the United States". *Los Ensayistas* 10–11 (1981): 129–38.
de Quesada y Miranda, Gonzalo. "El Directorio de Sociedades y la Guerra del 95". *Anuario del Centro de Estudios Martianos* 5 (1973): 190–99.
———. "Martí en Jamaica". *Anuario del Centro de Estudios Martianos* 5 (1973): 41–48.
Deschamps Chapeaux, Pedro. "Martí y la Sociedad Protectora de la Instrucción 'La Liga'". *Anuario del Centro de Estudios Martianos* 5 (1973): 61–71.
de Zéndegui, Guillermo. *Ambito de Martí*. Madrid: Escuela Gráfica Salesiana, 1954.
Diamond, Jared. *Guns, Germs, and Steel: The Fates of Human Societies*. New York: W.W. Norton, 1997.
Díaz Quiñones, Arcadio. "Martí: La guerra desde las nubes". In *José Martí: En los Estados Unidos. Periodismo de 1881 a 1892*, edited by Roberto Fernández Retamar and Pedro Pablo Rodríguez, 2119–47. Madrid: Allca XX, 2003.
Donahue, Francis. "Cuban de Tocqueville". *New Orléans Review* 3 (1979): 355–58.
Duno Gottberg, Luis. *Solventado las diferencias: La ideología del mestizaje en Cuba*. Madrid: Iberoamericana, 2003.
Escalona Chádez, Israel. *José Martí y Antonio Maceo: La pelea por la libertad*. Santiago: Editorial Oriente, 2004.
Esteban, Angel. *José Martí: El alma alerta*. Granada, Spain: Editorial Comares, 1995.
Estrade, Paul. *José Martí: Los fundamentos de la democracia en Latinoamérica*. Madrid: Ediciones Doce Calles, 2000.
Ette, Otmar. *José Martí: Apóstol, poeta, revolucionario: Una historia de su recepción*. Mexico City: Universidad Nacional Autónoma de México, 1995.
Ette, Otmar, and Titus Heydenriech, eds. *José Martí 1895/1995: Literatura, política, filosofía y estética*. Frankfurt: Vervuert Verlag, 1994.
Febles, Jorge. "Martí's Unmasking of Blaine in the First Segment of the *Escenas Norteamericanas* (1881–1886): The Idealist Defaces the Ideologue". *SECOLAS Annals* 22 (March 1991): 95–103.
Fernández-Armesto, Felipe. *Civilizations: Culture, Ambition, and the Transformation of Nature*. London: Macmillan, 2000.
Fernández Retamar, Roberto. *Ensayo de Otro Mundo*. Santiago, Chile: Editorial Universitaria, 1969.
———. *José Martí: La edad de oro. Edición crítica anotada y prologada por Roberto Fernández Retamar*. Mexico City: Fondo de Cultura Económica, 1992.
———. *José Martí: Páginas escogidas*. 2 vols. Havana: Editorial de Ciencias Sociales, 1985.

———. "Martí en su (tercer) mundo [Fragmentos]". In *Valoración multiple: José Martí. Edición al cuidado de Luis Toledo Sande*, 235–62. Havana: Fondo Editorial Casa de las Américas, 2007.

Ferrer, Ada. *Insurgent Cuba: Race, Nation, and Revolution, 1868–1898*. Chapel Hill: University of North Carolina Press, 1999.

———. "The Silence of Patriots: Race and Nationalism in Martí's Cuba". In *José Martí's 'Our America': From National to Hemispheric Cultural Studies*, edited by Jeffrey Belnap and Raúl Fernández, 228–49. Durham, NC: Duke University Press, 1998.

Ferrer Canales, José. "El negro en José Martí". In *Estudios Martianos: Memoria del seminario José Martí*, 109–18. Río Piedras: Universidad de Puerto Rico, 1974.

Flores Varona, Félix. *Traspasos de* La edad de oro. Havana: Centro de Investigación y Desarrollo de la Cultura Cubana "Juan Marinello", 2003.

Font, Mauricio A., and Alfonso W. Quiroz, eds. *The Cuban Republic and José Martí: Reception and Use of a National Symbol*. Lanham, MD: Lexington Books, 2006.

Fountain, Anne. *José Martí, the United States, and Race*. Gainesville: University Press of Florida, 2014.

———. *José Martí and US Writers*. Gainesville: University Press of Florida, 2003.

———. "Ralph Waldo Emerson and Helen Hunt Jackson in *La edad de oro*". *SECOLAS Annals: Journal of the Southeastern Council on Latin American Studies* 22 (March 1991): 95–103.

Franco, José Luciano. "José Martí y Juan Gualberto Gómez". *Anuario del Centro de Estudios Martianos* 4 (1972): 279–85.

Fraser, Howard M. "*La edad de oro* and José Martí's Modernist Ideology for Children". *Revista Interamericana de Bibliografía* 42, no. 2 (1992): 223–32.

García de la Torre, Armando. "José Martí and the Global Dimensions of Late Nineteenth-Century Nation Building". PhD dissertation, Washington State University, 2006.

García Guatas, Manuel. *La Zaragoza de José Martí*. Zaragoza, Spain: Institución "Fernando el Católico", 2004.

García Marruz, Fina. *El amor como energía revolucionaria en José Martí*. Havana: Centro de Estudios Martianos, 2003.

———. *Temas martianos: Tercera serie*. Havana: Centro de Estudio Martianos, 1995.

García Pascual, Luis, ed. *Destinatario José Martí*. Havana: Casa Editora Abril, 1999.

Gómez, Máximo. *Diario de campaña (1868–1899)*. Oviedo, Spain: Universidad de Oviedo, 2005.

González, Manuel Pedro. *José Martí: Epic Chronicler of the US in the Eighties*. Chapel Hill: University of North Carolina, 1953.

González, Manuel Pedro, and Ivan A. Schulman. *José Martí: esquema ideológico*. Mexico City: Editorial Cultural, 1961.

Gualberto Gomez, Juan. "Martí y yo". *Revista Bimestre Cubana*, February 1933. Reprinted in *Anuario del Centro de Estudios Martianos* 8 (1985): 279–80.

Guerra, Lillian. *The Myth of José Martí: Conflicting Nationalisms in Early Twentieth-Century Cuba*. Chapel Hill: University of North Carolina Press, 2005.

Gutiérrez, José Ismael. "José Martí y la traducción de cuentos para niños: Tradición y originalidad". *Hispanófila* 141 (2004): 31–46.

Hegel, Georg Wilhelm Friedrich. "World History", translated by T.M. Knox. In *German Essays on History*, edited by Rolf Sältzer, 63–72. New York: Continuum, 1991.

Helg, Aline. *Our Rightful Share: The Afro-Cuban Struggle for Equality, 1886–1912*. Chapel Hill: University of North Carolina Press, 1995.

———. "Race and Black Mobilization in Colonial and Early Independent Cuba: A Comparative Perspective". *Ethnohistory* 44, no. 1 (Winter 1997): 53–74.

Hidalgo Paz, Ibrahim. *José Martí: Cronogía, 1853–1895*. Havana: Editorial Ciencias Sociales, 1992.

———. "Reseña de los clubes fundadores del Partido Revolucionario Cubano". *Anuario del Centro de Estudios Martianos* 4 (1972): 208–30.

Hodgkinson, Virginia A., and Michael W. Foley, eds. *The Civil Society Reader*. Lebanon, NH: University Press of New England, 2003.

Hoffman, Stefan-Ludwig. *Civil Society*. New York: Palgrave Macmillan, 2006.

Holden, Robert H., and Eric Zolov, eds., *Latin America and the United States: A Documentary History*, 2nd ed. New York: Oxford University Press, 2011.

House, Laraine R. "José Martí y el ansia del amor puro". *Cuadernos americanos* 239, no. 6 (1981): 134–52.

Hughes-Warrington, Marnie, ed. *World Histories*. London and New York: Palgrave Macmillan, 2005.

Jiménez Grullón, Juan. *La filosofía de José Martí*. Santo Domingo: Biblioteca Nacional, 1986.

Jorge Viera, Elena. "Notas sobre la función de *La edad de oro*". In *Acerca de* La edad de oro, edited by Salvador Arias, 284–305. Havana: Centro de Estudios Martianos, 1989.

Jorrín, Miguel. *Martí y la filosofía*. Havana: UNESCO, 1941.

Le Riverend Brussone, Julio J. "Teoria martiana del partido político". In *Vida y pensamiento de Martí: Homenaje de la ciudad de la Habana en el cincuentenario de la Fundación del Partido Revolucionario Cubano, 1892–1942*, 83–110. Havana: Municipio de La Habana, 1942.

Lizaso, Felix. "Emerson visto por Martí". *Humanismo* 3, no. 23 (1954): 31–38.

———. *Martí, Místico del deber*. 3rd ed. Buenos Aires: Editorial Losada, 1952.

———. *Posibilidades filosóficas en Martí*. Havana: Molina, 1935.

Llaverías, Joaquín. *Los periódicos de José Martí*. Havana: Pérez Sierra, 1929.

Lolo, Eduardo. *Mar de espuma: Martí y la literatura infantil*. Miami: Ediciones Universal, 1995.

López, Alfred J. *José Martí and the Future of Cuban Nationalisms*. Gainesville: University Press of Florida, 2006.
———. *José Martí: A Revolutionary Life*. Austin: University of Texas Press, 2014.
López Mesa, Enrique. *José Martí: Editar desde New York*. Havana: Editorial Letras Cubanas, 2012.
———. *La comunidad cubana de New York: Siglo XIX*. Havana: Centro de Estudios Martianos, 2002.
López Morillas, Juan. *El krausismo español: Perfil de una aventura intelectual*. Mexico City: Fondo de Cultura Económica, 1956.
Lugo-Ortiz, Agnes. *Identidades imaginadas: Biografía y nacionalidad en el horizonte de la guerra (Cuba 1860–1898)*. San Juan: Editorial de la Universidad de Puerto Rico, 1999.
Mañach, Jorge. *El espiritu de Martí: Estudio preliminar y notas por Anita Arroyo*. San Juan: Editorial San Juan, 1973.
———. *El pensamiento político y social de Martí*. Havana: Edición Oficial del Senado, 1941.
———. *Martí, el apóstol*. 7th ed. Madrid: Espasa Calpe, 1998.
Manning, Patrick. "Methods and Materials". In *World Histories*, edited by Marnie Hughes-Warrington, 44–63. London and New York: Palgrave Macmillan, 2005.
Márquez Sterling, Carlos. *José Martí: Síntesis de una vida extraordinaria*. Mexico City: Editorial Porrúa, 1998.
Martí, José. *Antología mayor: Prosa y poesía*. Edited by Carlos Ripoll. Miami: Editorial Cubana, 1995.
———. *Diarios de campaña*. Edited by Mayra Beatriz Martínez. Havana: Centro de Estudios Martianos, 2014.
———. *En un domingo de mucha luz: Cultura, historia, y literatura españolas en la obra de José Martí*. Salamanca, Spain: Ediciones Universidad de Salamanca, 1995.
———. *José Martí: En los Estados Unidos*. Edited by Andrés Sorel. Madrid: Alianza Editorial, 1968.
———. *José Martí: Ideario separatista*. Edited by Felix Lizaso. Havana: Publicaciones del Ministerio de Educación, Dirección de Cultura, 1947.
———. *José Martí Reader: Writings on the Americas*. Edited by Deborah Shnookal and Mirta Muñíz. New York: Ocean Press, 1999.
———. *La edad de oro: Edición crítica de Eduardo Lolo*. Edited by Eduardo Lolo. Miami: Ediciones Universal, 2001.
———. *Lucía Jerez*. Edited by Mauricio Núñez. Heredia, Costa Rica: Editorial Universidad Nacional, 2013.
———. *Norteamericanos: Apóstoles, poetas, bandidos*. Edited by Marlene Vázquez Pérez. Havana: Centro de Estudios Martianos, 2009.
———. *Obras completas*. 27 vols. Havana: Editorial de Ciencias Sociales, 1975.

———. *On Education: Articles on Educational Theory and Pedagogy and Writings for Children from The Age of Gold by José Martí*. Translated by Elinor Randall. New York: Monthly Review Press, 1979.

———. *Our America: Writings on Latin America and the Struggle for Cuban Independence*. Edited by Philip S. Foner. New York: Monthly Review Press, 1977.

———. *Selected Writings*. Edited and translated by Esther Allen. New York: Penguin, 2002.

Martínez-Echazábal, Lourdes. "Martí y las razas (Martí and Race): A Re-Evaluation". In *Re-Reading José Martí (1853–1895): One Hundred Years Later*, edited by Julio Rodríguez-Luis, 115–26. Albany: State University of New York Press, 1999.

Massip, Salvador. "Martí, viajero". In *Vida y pensamiento de Martí: Homenaje de la ciudad de la Habana en el cincuentenario de la fundación del Partido Revolucionario Cubano, 1892–1942*, 187–231. Havana: Municipio de La Habana, 1942.

Maurya, Vibha. "Una visión india. El humanismo de José Martí y Mahatma Gandhi". *Anuario del Centro de Estudios Martianos* 10 (1987): 237–51.

McGetchin, Douglas T. "The Sanskrit Reich: Translating Ancient India for Modern Germans, 1790–1914". PhD dissertation, University of California, San Diego, 2002.

McKee Irwin, Robert. "*Ramona* and Postnationalist American Studies: On 'Our America' and the Mexican Borderlands". *American Quarterly* 55, no. 4 (Dec. 2003): 539–67.

McNeill, William. *The Rise of the West: A History of the Human Community*. Chicago: University of Chicago Press, 1963.

Méndez, M. Isidro. "Humanidad de Martí". In *Vida y pensamiento de Martí: Homenaje de la ciudad de la Habana en el cincuentenario de la fundacion del Partido Revolucionario Cubano, 1892–1942*. Havana: Municipio de La Habana, 1942.

Miller, Barbara Stoler, trans. *The Bhagavad-Gita: Krishna's Counsel in Time of War*. New York: Bantam Books, 1986.

Miller, Nicola. "The Historiography of Nationalism and National Identity in Latin America". *Nations and Nationalism* 12, no. 2 (2006): 201–21.

Mirabal, Nancy Raquel. " 'No Country But the One We Must Fight For': The Emergence of an Antillean Nation and Community in New York City, 1860–1901". In *Mambo Montage: The Latinization of New York*, edited by Agustín Laó-Montes and Arlene Dávila, 55–72. New York: Columbia University Press, 2001.

Molloy, Sylvia. "His America, Our America: José Martí Reads Whitman". *The Places of History: Regionalism Revisited in Latin America. Modern Language Quarterly: A Journal of Literary History* 57, no. 2 (1996): 369–79.

Montero, Oscar. "José Martí against Race". In *The Cuban Republic and José Marti: Reception and Use of a National Symbol*, edited by Mauricio A. Font and Alfonso W. Quiroz, 95–114. Lanham, MD: Lexington Books, 2006.

———. *José Martí: An Introduction*. New York: Palgrave Macmillan, 2004.

———. "Review of *The American Chronicles of José Martí. Journalism and Modernity in Spanish America*, by Susana Rotker". Translated by Jennifer French and Katherine Semler. *Hispanic Review* 70, no. 3 (Summer 2002): 473.

Nehru, Jawaharlal. *Glimpses of World History: Being Further Letters to His Daughter, Written in Prison, and Containing a Rambling Account of History for Young People*. London: Lindsay Drummond, 1939.

Núñez y Domínguez, José de J. *Martí en México*. Mexico City: Imprenta de la Secretaría de Relaciones Exteriores, 1933.

O'Brien, Patrick. "Historiographical Traditions and Modern Imperatives for the Restoration of Global History". *Journal of Global History* (March 2006): 3–39.

Olivio Jiménez, José. *La raíz y el ala: Aproximaciones críticas a la obra literaria de José Martí*. Valencia, Spain: Pre-Textos, 1994.

Ortiz, Fernando. "Cuba, Martí, and the Race Problem". *Phylon* 3, no. 3 (1942): 250–76.

———. "Martí y las razas: Conferencia pronunciada el día 9 de julio de 1941 en el salón de recepciones del Palacio Municipal de La Habana". La Habana: Publicaciones de la Comisión Nacional Organizadora de los Actos y Ediciones del Centenario y el Monumento de Martí, 1953.

———. "Martí y las 'Razas de librería'". *Anales de la Universidad de Chile* III, no. 89 (1953): 117–30.

———. "The Relations between Blacks and Whites in Cuba". *Phylon* 5, no. 1 (1944): 15–29.

Oullion, Juliette. "La discriminación racial en los Estados Unidos vista por José Martí". *Anuario Martiano* 3 (1971): 9–45.

Pappademos, Melina. *Black Political Activism and the Cuban Republic*. Chapel Hill: University of North Carolina Press, 2011.

Parker, Andrew. "Bogeyman: Benedict Anderson's 'Derivative' Discourse". *Diacritics* 29, no. 4 (Winter 1999): 40–57.

Pérez, Louis A., Jr. *Cuba: Between Reform and Revolution*. 3rd ed. New York: Oxford University Press, 2006.

———. *Cuba between Empires, 1878–1902*. Pittsburgh: University of Pittsburgh Press, 1983.

Pérez Nápoles, Rubén. *José Martí: El poeta armado*. Madrid: Algaba Ediciones, 2004.

Poey Baró, Dionisio. "Acerca del pensamiento antirracista de José Martí". *Anuario del Centro de Estudios Martianos* 16 (1993): 171–76.

———. "José Martí: 'Mi Raza' un siglo después". *Anuario del Centro de Estudios Martianos* 17 (1994): 81–93.

———. "Visión martiana del negro: Interiorización de una Mirada". *Anuario del Centro de Estudios Martianos* 21 (1998): 144–55.

Poyo, Gerald E. "Evolution of Cuban Separatist Thought in the Emigré Communities of the United States, 1848–1895". *Hispanic American Historical Review* 66, no. 3 (August 1986): 485–507.

Radhakrishnan, Sarvepalli, and Charles A. Moore, eds. *A Sourcebook in Indian Philosophy.* Princeton, NJ: Princeton University Press, 1957.

Rama, Angel. "La dialéctica de la modernidad en José Martí". *Estudios Martianos: Memoria del seminario José Martí y el departamento de estudios hispánicos, Facultad de Humanidades de la Universidad de Puerto Rico.* San Juan: Editorial Universitaria de Puerto Rico, 1971.

Ramírez Cañedo, Elier, and Carlos Joane Rosario Grasso. *El Autonomismo en las horas cruciales de la nación cubana.* Havana: Editorial de Ciencias Sociales, 2008.

Ramírez García, Rafael. *Martí-Maceo: Cartas cruzadas.* Santiago de Cuba: Editorial Oriente, 2003.

Ramos, Julio. *Desencuentros de la modernidad en América Latina (Literatura y política en el Siglo XIX).* Mexico City: Fondo de Cultura Económica, 1989.

Ratt, William D. "Ideas and Society in Don Porfirio's Mexico". *Americas* 30 (July 1973–April 1974): 32–53.

Renan, Ernest. "What is a Nation?" In *Becoming National: A Reader,* edited by Geoff Eley and Ronald Grigor Suny, 41–55. New York and Oxford: Oxford University Press, 1996.

Ripoll, Carlos. "Martí: Su último cumpleaños". *Diario las Americas.* 29 January 1987.

———. *Martí y el fin de una leyenda.* New York: Editorial Dos Ríos, 2007.

Rodríguez, Pedro Pablo. *Al sol voy: Atisbos a la política martiana.* Havana: Centro de Estudios Martianos, 2012.

———. *De las dos Américas (Aproximaciones al pensamiento martiano).* Havana: Centro de Estudios Martianos, 2002.

———. *De todas partes: Perfiles de José Martí.* Havana: Centro de Estudios Martianos, 2012.

———. *Un caudillo útil: San Martín en José Martí.* Havana: Centro de Estudios Martianos, 2012.

Rodríguez-Luis, Julio, ed. *Re-reading José Martí (1853–1895): One Hundred Years Later.* Albany: State University of New York Press, 1999.

Roig de Leuchsenring, Emilio. *Martí: Anti-Imperialist.* Havana: Ministry of Foreign Affairs, 1961.

———, ed. *Vida y pensamiento de Martí: Homenaje de la ciudad de La Habana en el cincuentenario de la fundación del Partido Revolucionario Cubano.* Havana: Municipio de La Habana, 1942.

Rojas, Rafael. *José Martí: La invención de Cuba.* Madrid: Editorial Colibrí, 2000.

Rotker, Susana. *The American Chronicles of José Martí: Journalism and Modernity in Spanish America.* Translated by Jennifer French and Katherine Semler. Hanover, NH: University Press of New England, 2000.

———. *Fundación de una escritura: Las crónicas de José Martí.* Havana: Casa de las Américas, 1992.

Sánchez Aguilera, Osmar. *Las martianas escrituras.* Havana: Centro de Estudios Martianos, 2011.

Sanguily, Manuel. *Brega de libertad*. Havana: Publicaciones del Ministerio de Educacion, 1950.

Santí, Enrico Mario. "'Our America', the Gilded Age, and the Crisis of Latinamericanism". In *José Martí's "Our America": From National to Hemispheric Cultural Studies*, edited by Jeffrey Belnap and Raul Fernández, 179–90. Durham, NC: Duke University Press, 1998.

Sardiña, Ricardo R. *Martí: El poeta*. Miami: Ediciones Universal, 1999.

Sarracino, Rodolfo. *José Martí en el Club Crepúsculo de Nueva York: En busca de nuevos equilibrios*. Guadalajara, Mexico: Universidad de Guadalajara, 2010.

Schnee, Walter. "Nationalism: A Review of the Literature". *Journal of Political and Military Sociology* 29 (Summer 2001): 1–18.

Schuler, Esther E. "José Martí, su critica de algunos escritores norteamericanos". *Archivo José Martí* 16 (Havana 1950): 164–92.

Schulman, Ivan A. *José Martí: Ismaelillo, Versos Libres, Versos Sencillos*. Madrid: Ediciones Cátedra, 1999.

———. "José Martí: Migraciones, viajes y la creación de la nación cubana". *Revista Iberoamericana* 69, no. 205 (October–December 2003): 927–33.

———. "Un nuevo mundo: Martí y la sociedad multicultural de los Estados Unidos". *Anuario del Centro de Estudios Martianos* 16 (1993): 252–66.

———. *Vigencias: Martí y el Modernismo*. Havana: Centro de Estudios Martianos, 2005.

Schultz de Mantovani, Fryda. "Introduction: *La edad de oro* de José Martí". In *José Martí: La edad de oro*, 9–33. San Salvador: Departamento Editorial Ministerio de Cultura, 1955.

Scott, Rebecca J. *Slave Emancipation in Cuba: The Transition to Free Labor, 1860–1899*. Princeton, NJ: Princeton University Press, 1985. Reprint, Pittsburgh: University of Pittsburgh, 2000.

Serra, Rafael. "Martí es la Democracia". *Anuario del Centro de Estudios Martianos* 5 (1973): 272–74.

Sherman, Paul. *Emerson's Angle of Vision*. Cambridge, MA: Harvard University Press, 1952.

Singer, Peter. *Hegel*. Oxford: Oxford University Press, 1983.

Stabb, Martin S. "Martí and the Racists". *Hispania* 40, no. 4 (Dec. 1957): 433–39.

Stearns, Peter. "Nationalisms: An Invitation to Comparative Analysis". *Journal of World History* 8, no. 1 (Spring 1997): 57–74.

Suárez León, Carmen. *Martí y Victor Hugo en el fiel de las modernidades*. Havana: Centro de Investigación y Desarrollo de la Cultura Cubana "Juan Marinello" and Editorial José Martí, 1997.

Suárez Suárez, Reinaldo. *José Martí contra Alphonse Karr: ¿De qué sirven vuestras leyes?* Santiago, Cuba: Editorial Oriente, 2009.

Thomas, Hugh. *Cuba or the Pursuit of Freedom*. New York: Da Capo, 1971.

Tinajero, Araceli. *Orientalismo en el modernismo hispanoamericano*. West Lafayette, IN: Purdue University Press, 2003.

Toledo Benedit, Josefina. *La madre de negra de Martí*. Havana: Casa Editorial Verde Olivo, 2009.
Toledo Sande, Luis. *Ensayos sencillos con José Martí*. Havana: Editorial de Ciencias Sociales, 2012.
———. "José Martí y Juan Gualberto Gómez: Toda la justicia". *Anuario del Centro de Estudios Martianos* 8 (1985): 52–92.
———. *Valoración multiple: José Martí. Edición al cuidado de Luis Toledo Sande*. Havana: Fondo Editorial Casa de las Américas, 2007.
Tone, John Lawrence. *War and Genocide in Cuba, 1895–1898*. Chapel Hill: University of North Carolina Press, 2006.
Tornadú, Noemí Beatriz. "Introducción y vocabulario". In *La edad de oro: Publicación de recreo e instrucción dedicada a los niños de América*, 5–20. Buenos Aires: Editorial Huemul, 1966.
Vázquez Pérez, Marlene. "Historia, recepción y literatura en *La edad de oro*". *Anuario del Centro de Estudios Martianos* 22 (1999): 120–32.
———. Introduction. In José Martí, *Norteamericanos: Apóstoles, poetas, bandidos*, ed. Marlene Vázquez Pérez, 11–50. Havana: Centro de Estudios Martianos, 2009.
———. *La vigilia perpetua: Martí en Nueva York*. Havana: Centro de Estudios Martianos, 2010.
Vásquez Vega, Miguel A. "Mística y poética en Martí: Lectura del poema V de *Versos Sencillos*". *Kañina* 4, no. 1 (1980): 49–54.
Vitier, Cintio. "Etapas en la acción política de Martí". In *Temas martianos*, edited by Cintio Vitier and Fina García Marruz, 19–82. Havana: Centro de Estudios Martianos, 2011.
———. *Vida y obra del apóstol José Martí*. Havana: Centro de Estudios Martianos, 2010.
Vitier, Cintio, and Fina García Marruz, eds. *Temas martianos*. Havana: Centro de Estudios Martianos, 2011.
Vitier, Medardo. "Dimensión filosófica [de José Martí], sobre todo en su sentido de la vida". In *Valoración multiple: José Martí. Edición al cuidado de Luis Toledo Sande*, 217–30. Havana: Fondo Editorial Casa de las Américas, 2007.
Whicher, Stephen E. *Freedom and Fate: An Inner Life of Ralph Waldo Emerson*. Philadelphia: University of Pennsylvania Press, 1953.
White, Hayden. *Metahistory: The Historical Imagination in Nineteenth-Century Europe*. Baltimore: Johns Hopkins University Press, 1973.
Zea, Leopoldo. *Dos etapas del pensamiento en Hispanoamérica: Del romanticismo al positivismo*. Mexico City: El Colegio de México, 1949.
———. Introduction. *José Martí: A cien años de Nuestra América*. Edited by Jesús Serna Moreno and María Teresa Bosque Lastra. Mexico City: Universidad Nacional Autónoma de México, 1993.

INDEX

abolitionism, and Cuban independence movement, 12, 104–5, 158
academic scholarship: diversity in interpretations, 20; Eurocentric constraints in understanding work of Martí, 16–17; on *Golden Years*, 35–36; on Martí as writer and poet, 17–18
Adventures of Tom Sawyer (Twain), 43
Africa, partitioning of by Europe, 11, 37–38
African diaspora: and biological determinism, 104, 190n4; cultural continuity, 12; and Martí, 141–42; poverty as consequence of oppression, 24–25; role of in independence movement, 24–25, 106; transnational perspective of Martí, 174–75
Afro-Cubans: Afro-Cuban culture, 121–25; colonial experience of racism, 107–13, 191–92n15; Martí as advocate for rights of, 88–89; multi-ethnic national identification, 12–13; *Patria* article on equality of, 119; population demographics, 122; racial hatred towards white Cubans, 106–7, 191n8, 192n19; violence against, 123–24
Aguilera, Antonio, 138–39
Aguilera, Francisco Vicente, 136
ahimsa, 91

Albertini, Rafael Díaz, 137
Alcott, Louisa May, *Little Women*, 43, 145
Alice in Wonderland (Carroll), 43
Alvarez, Agustín: *Transformación de razas en América* (*Race Transformation in America*), 110
Anderson, Benedict, 5–6; *Imagined Communities*, 6, 8
Anderson, Hans Christian, 43
Annam. See "Journey through the Land of the Annamese" (Martí)
Anthony, Susan B., 180n19
anti-colonial activism: "age of revolutions", 19; empowerment of colonial subjects, 55–56, 60; love and compassion, role of in resistance, 60; *marronage*, 122; of Martí, 1, 15–16, 18, 20, 123; resistance to foreign oppression, 56–58; Sepoy Rebellion, 19; Taiping Rebellion, 19
Antilles, 12
anti-racism: collaboration of Serra and Martí, 134; Cuba as "raceless nation", 88–89, 90; and Cuban independence, 103–4, 105, 108–9, 131–32, 141–42; in *Manifesto de Montecristi*, 100; paternalism, inherent racism of, 119–21; and pro-African-American

213

anti-racism (*continued*)
  activism, 25; promotion of non-European culture, 113–16; as spiritual mandate, 12, 21, 24, 80, 83, 116–17, 174–75
architecture: comparisons between Mayans and Gauls, 49–50; Eiffel Tower, 62; as historical source, 47; and indigenous technology, 50–52, 56; Parthenon, 61; religious dogma, rejection of, 58
Argentina, 110, 192n24; Martí as honorary consul general, 39, 74
Arguedas, Alcides: *Pueblo Enfermo (Sick Nation)*, 110
Arias, Salvador, 39
Arnold, Sir Edwin, 72, 73, 76
Arthur, Chester A., 145
Asia, and Western expansionism, 11
Aunt Judy's Magazine, 43
autonomistas, 9–10, 13; *Partido Liberal* (Liberal Party), 111–12

"balancing the world", 178; and anti-racism, 25; Cuban independence as exercise in, 28–29, 100, 102; Martí's conception of race, 117–19; political actions as humanitarian struggle for, 30–31
Ballón Aguirre, José, 72, 83
Bancroft, George, 52
Banderas, Quintín, 114; Cuban Liberation Army, 122
Batista, Fulgencio, 20
Bayly, C.A., 19
Beecher, Henry Ward, 81
Belnap, Jeffrey, 89
Berlin conference: partitioning of Africa by Europe, 11, 37–38
Besant, Annie, 72, 73, 75–76, 175

Bhagavad-Gita: as influence on Martí, 23, 175–77; karmic relationship, 81; *moksha*, 96; *prakriti*, and personal ambition, 77; in relation to war against Spain, 88, 89–90; sacrifice as purifying agent, 74–75; selflessness, and duty, 69–70, 187n4; Supreme Being, concept of, 77–79; war as sacred duty, 93, 95–96; war without hatred, 97–98
biographical essay(s): as hybrid chronicle, 152–53, 198n32; as pedagogical tools, 149–50
Blaine, James G., 39
Blanco, Ramón, 137, 138
Bolívar, Simón, 8, 9, 11, 46, 173
Bonilla, Gerónimo, 141
Bonilla, Juan, 113, 141
Boy's Own Magazine, 43
Breuilly, John, 5, 6
Bronson Alcott, Amos, 72
Buddhism, 59–60, 62–63, 74
Bulnes, Francisco: *El porvenir de las naciones hispanoamericanas (The Future of Latin American Nations)*, 110
Burnett, Frances Hodgson, *Little Lord Fauntleroy*, 42

Calhoun, Craig, 5
Cantù, Cesare, 47
Carbonell, Néstor L., 40
Caribbean: association with Antilles, 12; geopolitical value, 13–14; as "globalized space", 29–30, 98–99; impact of Haitian revolution on, 106–7; significance of in Cuban liberation, 30; as source of European wealth, 29; spiritual unity with Cuba, 98–99; and US expansionism, 11, 12, 13–14, 26, 28, 147, 150
Carroll, Lewis, *Alice in Wonderland*, 43

caudillismo, 10; *caudillo* qualities, 173; concerns over, 94–95, 150; and meeting at *La Mejorana*, 130–31; remedies against, 21
Central Directorate of the Societies of the Coloured Race in Cuba, 139–41
Centre for Martí Studies, 35
Century Magazine, 146
Chatterjee, Partha, 6
children's journals, 41–45; messages for children, 43; transmission of civic values, 177; value of non-Western history, 47–48. See also *Golden Years (La Edad de Oro*, Martí)
científicos, 110, 111
Cirujeda, Francisco, 112
civic values: childhood education, and political consciousness, 34–36; training and teaching of, 164; transmission of, 63, 64–66, 177
Civil War (US), 120; Grant, positive/negative qualities of, 161–66; imagery, 152–53; as noble crusade, 156–57, 158; parallels with Cuban independence, 156–60; relevance for Martí, 25–27, 147–48; as spiritually purifying mechanism, 160–61; transmission of right government, 146–47
Civilisation and Barbarism (Sarmiento), 110
"civilization vs. barbarism" debate, 51–53, 110–11, 114
colonial absolutism, 103–4
colonialism: as bonds of dependence, 9–10; critique of colonial cultural stereotypes, 54–55; and European "civilizing mission", 22, 24–25, 27, 47–48, 53; European expansion into Africa and Asia, 11, 37–38; and European racial superiority, 113; master/subject relationship, 56–57; resistance against, 3, 56–58; scaffold as symbol of power, 15, 91. *See also* anti-colonial activism
"Con todos y para el bien de todos" ("For All and for the Good of All", Martí speech), 109–10, 192n23
Congress of Panamá, 46
Conspiración de la Escalera (Ladder Conspiracy), 107–8
Cooper, Peter, 145
Costa Rica, 128–29
critical thinking, importance of, 58–59
Crombet, Flor, 85, 112; on Antonio Maceo, 125; Cuban invasion plan, 129–30; Cuban Liberation Army, 122
Cuba: abolition of slavery, 12, 106; *autonomistas*, 9, 10, 13, 111–12; black participation in government, 111–12; Cuban Revolutionary Party (Partido Revolucionario Cubano, PRC), 7, 18, 180n19; history as national story, 26–27; independence as "necessary war", 27; independence movement, 12, 94–95; *La Guerra Chiquita* (the Little War), 71, 126, 129, 137; *La Guerra Grande*, 109, 114, 126; Ladder Conspiracy, 107–8; *marronage*, 122; Movement of Purnio, 128; multi-ethnic national identification, 12–13; national self-determination, 57–58; Pact of Zanjón, 129; Partido Independiente de Color (Independent Party of the Coloured), 18; peace treaty, Cuban War of Independence, 13–14; population demographics, 122; press censorship, 42–43, 58; "Protest of Baraguá", 126; as "racelesss nation", 88–89, 90; scaffold as symbol of power, 15, 91; as sovereign republic, 13–14; Ten Years' War, 26, 94; US annexation of,

Cuba (*continued*)
    39–40, 183n21; violence against Afro-Cubans, 123–24; Yara uprising, 106
Cuban diaspora, 108, 109–10, 189n6, 192n23
Cuban Liberation Army, 30, 125–26, 127, 195n75; call to arms, 141; leadership role of black Cubans, 122
Cuban Revolutionary Committee, 92–93
Cuban Revolutionary Party (Partido Revolucionario Cubano, PRC), 18; establishment of, 40; as gender neutral, 7, 180n19; Gómez-Maceo Plan, 128; membership composition, 134; *Patria*, 39
Cuban War of Independence: conflict over civilian government, 146–47, 197n14; declaration of war, 141; invasion plan, 129–30; meeting at *La Mejorana*, 130–31; parallels to US Civil War, 147–48, 156–60; US intervention, 1, 38, 89
Cubanidad, as national identity, 105
cultural diffusion, 53
cultural exchange, 48, 61–62

Da Costa Gómez, Aaron, 41, 44, 183n30
Dana, Charles, *The Life of Ulysses Grant*, 146
Darío, Rubén, 41
de Azcárate, Nicolás, 136, 138
de Céspedes, Carlos Manuel, 106, 192n19
de la Torre, Mildred, 111
de Las Casas, Father Bartolomé, 59
de Quesada, Gonzalo, 37, 72, 83, 90, 155
de San Martín, José, 173
de Viondi, Miguel, 136, 138
Defoe, Daniel, *Robinson Crusoe*, 43
democracy, in Cuban independence movement, 12
desires, and personal ambition, 77–79, 95–96
despotism, and corrupt government, 166–67
destiny, and heroic figures, 155–56
Diarios de Campaña (Martí), 116, 130
Díaz, Porfirio, 3
Díaz Quiñones, Arcadio, 147
dictatorships. See *caudillismo*
divinity: of humanity, 80, 117, 150; of nation-state, 14, 16–17, 21, 23–24, 175–76
Domínguez, Fermín Valdés, 73
Dominican Republic, treaty of annexation, 168–69
Douglas, Frederick, 120

Ecuador, 110, 192n24
education, advocacy of, 92
Eiffel Tower, 62
El Avisador (newspaper), 143
El Camarada (*Buddy*, children's journal), 42
El Museo de la Juventud (*Museum for Youngsters*), 42
El País (the *Homeland*, newspaper), 112
El Partido Liberal (newspaper), 39, 74, 76, 145
El porvenir de las naciones hispanoamericanas (*The Future of Latin American Nations*, Bulnes), 110
"El presidio político en Cuba" (Martí), 3
elegance, 61
Emerson, Ralph Waldo, 145, 175; and Hindu philosophy, 72–73; influence on Martí, 42; Martí's essay on, 70–71, 73, 75, 80–83, 117
Épinal graphic studios, 44
Escalona Chádez, Israel, 128
Estrada Palma, Tomás, 13

Estrázulas, Enrique, 44
ethnicity: and ethnocentric doctrines of nationalism, 3–4, 7
ethnie theory of nationalism, 5
ethnocentrism, and intercultural exchange, 61–62
European society: admiration of European cultural expressions, 48, 185nn61–62; cultural norms, adoption of, 51–52, 113–16; cultural stereotypes, 54–55; non-superiority of, 22, 24–25, 35, 54–55, 65–66; and pre-colonial indigenous technology, 50–52; and racial oppression, 113; and value of non-Western history, 47–48
Evening Telegraph (newspaper), 119
exceptionalism, 52
expansionism: European partition of Africa, 11, 37–38; manifest destiny of US, 38; Martí on US expansionism, 37; of US into Cuba, 39–40, 64, 183n21; of US into Latin America/Caribbean, 11, 12, 13–14, 26, 28, 147, 150, 168–69, 183n21; Venezuela-British Guiana border dispute, 38

fanaticism, 162
Fernández, Raúl, 89
Fernández Retamar, Roberto, 11, 48–49, 52, 64
"For All and for the Good of All" (Martí speech), 109–10, 192n23
forgiveness and reconciliation, 25, 170; as nation-building value, 148, 153–55, 198n40
Fountain, Anne, 72, 105, 109, 114
Francia, José Gaspar Rodríguez de, 110, 192n24
freedom of religion, 159
freedom of self defense, 159
freedom of speech, 159
freedom of the press, 159
Freemasonry: influence on Martí, 175; and Mexican nationalism, 9

Gandhi, Indira, 36
Gandhi, M.K. "Mahatma", 27; *ahimsa*, 91; comparison to Martí, 24, 91–92, 176, 181n42; *patria*, divine conception of, 14; *swaraj*, 28, 91–92
García Marruz, Fina, 33, 40, 60, 63, 64
Garfield, James A., 145
Garifuna population, description of, 117–18, 123, 193–94nn50–51
Garnet, Henry, 120
Gellner, Ernest, 5, 6
gender roles, polarization of, 56
"General Grant" essay (Martí), 150–53; background, 143–45, 196–97nn3–5; as "discourse of forewarning", 147; funeral, 146, 148, 154–55, 198n40; nation-building values, themes of, 148, 153–60; sources, 146
God Consciousness, 77–79, 85–87, 100–102
God *patria*, 90–92, 96–97, 175–76
Golden Years (*La Edad de Oro*, Martí), 182n3; civic values, transmission of, 34–36, 63, 64–66, 177; "civilization vs. barbarism" debate, 51–53; criticisms of, 40; distribution, 41; financial support, 41, 44, 183n30; graphic techniques, 44; humanitarianism, 60–66; ideological themes, 35; inspiration and context, 36–41; intergenerational writings, 33–34; models for, 42, 46–48; national pride, 45–46; national self-determination, 48–58; nation-building values of, 22; non-superiority of European civilization, 22, 35, 116;

Golden Years (continued)
  pedagogical intent, 40–41; personal self-determination, 58–60; polarization of gender roles, 56; reviews of, 41; sources of inspiration, 43–44; value of older traditions, 50–52, 64. *See also* "Journey through the Land of the Annamese" (Martí); "The Story of Humanity, Told through Its Houses" (Martí)
Gómez, Máximo, 30, 85, 94, 99, 164; conflict over civilian government, 146–47, 197n14; Cuban Liberation Army, 122, 125
González, Manuel Pedro, 74
Gothic architecture, 58
governance: knowledgeable governance, 25, 148, 166–71; and nation building, 145; need for humility in, 167
Grajales Coello, Mariana, 126, 127, 129
Gran Colombia, 8, 9
Grant, Jesse R., 146
Grant, Ulysses S., 52; as *caudillo*, 150, 173; financial scandals, 145, 151; funeral, 146, 148, 154–55, 198n40; as personification of US national character, 151–52; as political opportunist, 165–66; as positive/negative model, 147–48, 161–66; redemption in death, 169–70, 171; relevance of US Civil War to Martí, 25–27. *See also* "General Grant" essay (Martí)
"great man" narrative, 169, 170, 171; and Martí, 172–73
Greek art and architecture, 58
Greenfeld, Liah, 5
Gualberto Gómez, Juan, 25, 107–8, 112, 126, 136–41; *La Fraternidad* (Fraternity, newspaper), 139; *La Igualdad* (Equality, newspaper), 139–40

Gulliver's Travels (Swift), 43
Gutiérrez Nájera, Manuel, 41
Guzmán Blanco, Antonio, 71

Haiti: impact of Haitian revolution on Caribbean, 106–7; rhetoric of inclusion, 7; support of Cuban independence, 9
Harper's Young People, 42, 43
hatred: rejection of, 60, 163; war without hatred, 27, 85, 91–92, 97–102
Hegel, G.W.F.: history as progression of freedom, 47–48, 65, 66, 149–50
Henríquez Carvajal, Francisco, 36
Hidalgo, Miguel, 8
Hindu philosophy: *Atman*, 73–74; *Bhagavad-Gita*, 23, 69–70, 74–75, 77–79, 81, 187n4; and construction of nation, 24; influence on Martí, 16, 21, 22–24, 69–71, 96–97, 116–17, 175–77, 181n41; Krishna's advice to Arjuna, 69–70, 75, 78–79, 97–98, 176–77; *moksha*, 75; *prakriti*, and personal ambition, 77–79; reincarnation, 81, 83; in relation to war against Spain, 88, 89–90; sacrifice as purifying agent, 73–76, 175–77; and Transcendentalism, 79, 82–83; value of education, 76
historical narratives: "civilization vs. barbarism" debate, 51–53, 110–11, 114; global history, Martí's knowledge of, 34–35, 65, 182n4; non-superiority of European civilization, 22, 24–25, 35, 48; political implications in, 50; value of non-Western history, 47–48, 64
history, as national story, 26–27
Hobsbawn, Eric, 7
Huckleberry Finn (Twain), 43
Hugo, Victor, *Mes fils*, 22
humanitarianism, 22, 60–66; in

"balancing the world", 30–31; civic values of, 60–66; sacrifice as purifying agent, 73–76; and selflessness, 35, 62–63
humanity: league of nations as means of securing freedom, 45–46
Hunt Jackson, Helen, *Ramona*, 118
Hutchinson, John, 6

Imagined Communities (Anderson), 6, 8
imperialism: and expansionism of colonial powers, 11; partitioning of Africa by Europe, 11, 37–38; resistance to foreign oppression, 56–58
independence movement(s): "age of revolutions", 19; Annamese, 55–56; anti-colonial activism of Martí, 1, 15–16, 18, 20, 136–38; *caudillismo*, concerns over, 94–95; forgiveness and reconciliation, 25; global influences on Martí, 21–29; humanitarian spirit of, 27; leadership role of black Cubans, 122; personal freedoms, 25; sacrifice and selflessness, 25
India: Sepoy Rebellion, 19; tradition of tolerance, 7
indigenous peoples: comparison to European civilizations, 48–50, 54–56; and cultural exchange, 48; defence of, 30; discrimination against, 118; downplaying of indigenous cultures, 112–13; indigeneity, promotion of, 10, 50–52, 56–57; non-Western indigenous archetypes, 66; pre-colonial indigenous technology, 50–52, 56
Ingenieros, José, *Sociología argentina* (*Argentine Sociology*), 110
Ismaelillo (*Little Ishmael*, Martí), 71

Jackson, Helen Hunt, 42; *Ramona*, 10
James, Jesse, 145

Journal Hebdomadaire, 46
"Journey through the Land of the Annamese" (Martí), 35–36, 38, 40–41; Buddhist principles, promotion of, 59–60, 62–63, 74; critique of colonial cultural stereotypes, 54–55; graphic techniques, 44; humanitarianism, 62–63; Jain folk tale, 58–59; national pride, 45–46; national self-determination, 53–58; personal self-determination, 58–60
Juvenile Miscellany, 43

Kant, Immanuel, 45
King, Martin Luther, Jr., 27, 28
knowledgeable governance. *See* governance
Krause, Karl C.F., 70, 83, 175

La Fraternidad (*Fraternity*, newspaper), 139
La Guerra Chiquita (the Little War), 71, 126, 137; Pact of Zanjón, 129
La Guerra Grande, 109, 114, 126
La Igualdad (*Equality*, newspaper), 139–40; Plácido as martyr and race hero, 107–8
La Liga Antillana, 133
La Liga (the League), 40, 133–34; "Vázquez, friend of *La Liga*", 121
La Nación (newspaper), 39, 74, 143, 145; Martí on humanity, 80; Martí on US expansionism, 37; Sheridan essay, 149
La Niñez (*Childhood*), 43
La Opinión Nacional (newspaper), 39, 70, 71, 145
La Opinión Pública (newspaper), 145
La República, 145
"La república española ante la revolución cubana" (Martí), 3

Laboulaye, Édouard René Lefebvre de, 43
Ladder Conspiracy, 107–8
Latin America: *caudillismo*, 10, 109–10, 192n24; "civilization vs. barbarism" debate, 51–53, 110–11, 114; European cultural norms, adoption of, 51–52, 113–16; and indigeneity, 10; nationalism discourse in, 6–12; pan-Latin Americanism, 1, 36–38; pan-regional framework of study, 17–18; rhetoric of inclusion, 7; and US expansionism, 11, 12, 13–14, 26, 28, 147, 150; views on race, 107–13, 191n9
league of nations, 45–46
Lee, Robert E., as counterbalance to Grant, 162–63
Legrand, P., "L'Habitation humaine", 46
L'Exposition de Paris de 1889, 44, 46
Life of Ulysses Grant, The (Dana), 146
Liga de Instrucción, 133
literary journalism, 42
Little Women (Alcott), 43
Lolo, Eduardo, 41–42
Lomnitz, Claudio: *nación*, connotations of, 9–10
Los Niños (*Children*), 42
Louverture, Toussaint, 46
love, as revolutionary energy, 60
Lugo-Ortiz, Agnes, 107–8, 115

Maceo, Antonio, 25, 85, 112, 121; conflict over civilian government, 146–47, 197n14; correspondence with Martí, 127–29; Cuban Liberation Army, 122, 125–26, 127, 195n75; death of, 126; and *Guerra Grande*, 126; meeting at *La Mejorana*, 130–31; in New York City, 94, 126; "Protest of Baraguá", 126
Maceo, José, 129, 130

Maceo, Marcos, 126
Machado, Gerardo, 20
Machiavelli, Niccolò, 47–48
Madero, Francisco, 181n41
manifest destiny, 38
Manifiesto de Montecristi, 97–102; anti-racism, 100, 121; as Caribbean document, 29–30; Cuba as nation of diverse origins, 92; as declaration of independence, 85–87, 175–76; divinity of nation-state, 23–24; European cultural norms, adoption of, 115; and European racial superiority, 114; forgiveness and reconciliation, 25, 148, 153–55, 198n40; and freedom in the Americas, 192n23; purpose of war for independence, 98–99; and Spanish colonial rule, 28–29; spiritual unity between Cuba and the Caribbean, 98–99
Mantilla, Carmen, 44
Mantilla, María, 32, 44, 61, 116, 194n69
Mantilla Miyares, Carmen, 116
Mantilla Sorzano, Manuel, 116
Márquez Sterling, Adolfo, 137
Martí, José: as absent father, 44, 71; admiration of European cultural expressions, 48, 185n61, 185n62; on Annie Besant, 75–76; anti-colonial activism, 1, 15–16, 18, 20, 39; assassination attempt on, 141–42; comparison to Gandhi, 24, 91–92, 176, 181n42; "Con todos y para el bien de todos" (speech), 109–10, 192n23; conflict over civilian government, 146–47, 197n14; correspondence with Maceo, 127–29; correspondence with Serra, 135; death of, 3, 131; deportation to Spain, 1, 3, 15, 30, 79–80, 137–38; existential doubts of, 67–69, 72; global history, knowledge of, 34–35,

65, 182n4; global influences, overview, 21–29; as honorary consul general, 39; inclusion as gender neutral, 7, 180n19; independence, and national liberation, 4; indigeneity, promotion of, 10; knowledge of global history, 34–35, 182n4; *La Liga* (the League), 40, 121, 133–34; life outside of Cuba, 15–16; as nation builder, 7–9; nationalism, and cross-ethnic fraternity, 5; in New York City, 3, 13, 39, 71, 123–24, 132–33, 138; pan-Latin Americanism, 36–38; *patria*, 4, 14, 16–17, 179n3; personal struggles, 27–28, 70–71, 74; on race, and racial prejudice, 4; racial idealism of, 113–17; Rafael Mendive as mentor, 15, 34; return to Cuba, 136–38; teleological framework of beliefs, 47–48; transparency of private/public life, 18; *weltaunschauung*, 63

Martí, José: writings: academic scholarship, 17–18; biographical essays, 145; Caribbean testament, 36; *Diarios de Campaña*, 116, 130; Emerson essay, 70–71, 73, 75, 80–83, 117; as foreign correspondent, 39; *Ismaelillo* (*Little Ishmael*), 71; "Mi raza" ("My Race"), 103, 120–21, 140; "My Black People", 124–25, 194n69; "North American Scenes", 143, 145; "Nuestra América" ("Our America"), 36, 52, 114; personal notebook, 81, 109, 124–25, 194n69; poetry on "men of the earth", 151, 198n28; "Political Prison in Cuba", 3; Sheridan essay, 149, 164; "The Spanish Republic Faces the Cuban Revolution", 3; translation work, 10, 22, 182n3; "Vázquez, friend of *La Liga*", 121; "Vindication of Cuba", 39; "Yugo y Estrella", 67, 186–87n1. *See also*

"General Grant" essay (Martí); *Golden Years* (*La Edad de Oro*, Martí)
"Martí es la Democracia" (speech), 134–35, 195–96n94
Martínez-Echazábel, Lourdes, 113, 114
Maurya, Vibha, 91, 92
Mayans, comparison to Gauls of Europe, 48–50
Mazzini, Giuseppe, 45
McNeill, William, 53
Mendive, Rafael, María, 14, 34, 64
Mercado, Manuel, 38, 40–41, 43, 44, 57, 149, 158
Mes fils (Hugo), 22
metaphysics, 83
Mexico: and Freemasonry, 9; racialized political discourse, 110; under Spanish colonialism, 8
"Mi raza" ("My Race", Martí), 120–21, 140
Michelet, Jules, 27, 152–53, 169
Miller, Nicola, 6–7
Mirabel, Nancy Raquel, 12
miscegenation, 111, 117–18, 193n50, 194n51
Mistral, Gabriela, 91
Miyares Peoli, Carmen, 116
modernismo, 17, 42
Montero, Oscar, 76
Morúa Delgado, Martín, 112
"My Black People" (Martí), 124–25, 194n69

nación, connotations of, 9–10
Napoleon, 12
nation building, holistic approach to, 18–19, 20
national self-determination, 22; empowerment of colonial subjects, 55–56; "Journey through the Land of the Annamese", 53–58; as moral value,

national self-determination (*continued*) 35; promotion of democratic values, 54; "The Story of Humanity, Told through Its Houses", 48–53

nationalism: as construct of ruling elites, 45; emergence of modern nationalism, 4–5; ethnocentric doctrines of, 3–4; exclusionary politics of, 14, 45; and gender stereotypes, 21; as internalized sentiment, 45; in Latin America, 6–12; of Martí, 45–46; modern theories of, 3–6; multi-ethnic national identification, 12–13; as political construction, 7; and print-capitalism, 5–6, 7, 8; and racial exclusion, 53; and secularization, 9; Third World nationalism, 6

nation-state: divinity of, 14, 16–17, 21, 23–24, 87–88, 96–97; God *patria*, 90–92, 175–76; hybrid conception of, 11–12; leadership qualities, 168; as political construction, 7; as republic and nation, 8–9; soul as spiritual principle, 90

nativism, 50, 55

"Negros y blancos" ("Blacks and Whites", Sanguily), 108, 191–92n15

Nehru, Jawaharlal, 36, 66

New York Evening Post: "Vindication of Cuba", 39

New York Herald, 1, 3, 20

New York Sun, 74

"North American Scenes" (Martí), 143, 145

"Nuestra América" ("Our America", Martí), 36, 52, 114

Ortiz, Fernando, 103–4, 111, 118, 140, 174, 190n4

Pan-American Monetary Conference, 37, 38, 182n11

pan-Latin Americanism, 1, 36–38

Pappademos, Melina, 112, 114–15

Paraguay, 110, 192n24; Martí as honorary consul general, 39, 74

Paris World's Fair, 62; *L'Exposition de Paris de 1889*, 44, 46

Parthenon, 61

Partido Independiente de Color (Independent Party of the Coloured), 18, 89, 189n6

Partido Liberal (Liberal Party), 111–12

Partido Revolucionario Cubano (PRC). *See* Cuban Revolutionary Party

paternalism: hierarchical bonds of colonialism, 9; inherent racism of, 119–21

patria: concept of, 4, 179n3; divinity of nation-state, 14, 16–17, 21, 23–24; and God Consciousness, 77–79, 87–88, 100–102; God *patria*, 90–92, 96–97; as spiritual call to duty, 93–94; unity with humanity, 87–88, 172

Patria (PRC newspaper), 39, 119, 140

patriotic duty, as journey of purification, 16–17

Pedroso, Paulina, 120–21, 141

Pedroso, Ruperto, 141

Pellerin, Nicolas, 44

Perrault, Charles, *Tales and Stories of the Past with Morals*, 43

personal freedom, 25, 170; as nation-building value, 148, 156–60

personal self-determination, 22, 58–60

Phillips, Wendell, 120, 132

Plácido: Ladder Conspiracy, 107–8

"Political Prison in Cuba" (Martí), 3

positivism, doctrine of: and racialized political discourse, 110–11

poverty, as consequence of oppression, 24–25
print-capitalism, and nationalism, 5–6, 7, 8
Pueblo enfermo (*Sick Nation*, Arguedas), 110

race: anti-racism, and Cuban independence, 103–4; biological determinism, 104, 190n4; as cause of economic disparity, 110–11; as cultural distinction, 118–19; and doctrine of positivism, 110–11; as justification for racial oppression, 110–13; Latin American views on, 107–13, 191n9; Martí on, 4, 21; Martí's conception of, 117–19; as social construct, 106, 174, 191n8; whiteness as matter of culture, 113
racial ideologies: colonial experience of racism, 107–13, 191–92n15; colonial policies towards non-Europeans, 51–52; critique of colonial cultural stereotypes, 54–55; elimination of, 24–25; and ethnocentric doctrines of nationalism, 3–4; and European "civilizing mission", 22, 24–25, 27, 47–48, 53; and indigenous peoples, 10, 113; miscegenation, and European racial superiority, 111, 113; pseudoscientific Darwinism, 113; racial hatred between white and black Cubans, 106–7, 191n8, 192n19; undermining of, 12. *See also* anti-racism
Ramage, James, 147–48
Ramona (Hunt Jackson), 10, 22, 118
Rawlins, John Aaron, 168
reconciliation, and forgiveness, 25, 148
Reformes dans les îles de Cuba et Porto Rico (Valiente y Cuevas), 43

reincarnation, 23, 81–84, 161, 177
religious expansionism, 9; *Carlistas*, 77; comparison of Buddhist monks to Catholic missionaries, 59–60; religious dogma, rejection of, 58–60
Renaissance architecture, 58
Renan, Ernest, 45, 90, 92
Revue de L'Exposition Universelle de 1889, 46
Robinson Crusoe (Defoe), 43
Rodríguez, Pedro Pablo, 4, 5, 13, 48, 64, 178
Rojas, Rafael, 181n41
Rojas, Ricardo, 26
Roloff, Carlos, 130
Roman Catholic Church, 77
Romantic historians, 27, 152–53; "great man" narrative, 169, 170
Rosas, Juan Manuel de, 110, 192n24
Rubens, Horatio: Teller Amendment, 13

Saco, José Antonio, 15, 108
sacrifice and selflessness, 25, 170, 176–77; as nation-building value, 148, 155–56
Sáenz Peña, Roque, 37
salvation, and redemption, 74–75
Sánchez, Serafín, 129–30
Sanguily, Manuel: racism against Afro-Cubans, 108, 191–92n15
Sarmiento, Domingo, 52, 114; *Civilisation and Barbarism*, 110
Sarracino, Rodolfo, 39
Schulman, Ivan, 92, 145
self-determination: and civic values, 22, 65, 66; at national level, 35, 48–58; personal level, 35, 58–60; war as ethical right of, 94
selflessness, 35, 62–63; and duty, 69–70, 187n4; redemptive nature of, 95–97; and sacrifice, 148, 155–56, 170; sacrifice

as purifying agent, 73–76, 175–77; war as spiritual call to duty, 92–94
Sepoy Rebellion, 19
Serra, Rafael, 25, 96, 126, 132–36, 140, 176; correspondence with Martí, 135; "Martí es la Democracia" (speech), 134–35, 195–96n94
Sheridan, Philip, 149, 164
slavery: abolition, and independence movement, 104–5, 158; abolition of in Cuba, 12, 106; and social exclusion post-abolition, 174
Smith, Anthony, 5, 6
social mobility: and adoption of white culture, 24, 25
societal development: cross-cultural exchanges, 53; role of environment in societal complexity, 52
Sociología argentina (*Argentine Sociology*, Ingenieros), 110
soul, as spiritual principle of nation, 90
Spain: *autonomistas*, 9–10; censorship by, 42–43, 58; colonial absolutism of, 103–4, 190n4; colonial religious expansionism, 9; colonial rule of, 3, 15, 28–29; deportation to, 1, 3, 15; Ladder Conspiracy, 107–8; peace treaty, Cuban War of Independence, 13–14; scaffold as symbol of power, 15, 91
"The Spanish Republic Faces the Cuban Revolution" (Martí), 3
spirituality: and anti-racism, 80, 174–75; divinity of the nation-state, 88, 90–92; God Consciousness, 77–79, 87–88, 100–102; in "Journey through the Land of the Annamese", 79; reincarnation, 81–84; true nature of the soul, 77–81. *See also* Hindu philosophy; Transcendentalism
St Nicholas, 42, 43

Stabb, Martin, 111
"The Story of Humanity, Told through Its Houses" (Martí): commonality of humanity, 49–53; cultural norms, adoption of, 51–52; graphic techniques, 44; national pride, 45–46; national self-determination, 48–53; origins and context, 46–48; pedagogical intent of, 35–36, 38, 40–41; personal self-determination, 58; religious dogma, rejection of, 58, 59; value of friendship, 61, 62
Stowe, Harriet Beecher, *Uncle Tom's Cabin*, 10
Suárez León, Carmen, 18
Suárez Suárez, Reinaldo, 15
Sumner, Charles, 168
swaraj, 91–92
Swift, Jonathan, *Gulliver's Travels*, 43

Taiping Rebellion, 19
Tales and Stories of the Past with Morals (Perrault), 43
technology: pre-colonial indigenous technology, 50–52
Teller Amendment, 13
Ten Years' War, 26, 94
Third World nationalism, 6
Thoreau, Henry David, 46, 72, 73, 83
Tone, John Lawrence, 45, 184n49
Transcendentalism: divine spark within individuals, 73–74; and Hindu philosophy, 79, 82–83; influence on Martí, 16, 23, 42, 46, 70–71, 175
Transformación de razas en América (*Race Transformation in America*, Alvarez), 110
Twain, Mark: *Adventures of Tom Sawyer*, 43; *Huckleberry Finn*, 43

Uncle Tom's Cabin (Stowe), 10
United States: African-American population, exclusion of, 118, 123; annexation of Cuba, 39–40, 183n21; Caribbean/Latin American expansionism, 11, 12, 13–14, 26, 28, 147, 150, 168–69, 183n21; discovery of Cuban invasion plan, 129–30; exceptionalism, 52; freedoms of, 159–60; intervention in Cuban War of Independence, 1, 38, 57, 89; manifest destiny, 38; Martí on US expansionism, 37; "No Transfer" doctrine, 183n21; Pan-American Monetary Conference, 37, 38, 182n11; as positive model, 150; and proper governance, 167; racial politics, 105, 109, 115, 119–20; Teller Amendment, 13. *See also* Civil War (US)
Uruguay, 39, 74

Valdés, Gabriel de la Concepción (Plácido), 107–8
Valdés Domínguez, Fermín, 131
Valiente y Cuevas, Porfirio, *Reformes dans les îles de Cuba et Porto Rico*, 43
Varela, Felix, 14
Varona, Enrique José, 41
"Vázquez, friend of *La Liga*" (Martí), 121

Vázquez Pérez, Marlene, 47
Veintimilla y Villacís, Ignacio de, 110, 192n24
Vico, Giambattista, 47
Vietnam. *See* "Journey through the Land of the Annamese" (Martí)
Vitier, Cintio, 40
Vitier, Medardo, 47–48

war: as mechanism of spiritual purification, 160–61; and personal freedom, 157–58; as sacred duty, 91–92; as spiritual call to duty, 92–94, 101–2; without hatred, 27, 60, 85, 91–92, 97–102
War of Independence (Cuba). *See* Cuban War of Independence
weltaunschauung: Annie Besant, 76; of Martí, 63
White, Hayden, 152
Whitman, Walt, 72, 73, 81, 82, 145
Wilson, Woodrow, 46
women: inclusion of, 7, 21, 180n19; polarization of gender roles, 56

"Yugo y Estrella" (Martí), 67, 186–87n1

Zayas Bazán, Carmen, 136
Zea, Leopoldo, 11

www.ingramcontent.com/pod-product-compliance
Lightning Source LLC
Chambersburg PA
CBHW032004220426
43664CB00005B/136